Dick Douwes is Professor of History at the Erasmus School of History, Culture and Communication, Erasmus University Rotterdam. He has previously taught at the universities of Nijmegen and Leiden and holds a PhD from Nijmegen University (Radboud University). From 1994 to 1998 he was coordinator of the programme Indonesian-Netherlands' Cooperation in Islamic Studies (INIS) at Leiden University. From 1998 he was academic coordinator – later executive director – of the International Institute for the Study of Islam in the Modern World (ISIM) and editor of the ISIM Newsletter/Review and ISIM Papers series. His research interests are late Ottoman history in Syria and religious plurality in the Middle East, as well as Muslims in Western Europe.

The Ottomans in Syria

A History of Justice and Oppression

Dick Douwes

I.B.TAURIS
LONDON · NEW YORK

New paperback edition published in 2017 by
I.B.Tauris & Co. Ltd
London • New York
www.ibtauris.com

First edition published in 2000 by I.B.Tauris & Co. Ltd

ISBN: 978 1 78453 734 0
eISBN: 978 1 78672 177 8
ePDF: 978 1 78673 177 7

A full CIP record for this book is available from the British Library
A full CIP record is available from the Library of Congress

Library of Congress Catalog Card Number: available

Contents

Preface vii
Introduction 1
1 Inland Syria; the fringes of cultivation 14
2 The office-households of the province 44
3 Local participation in the administration 63
4 Provincial alliances and factions 85
5 Local politics and violence 104
6 The fiscal regime 125
7 The logic of injustice; fiscal and financial policies 152
8 The Egyptian experience 188
Conclusions 211
Glossary 218
Annexes 222
Bibliography 231
Index 241

Preface

My interest in Syria dates from the late 1970s when I first visited the country as a student. My PhD research in the Centre for Historical Documentation in Damascus was conducted in the late 1980s and early 1990s with the generous support of the Netherlands' Organization for Scientific Research (NWO) and resulted in a PhD thesis which I defended in 1994. This PhD thesis formed the basis of this book that, due to changes in career and research interests took longer to mature than expected. However, this delay allowed for additional research on inland Syria and for a better reflection of earlier research results and its interpretation.

Acknowledgements

In the long process many people assisted and inspired me, contributing in one way or the other to this work. Mahmud Amin from Tell Dara introduced me to the history of the repopulating of each individual village in the area to the east of Hama. He and his family offered me hospitality and entertainment for several months. Norman Lewis contributed much to my understanding of the relationships between nomads and settlers introduced me to various sources, in particular travel accounts. I treasure the days I spent with him, and with Rosemary, in Croydon. Abdul-Karim Rafeq was always willing to share his expertise with me. Moreover, he commented in detail on my PhD thesis thus saving me from the repetition of some mistakes and making a number of valuable suggestions. All remaining errors and mistakes are to be blamed on me. I offer them my sincere gratitude.

Others to whom I owe thanks are Camilla Adang, Adnan Bakhit, Monique Berhards, Sarab Atasi, Gilbert Delanoue, the late Marion Farouk Sluglett, Fakhry Kaylani, Josua Landis, Gabrielle Landry, Richard van Leeuwen, Brigitte Marino, Nadine Meouchy, John Nawas, Jean-Paul Pascual, Eugene Rogan, Peter Sluglett, Umar Najib Umar, and Christian Velud. I would also like to thank the staff of the Centre for Historical Documentation, in particular Daʿad al-Hakim. I was also fortunate to have the support from friends and colleagues from the

Department of Middle East Studies of Nijmegen University, above all from Kees Versteegh, who always kept faith in me, and Erik-Jan Zürcher, who was also instrumental in securing the financial support of the International Institute of Social Studies, Amsterdam for this publication. I owe both special thank for their continuous encouragement. I would also like to thank my colleagues and friends at the International Institute for the Study of Islam in the Modern World, at the Indonesian-Netherlands' Cooperation in Islamic Studies and the International Institute for Asian Studies, in particular Wim Stokhof, who allowed me but little time to build on past experiences, but who offered me the opportunity to have new ones.

Note on Transliteration

Because this study is mainly based on Arabic documentary and literary sources the large majority of names and technical terms are transliterated according to the convention for Arabic used in the International Journal of Middle East Studies. Turkish administrative terms that are derived from Arabic have also been given this transliteration. For other Turkish terms the modern standard Turkish spelling has been employed, except that the tendency to change the final consonants d and b into t and p has not been followed. Place names are given in their more familiar English form, albeit that smaller, less well-known places appear in transliteration.

Introduction

'And they imposed a reign of injustice which was beyond description; even the rains stopped because of the injustice done.'

Muhammad al-Makkî, *Târîkh Hims*

The forces of order in traditional society harboured the antipodes of justice and benevolence: injustice and oppression. Both rulers and subjects were generally well aware of this contradiction that ruled society.[1] This awareness is manifest in the literary and documentary sources. Chroniclers complain about a wide range of unjust measures imposed by the agents of the state; superiors warn their inferiors to refrain from such acts; court historians concede that inequitable measures had become part of the system, and even had to become part of it because their inclusion was considered an undesirable, but inevitable stage in the life-cycle of empires.[2]

The Ottoman state

The main contradiction ruling traditional states like the Ottoman Empire concerns the recurrent disparity between the needs of the state and the inadequacy of resources of the territories over which it ruled. Notwithstanding the achievements of the Ottomans in organizing a complex administration, which encompassed vast and diverse territories, the capabilities of a pre-industrial state like the Ottoman were limited.[3] In these states coercion constituted a vital policy instrument, since other methods of persuasion often failed. Although coercion was

[1] Chaudhuri, *Asia*, pp. 71–72

[2] Ibn Khaldûn's (*Muqaddima*) concept of the ages of the state, which holds that the once high standards of rule are bound to be abandoned in the fourth stage, strongly influenced Ottoman court historians. Mustafa Naima, for instance, believed that the Ottoman empire had entered this stage at the time of the second failure to capture Vienna (1683). See Thomas, *Naima*, pp. 77–80

[3] Much has been written on the pre-industrial or pre-modern state. I have drawn in particular on Chaudhuri, *Asia*; Gellner, *Nations* and *Plough*; Tilly, *Coercion*; Crone, *Pre-industrial*; Eisenstadt, *Systems*; and Wittfogel, *Despotism*.

not by definition unjust, it could easily be regarded as such by the subjects of the state, in particular when they suffered from violent acts causing damage, loss and grief. The mere threat of harmful action, or symbolic punitive exercises, sufficed to keep the awareness of the potential damage alive.[4] The preservation of the state depended to a considerable extent on the application of force. It was an indispensable tool to impose the material claims of the state on the population. However, the exploitation of the resources of its territories could not be pursued with success when the state lost its legitimacy. The Ottoman court historian Mustafa Naima considered it the ideal that the subjects felt both dread of and affection for the sultan.[5] Evidently, coercion was deemed to be complementary to legitimacy, and not necessarily inconsistent with legitimate power, as long as it was the privilege of the state.

The Ottoman concept of the state, *devlet* (Arabic *dawla*) was not an impersonal abstraction. It denoted the dynastic rule of each individual head of the House of Osman, the sultan, and, by extension, the institutions created to protect his rule and to administer the territories under his rule, the dynastic patrimony. The army constituted the main supportive institution; troops often were referred to as *dawla* in local texts.[6] Those who protected the rule of the sultan and administered the territories enjoyed a number of privileges, but they were considered the sultan's slaves. The ruling class, then, constituted a servile elite. This ruling class was referred to as *askeri*, the military, but included the

[4] Charles Tilly (*Coercion*) includes Ottoman rule, in my view correctly, in the category of the coercive-intensive mode. Tilly does not relate coercion to the question of legitimacy. Ernest Gellner (*Plough*, pp. 146–47) equates coercion with power. He argues that coercion and legitimacy (and conviction) are complementary elements of the mechanism which imposes structure on society (p. 18). Tilly defines coercion as '. . . all concerted application, threatened or actual, of action that commonly causes loss and damage' (*Coercion*, p. 19). His definition roughly equals Gellner's concept of primary coercion; the physical threat (*Plough*, p. 146). Obviously, neither Tilly nor Gellner follow Max Weber's definition of coercion, i.e. the antithesis of authority; power which is regarded illegitimate by those over whom it is exerted (Tischler, et al, *Introduction*, p. 455).

[5] Thomas, *Naima*, p. 88

[6] The inhabitants of Damascus referred to the two main military formations of Damascus, the imperial and local janissaries, as *dawlat al-qalʿa* (The Troops of the Citadel) and *dawlat* Dimashq (The Troops of Damascus) respectively, see Barbir, *Ottoman*, p. 90

bureaucrats as well. They were the Ottomans. The subject classes, the *reaya* or flocks, were free, but entrusted by God to the care of the sultan, as was most of the land they worked.[7]

The authority of the sultan was absolute. No formal limitations on his power existed, but the inclusion of the divine law, the *shar*ᶜ, in Ottoman ideology did put some restraints on the sultan's power. The association of the sultanic authority with religious law was derived from the pre-Islamic traditions, in which royal authority and religious order had been made mutually dependent. In the Ottoman concept of government the Islamic law constituted the foundation of the state, but this law could not be upheld without sultanic support. Well into the nineteenth century two complementary principles of government dominated Ottoman political thinking: the Circle of Justice and the Bounds. Apart from the association of royal authority with religious law, the first doctrine maintains that the survival of the state depends on the prosperity of the subjects, in particular the peasantry. They pay the taxes which enable the sultan to maintain the military and the bureaucratic apparatus. The prosperity of the subjects depends on justice and it is the function of the sultan to render justice. In the view of Ernest Gellner this 'simple and elegant political theory . . . sums up, lucidly and adequately, the general condition of agrarian society'.[8] The second doctrine holds that the separation between the *askeri* and the *reaya* is fundamental for the proper functioning of the state, basically because the *askeri* class did not pay taxes.[9] Moreover, the idea of the bounds reflected the conservative approach of the Ottomans toward the sources of revenue; the protection of the productive units of the peasant communities and artisanal groups, not only following fiscal considerations, but also in view of the provisioning of the armies and the cities.

[7] See on the Ottoman concept of the state, Findley, *Bureaucratic*; Gerber, *State*; Göçek, Rise, pp.20–26, Inalcik, *Ottoman*, pp. 65–75; Itzkowitz, *Men*; Keyder, *State*, pp. 7–23; pp. 5–19; Shaw, *History*, vol. 1, pp. 164–65

[8] Gellner, *Plough*, p. 156. The full circle was as follows: There can be no sultanic authority without the *askeri*; there can be no *askeri* without wealth, the *reaya* produce wealth; the sultan keeps the *reaya* prosperous by making justice reign; justices requires harmony in the world; the world is a garden; its walls are the state; the foundation of the state is the religious law; there is no support for the religious law without sultanic authority. See Itzkowitz, *Men*, pp. 23–24 and Thomas, *Naima*, p. 78

[9] This is the principle of the *hudud* (Arabic *ḥudûd*) which was not restricted to the functioning of the state, but considered valid for society at large.

The rule of justice

In the political context justice meant the protection of the subject classes against abuse of the power which was delegated by the sultan to his servants, the *askeri*. Above all, the subject classes had to be protected against their illegal financial demands.[10] This notion was certainly linked to the consideration that the subjects should be left with sufficient means to continue their economic activities, but more importantly, it was aimed at the maintenance of the personal and absolute power of the sultan and his inalienable right to the (entire) revenue.

These basic political principles were not Islamic in the sense that they predated Islam by centuries; moreover, they found little support in Islamic legal writing. But in earlier Muslim political writing – as early as the eighth century when Ibn al-Muqaffaᶜ even advised the caliph to subordinate the *sharᶜ* to his royal authority[11] – the association of political authority and divine patronage was a common feature of the political ritual and discourse.

The concept of justice (*ᶜadl* or *ᶜadâla*), too, predates Islamic times, but this ancient concept had found wide use in Islamic legal writing. In the Islamic tradition, justice normally signified upholding and obeying the (religious) rules and laws; subsequently, a just ruler abides the law.[12] In this broad meaning the concept expressed the great stress in the Islamic tradition placed on having good morals, of the prevalence of good over evil. In the same long tradition, the antonyms of justice were tyranny and (moral) corruption, often referred to as *ẓulm* and *fasâd* in the documents and chronicles of Syria.[13] Acts of *ẓulm*, *maẓâlim*, comprised in particular abuses of power. The traditional institution to hear and redress complaints of such acts was likewise called *maẓâlim*; the practice of petitioning in the Ottoman empire was predicated on this time-honoured custom, which is often seen as the rendering of 'secular' justice, in the sense that the cases were not – or only to a limited extent

[10] Darling, *Revenue-raising*, pp. 282–83; Findley, *Bureaucratic*, p. 18; Inalcik, *Ottoman Empire*, p. 66

[11] EI2, p. 884

[12] A more technical meaning of *ᶜadl* concerns the prescribed qualities of a witness, a subject on which extensive legal writing exists.

[13] Other frequently used (near) equivalents are *jawr* and *taᶜaddî*, often in combination with *ẓulm*. The common antonym of *ᶜadl* of the (classical) legal texts, *fisq*, hardly occurs in these text, but is used in contemporary legal writing.

– considered in the light of the precepts of the Islamic law, albeit that the qâḍî was often involved in the handling of a case.[14]

The Ottomans were careful not to separate sultanic from divine rule. While most specialists of the divine law, the ulema, acquiesced to the sultan's prerogatives to legislate, others expressed some criticism, but it was extremely rare for a member of the learned class to draw the conclusion that the Ottoman sultanate was, in fact, a corrupt form of political authority.[15] The persistence of a – much milder – critical trend demonstrated that no consensus came about among the ulema over the ultimate legitimacy of the sultan's prerogatives. Nevertheless, by the eighteenth century it had became normal practice that legislation in the fields of public order and revenue extraction evolved by and large within the domain of the sultan.

The province

Another restraint on the absolute claims of the sultan was the delegation of power; it constituted a major dilemma in an autocratic state like the Ottoman empire. Considerable powers had to be delegated to those who served in the provinces. The ability to control the office-holders in the provinces was limited, in particular because local power groups had been increasingly engaged in provincial administration in the course of the seventeenth and eighteenth centuries. In other words, local elements had gained access to the *askeri* class. As a result, the separation between the *askeri* and *reaya* classes had not only become blurred, but the enlargement of the *askeri* class posed a danger to the functioning of the state to the well-being of the *reaya*, or rather to their productive qualities, because the material claims on the subjects increased. Moreover, the danger existed that the agents of the state were able to acquire an independent power base in the province. Locally recruited nominees already had a power base and were liable to strengthen their position. Non-local nominees regularly succeeded in creating a power base in the province. The outcome was the fragmentation of power.

The collection of revenue and the protection of production formed

[14] See, on the development of the institution in the pre-Ottoman period, Nielsen, *Secular*. See, for petitioning in relation to taxation in sixteenth and seventeenth centuries, Darling, *Revenue-raising*, 246–80; see also Gerber, *State*, pp. 66–78

[15] See, for instance the outspoken criticism of ʿAlî al-ʿUmarî of eighteenth century Mosul, Khoury, *State*, pp. 173–78

the main responsibilities of the provincial office-holders. Given the recurrent inadequacy of the provincial resources, competition for revenue was intense, not only amongst the local power groups, but also between these and the central authority. The central state had adopted a position towards the extraction of revenue which posed a moral dilemma. It did not necessarily object to unjust measures in the process of collecting revenue, provided that its own material demands were fulfilled. After all, '. . . most governments preferred material to moral satisfaction.'[16] In this respect the government can be defined as 'an institution which prevents injustice other than such as it commits itself.'[17] The ideal, or myth, of a just and benevolent sultan facilitated the disciplining of the office-holders. In order to preserve its moral hold on the population the central authority imposed, or more often threatened to impose, sanctions on those who perpetrated acts of injustice. This latter policy served as an important instrument to contain power groups in the province and to impose the central state's financial claims on them. This was not the only method to safeguard the interests of the central state. Various instruments were employed in order to contain the power of provincial office-holders, like the rotation of the senior offices and the separation of authority. Each of these instruments had its limitation and their efficiency depended on circumstance.

Some of the dilemmas facing the central authority were embedded in the provincial administration as well. The senior provincial office-holders depended on the services of the body of officials, officers and tax farmers to whom power had to be delegated. Within the confines of provincial rule the mechanisms of control were often inadequate. The containment policies of the central state could produce or stimulate political fragmentation in the province, in particular when senior office-holders were interchangeably recruited from competing local power groups. The limitations imposed by the central authority on the office-holders in the province could seriously restrict their abilities and force them, more often than not, to use more informal methods, including some which were not sanctioned by law, to strengthen their control of local affairs. The extent to which strictly coercive means were applied varied, but for the population at large the degree of coercion greatly influenced the perception of rule as being just or oppressive.

[16] Wittfogel, *Despotism*, p. 72

[17] Gellner, *Plough*, p. 239. The quotation is Gellner's interpretation of Ibn Khaldûn's definition of government.

The Syrian interior

Inland Syria was divided over two large provinces; the north was administrated from Aleppo and the central and southern areas from Damascus. In this monograph the emphasis is on the latter province, in particular on the district of Hama, a principle cereal producing area which enjoyed a special relation with the governorship of Damascus. It concerns the history of a long stretch of land, along the Sultanic Road, which connected Anatolia with Aleppo, Damascus and the holy land of the Hijaz, a zone in which sedentary and nomadic modes coexisted. The eighteenth century, in particular the latter part, witnessed several changes and shifts which had an impact upon the social and economic order: overland trade decreased in importance and changed in direction; trade with Europe, after a strong upsurge, declined rapidly toward the closing of the century; the migration patterns of several large Arabian beduin tribes shifted to the north and came to include all of inland Syria and the political point of gravity shifted from Damascus to the coastal town of Acre, the centre of the province of Sidon, a change which was part of a larger regional transformation which eventually resulted in the coming of dominance of Egypt.

Due to repeated heavy defeats at the hands of European powers and to the changing military needs which put a strain on the empire's resources, social and political order became increasingly tested, leading to a long chain of revolts in many parts of the Ottoman domains.[18] In the late eighteenth and early nineteenth centuries invasions and revolts combined with an intense competition between local factions located in inland and coastal Syria generated strongly coercive responses to problems of maintaining order. In the 1810s this provincial factionalism acquired a more narrow and petty local nature and by the 1830s, local factionalism was by and large suppressed. This latter development was not the logical outcome of an internal evolution; in 1831 the reformist governor of Egypt, Muḥammad ʿAlî Pasha, rebelled against the sultan and by July of 1832 his armies had occupied all of Syria and much of Anatolia. For nearly a decade Syria witnessed an unprecedented degree of direct, but highly coercive rule. Muḥammad ʿAlî Pasha is regularly regarded as the first, at least would-be, modern ruler in the Eastern Mediterranean; the first to formulate new answers to old problems, among them being the predicament of the delegation of power and the deficiency of the resources. For Syria his policies failed to accomplish

[18] Khoury, *State*, pp. 5–6

these goals and its resources were over-exploited. With the evacuation of the Egyptian troops, inland Syria returned to older habits.

This study deals with a set of related questions concerning the capabilities of the various actors on the provincial level and the limitations put upon them arising from their mutual relations and their dependence on central authority. The composition, recruitment and career patterns of local office-holders, in particular the military, will be traced, also, to illustrate that they had to perform their tasks under – more often than not – difficult conditions. The methods of exploitation of the resources, of revenue extraction, are central to their functioning as well as to societal order at large, but are of particular relevance in the rural setting, in the lives of the most important group of producers, the peasantry. Access to and control of the agricultural production and its distribution underpinned the local order.[19]

Sources

The narratives contained in this study are primarily based on local sources, in particular on local chronicles and on the records of the court of Hama. In addition to the local material, use has been made of contemporary observations of some Europeans, mostly travellers, but sometimes commercial and political agents.[20] The chronicles encompass writings from the interior, in particular Damascus, and from coastal Syria, especially the Lebanon.

Four chronicles deserve a short introduction here:

> *Lubnân fî ʿahd al-umarâ' al-Shihâbiyyîn* by Ḥaydar Aḥmad Shihâb (1761–1835), edited by A. Rustum and F. al-Bustânî. The edited text comprises the last to parts of the voluminous manuscript of this Lebanese emir. The original title of the manuscript appears to have been *Ghurar al-ḥisân fî dhikr abnâ' al-zamân*.[21] The history of the Shihâb family and of Mount Lebanon forms the centrepiece of this manuscript, but it contains much information on developments in inland Syria.

[19] Doumani, *Rediscovering*, pp. 2–4

[20] Many of the literary sources, see below and the bibliography, with the most important exception of one important Damascene chronicle, *Târîkh Ḥasan Aghâ al-ʿAbd*, formed the basis of the unpublished PhD thesis of Koury, *The Province of Damascus*, 1785–1831

[21] Rafeq, *Province*, pp. 325–27

Târîkh ḥawâdith al-Shâm wa-Lubnân, also known as *Târîkh Mikhâ'îl al-Dimashqî*, first edited by L. Maᶜlûf and published in *al-Mashriq* in 1912. In 1982 an edition by A. Gh. Sabânû was published in Damascus. The author of the manuscript is referred to by its copyist as *Mikhâ'îl al-Dimashqî*, but this might well have been a pseudonym. The manuscript is made up of three parts and was completed in 1843.

Târîkh Ḥasan Aghâ al-ᶜAbd, edited by Y. J. Nuᶜaysa and published in 1979. The manuscript and its edition have received little attention so far. The original manuscript was part of the vast collection of the Ẓâhiriyya library in Damascus, but only a xerox copy has survived. The Damascene Ḥasan Aghâ is the author of the untitled and incomplete manuscript. The little we know about him is derived from the manuscript itself and from a few scattered references in some other chronicles. Ḥasan Aghâ was an official who was involved in the repair of fortresses along the caravan road to the Hijaz. In the early 1820s he acted as governor of the Biqa district. The edited text covers events in the province of Damascus from 1772–1826.

Târîkh Hims, by the religious sheikh Muḥammad ibn Makkî ibn Khânqâh, a native of Homs, the twin town of Hama. The untitled manuscript is kept in the library of the American University of Beirut. It was edited by ᶜUmar N. al-ᶜUmar and published in Damascus in 1987. The work is of interest because it is one of the very few chronicles which have survived from places other than Damascus, Aleppo, and Lebanon. The chronicle sheds some new light on the circumstances in which the Homs and Hama area at the time of the emergence of the famed ᶜAẓm family, which played a prominent role in eighteenth and early nineteenth-century Syria.

The records of the Hama court (*maḥkama sharᶜiyya*) contain four broad categories of documents; firstly, copies of judicial deeds issued by the court in which a summary of a law suit and sentence is given (*ḥujja*); secondly, copies of notarized deeds concerning a variety of transactions, but in particular sale contracts and inheritances, as well as documents related to the administration and lease of religious and family foundations (*waqf*); thirdly, copies of edicts emanating from the provincial governor, his council, or from the imperial council in Istanbul (*buyuruldu*); and fourthly, tax tabulations and surveys, as well as auditor reports of the finances of individual office-holders.[22]

[22] See, on the use of court records as a source for local (social and economic) histories, p. 125–126 and Doumani, *Palestinian*; Glasman, *Documents*; Layish, *Sijill*; Mandaville, *Ottoman*; Mannaᶜ, *Sijill*; Marcus; Middle East, pp. 6–11; Rafeq, *Registres* and *Law-court*; Reilly, *Sharîᶜa*.

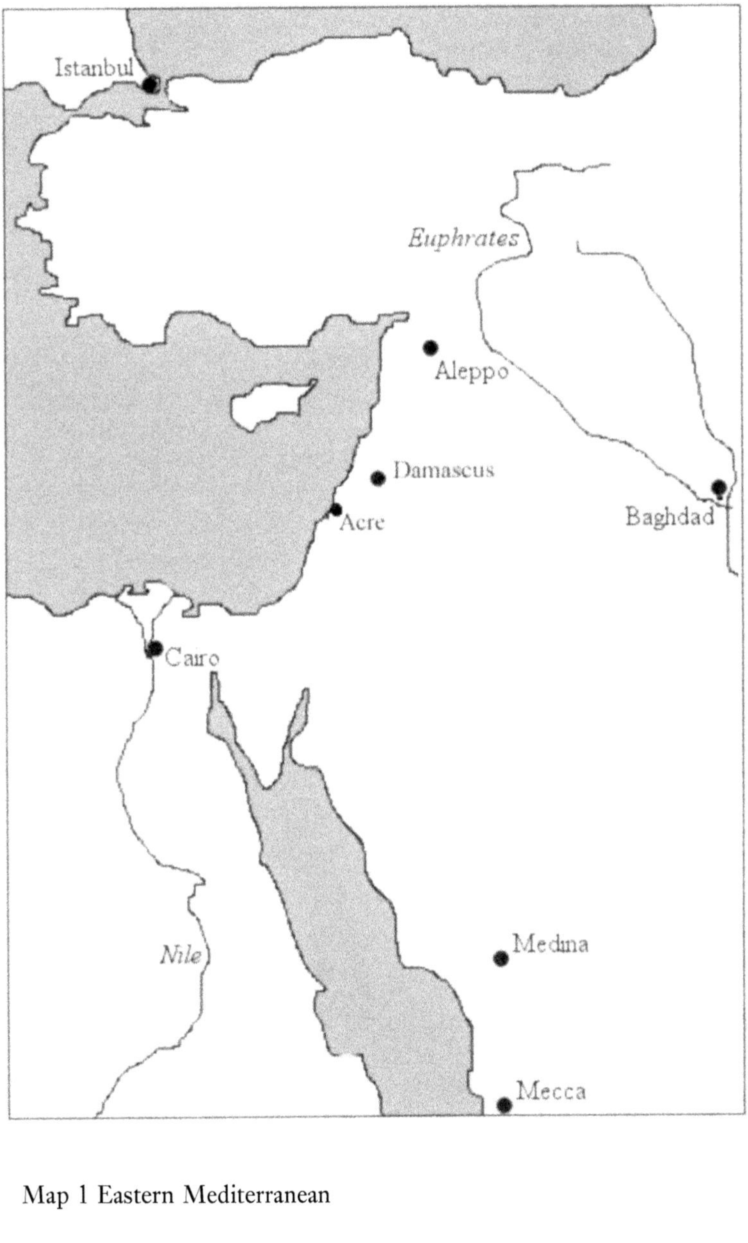

Map 1 Eastern Mediterranean

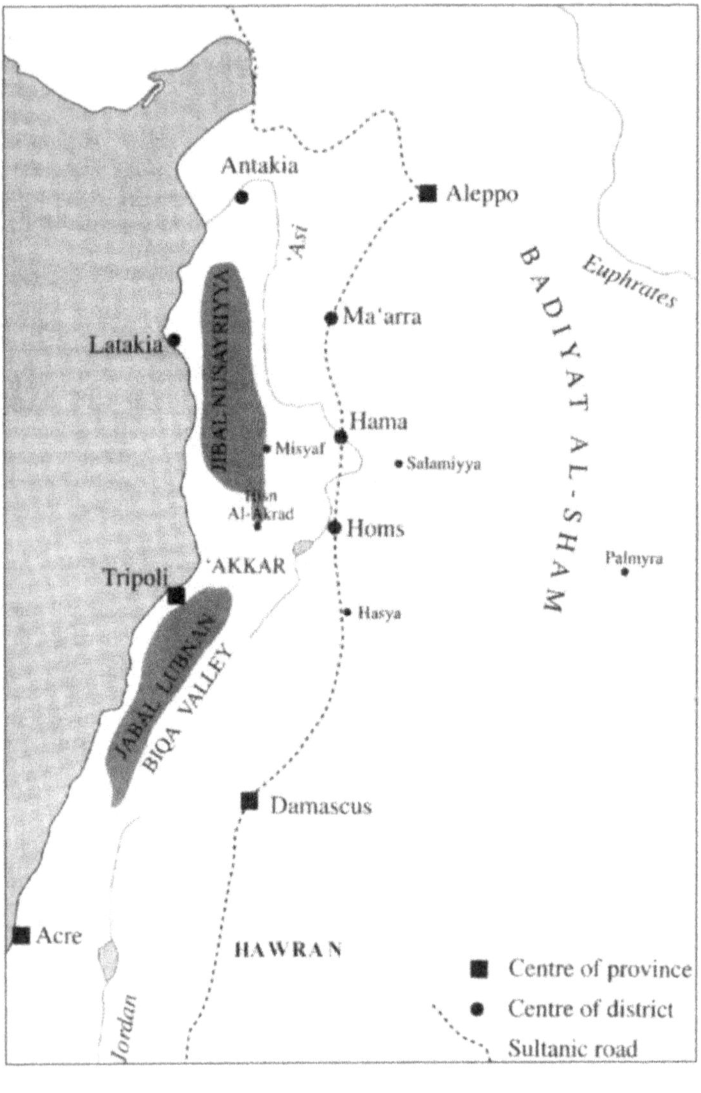

Map 2 Inland Syria

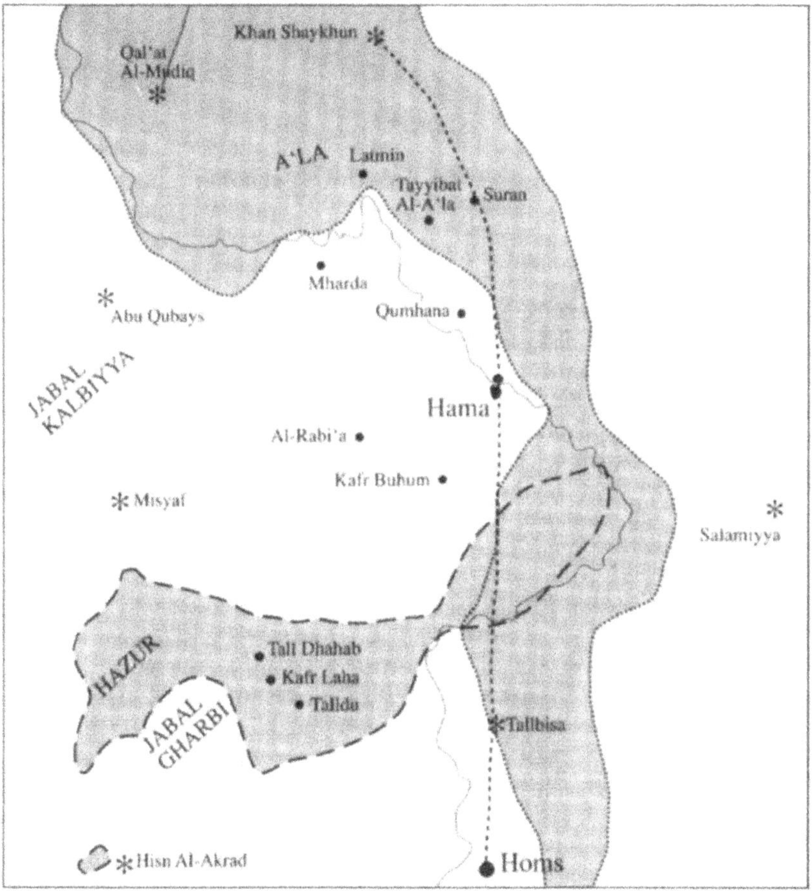

Map 3 The Hama area

1. Inland Syria; the fringes of cultivation

A frontier village of the eighteenth and nineteenth centuries

In 1866 Shâḥûd, son of Sulaymân, from the village of Murayj ad-Durr had his two cousins ʿAlî and Muḥaymid summoned to court in the nearby town of Hama. Shâḥûd claimed his share of the flock of the family. His grandfather Muḥammad had passed away some 28 years ago, when Shâḥûd was three years old. By then, his father Sulaymân had already died. His father had two brothers; one had left the village long ago, never to return; the other, ʿÎsâ, had taken care of the livestock of Shâḥûd's grandfather. Later, the two sons of ʿÎsâ inherited all, refusing Shâḥûd his legal share. The cousins denied the claim; their entire flock had been built through their own efforts. At the time of their grandfather's death, the governor of Hama, Faraj Aghâ, came to the village and extorted half of his sheep. Soon after, ʿAnaza beduin robbed what had remained, including all of his cows. Because Shâḥûd had not contributed to the upkeep of the new flock, they argued, he had not acquired any rights. The village headman, and those of two neighbouring villages, corroborated the account of the cousins. Subsequently, the judge dismissed Shâḥûd's charge.[1]

Murayj al-Durr – Little Pearl Valley – was one of the few villages situated on the east bank of the ʿÂṣî river. This village of farmers and herdsmen marked the transition from a sedentary to a nomadic lifestyle. From the perspective of the peasants the village was situated on the fringes of the precious cultivated land of inner Syria; from the viewpoint of the nomads, it was located in the highly valued periphery of the Syrian Desert. Murayj al-Durr and its twin village Îghûr on the opposite side of the river, were inhabited – at least in part – by Turcomans of the Jaliqliyya tribe, descendants of nomadic tribesmen who had

[1] SMH 60, p. 284, 7 Rajab 1283

been forced to settle some 140 years earlier. Over a dozen villages south of Hama had been populated by Turcomans at the time, presumably villages which had been deserted in the wake of rural and tribal unrest. On the southern fringes of their former migration cycles – which connected winter grazing on Syrian steppes to summer grazing on Anatolian highlands – the migrant herdsmen were turned into frontier peasants. In return for military services and because of the risk of nomadic attack, they paid fewer taxes than the other peasants in the region, whom they were to protect against nomads and their herds. Resistance to sedentarization lasted for some time, but at a certain point the Turcoman tribesmen started to appreciate settled life and even occupied a number of other prosperous, non-frontier villages, expelling their original inhabitants.

In the days of Shâḥûd's grandfather the military value of the sedentary Turcomans had declined. Murayj al-Durr now depended for trade and protection on the town of Hama and on beduin tribes. As frontier peasants, the villagers continued to receive favourable fiscal treatment, by now, perhaps, in reward for their endurance only. In years of dearth local authorities also provided the village with sowing-seed and draught animals in order to keep it productive.[2] The authorities, however, were not merely benevolent; the sowing-seed was added to the impending levies in kind and the value of the cows or oxen was added to the tax arrears. Governors who were in need of cash or kind and in need of an excuse, easily found one: the levying of tax-arrears. The proficient Faraj Aghâ, the governor of Hama whose alleged rapacity appears to have contributed to the miserable fate of Shâḥûd, indeed, had a reputation of being more demanding than others were.

Beduin formed another receiving party. Most villages, but in particular frontier villages, paid protection money to one or more tribes. At the time of Shâḥûd's birth various tribal sections of the ᶜAnaza beduin had only recently extended their range of migration towards the area of Hama. They clashed with each other, and with other tribes and villagers. In the process of – regularly violent – bargaining over water and grazing rights, legal ownership of herd and flock was uncertain. Villagers left their homes, some temporarily others for good. Normally, frontier villages survived or revived after a period of what was officially called 'inactivity'. Murayj al-Durr impoverished, but no records exist indicating that it was ever entirely

[2] SMH 43, p. 354, 20 Rabîᶜ I 1238

deserted after Turcomans had repopulated it. In times of relative prosperity new settlers came to village, not all of them Turcoman. Due to an influx of migrants, the village was about to loose its Turcoman identity at the time of Shâḥûd's appeal to the judge. New settlers were arriving from the coastal mountains, many of them Alawites, then called Nuṣayrîs. A decade later Circassian refugees from the Caucasus settled near the village. By then Murayj al-Durr was no longer located on the edge of sedentary Syria; new frontier villages had been established further to the east.

The ancient inland plains

The inland plains of Syria are contained by mountains to the west and deserts to the east and south. In Ottoman times – and before – the area in between the Euphrates River and the Hijaz was usually called Bilâd al-Shâm, the Land of Sham. Until today Shâm is the popular name of the city of Damascus. Mountains separate the plains from the Mediterranean coast. These mountains consist of a coastal range and an adjoining range stretching from southern Anatolia to the Gulf of Aqaba. A succession of valleys divides the two mountain ranges, among them the Ghâb, Biqa and Jordan valleys. Because of gorges, ravines and ridges the mountains were not easily passable, in particular those closer to the coast in what is today Lebanon and coastal Syria, but a number of depressions and passes served as corridors, connecting the ports of Latakia, Tripoli, Beirut, and Acre with the inland cities of Aleppo, Hama, Homs, Damascus, and Nablus.[3]

The inland cities served as 'desert ports'; they 'gave access to the desert and [. . . .] the lands beyond'.[4] Caravans embarked from these cities to Mosul and Baghdad in the east, and to Medina and Mecca in the south. Nomads called at these ports in order to trade their products for wheat, coffee, weaponry, and other necessities of life. The Syrian Desert was – at the time – not a 'typical' desert. This northern extension of the great Arabian desert comprised extensive tracts of steppe and pasture. The eastern and northern fringes received a fair amount of rain, while in the dryer zones some locations were well watered by springs and wells, or even by permanent rivers, in particular the Euphrates. (At present, these fringes and locations have been brought into cultivation.) The local name of the Syrian Desert is Bâdiyat al-Shâm; the word *bâdiya*

[3] Referred to as 'dry ports' by Doumani, *Rediscovering*, p. 23

[4] Petran, *Syria*, pp. 19–20

denoted wasteland, not necessarily scarcely vegetated arid land. To the east and, in particular, the south, water and vegetation became scarce, but even the dryer part of the Syrian Desert, the Hamad, supported nomadic life during winter.

Squeezed between the mountains and the desert lay nearly treeless but fertile plains. Here the long summers are hot and dry, and the short winters cold and moist. Some patches of forest and brushwood survived on hilly elevations and plane trees sometimes marked the location of wells and streams. Natural vegetation was dominated by perennial shrubs, thistles and grasses. Wheat and barley were sown in winter and ripened in spring. By June, the summer heat scorched most vegetation. To the south of Homs, a range of wind-eroded mountains runs eastwards to the oasis of Palmyra. These barren mountains separate the wider northern plains from the Damascus oasis and the plains and hills of the Hawran and the Balqa. Already sparse in most northern areas, rainfall diminishes quickly towards the south.

Surface water is rare. The only permanent rivers of some substance are the ᶜÂṣî and Barâdâ. The ᶜÂṣî River owes its name, the Rebel, to its unique flow in the wider region; contrary to the other rivers it flows from south to north. The river meanders through the Homs and Hama area. In the Ghâb and ᶜAmq valleys the water was soaked into long stretched marshlands, before it makes a sharp curve to water the coastal strip of Antioch. The Barâdâ River is much shorter, but not less important; it feeds the large oasis of Damascus. Most rivers and rivulets are fed by winter rains in the western mountains and many dry up, or nearly so, in summer, including the Golden River of Aleppo. The availability of surface water did only partly determine the distribution of population and the pattern of migration of pastoral nomads. Much of inland Syria was blessed with subterranean water feeding springs and wells. In some areas subterranean canals, *qanâwât*, were used to collect seepage-water from porous and soft rock. When no longer attended to, some old canals provide for sufficient water for some ponds and marshes, as for instance near the deserted town of Salamiyya (the Byzantine Salaminias) to the east of Hama.

The plains were dotted with the *khirba*s, the – often ancient – ruins of villages and towns. Salamiyya was one the larger ruins, some twenty kilometres to the east of Murayj al-Durr, in what was now steppeland. Together with two other ruined sites, Salamiyya had been a town of importance in the Byzantine period, when it was famous for its high quality of hard wheat. Nearby Andarîn (Androna) produced wines which were in high demand.[5] Salamiyya had been inhabited for some time in the eleventh and twelfth centuries when it served as a retreat for a community of dissident and militant Muslims, the Ismailis of the New Call (to God), known as the Assassins in European writing. More quietist heirs to this famed group settled again in this spot around 1850, pioneering the repopulation of numerous old settlements in the closing decades of Ottoman rule over inland Syria. But for much of the intervening centuries Salamiyya served as a stronghold of the dominant tribal group of the *ᶜarab* of the northern plains: the Mawâlî.

In the eyes of many Europeans who passed through the area in the Ottoman centuries the reminders of former agricultural splendour indicated that the present inhabitants and their rulers failed to fully appreciate the value of this old classical land. Most of the ruins dated back to pre-Islamic times, in particular to the late fifth and early sixth centuries, when irrigated farming spread rapidly.[6] The high density of settlements had been made possible by high investments in irrigation. In the closing decades of Byzantine rule over Syria, agriculture in inner Syria contracted. During the reign of the territorial heirs, the Umayyad caliphs of Damascus, the irrigation systems were well kept, often as dynastic holdings, but probably at the point of diminishing returns. With the end of the empire in Syria, in the middle of the eighth century, many irrigation works and settlements on the inland plains were abandoned.[7] The regional political and economic centre of gravity shifted eastwards, to Baghdad, and later to Cairo and eventually Istanbul. It seems that most rulers of Syria were confronted with the question of how to keep land in production, and all the more so because of the earlier capital intensive agricultural expansion.[8] The distribution of the population continued to fluctuate. In the wake of later wars or invasions, or of natural calamities like the plague, drought and locust, villages were evacuated but, it seems, only few for good. In times of crisis many peasants found refuge in fortified villages or in the towns and cities, but most returned to their land or went to alternative places when conditions improved. The Mongol invasions were strongly felt in Syria, but it is uncertain whether they caused the lasting depopulation of many settlements, except for the northern fringes of inland Syria, which acquired a strong pastoral profile in the late medieval period

[5] E. Litmann, *Zur Frage*

[6] A. Cameron, *Mediterranean*, pp. 176–182

[7] Hodgson, *Venture*, vol. 1, p. 286

[8] *Ibid*, vol. 2, p. 391

following the 'nomadization' of parts of Southern Anatolia and the Jazira region to the east of Aleppo.

Fluctuations in the climate may well have contributed to shifts in the use of land, but it appears that in the long run, in most of inland Syria no major changes occurred in the distribution of the sedentary population after Arab geographers produced their first major descriptions in the late Middle Ages, with the exception of the Euphrates area where, notwithstanding the presence of a large permanent river, sedentary farming continued to contract well into the Ottoman period. Notwithstanding their nomadic origins, the Ottomans depended, as did their predecessors, to a great extent on agricultural production and trade; from their point of view the nomadic groups constituted a problem; their mobility and social-political structure made them difficult to control.[9] The nomads were tied to local and regional economies, but instances of raids on villages or caravans or even pilgrims continued to rouse the concerns of the Ottoman authorities, as well as of villagers, traders, and pilgrims. The main concern of the Ottomans was to see to the production of sufficient supplies for the cities, the armies and the pilgrims, in particular wheat and barley of which Syria produced some of the best qualities. Given the mere size of cities like Aleppo and Damascus, local agricultural production appears to have been in matching with local demands for most of the time; there are no indications of regular imports of wheat and barley, albeit that in some years food stuffs were imported from Egypt or Anatolia in order to counter local shortages. Increase in demand following population growth in the Aleppo area in the sixteenth century brought about an extension of cultivation in the area.[10] Famine was not unknown to the area, but even in years of harvest failures, stock supplies of wheat often prevented mass starvation. In 1803 mice, heavy rains and severe cold caused crop failures, but the wheat from the Hawran to the south of Damascus prevented the prices from skyrocketing.[11] Crop failure, however, could prepare the way for epidemics. In times of diminishing agricultural production the diet of the rural population was very poor; villagers reaped some of the wheat before it had ripened and concealed it in caves.[12] In some years, starvation on a larger scale occurred, for instance

[9] See, on patterns of settlement in the Ottoman empire in general, *Economic*, vol. 1, pp. 155–178

[10] Venzke, *Question*

[11] Munayyir, *Durr*, p. 142

[12] Volney, *Voyage*, vol. 1, pp. 377–79

in 1787 and 1792; typically famine was followed by the plague.[13] Sequences of bad weather, locusts, famine, and the plague were common and sometimes culminated in severe subsistence crises; one of the worst years was 1827 when, after a year in which locusts devoured the standing crops and the rains failed to come, inland Syria was hit by one of the worst plagues in its history. Famine spread all over the area; *ᶜarab* tribesmen were driven out of the desert and besieged the town of Hama, being desperately in need of food.[14] Instances of plague and famine occurred well into the 1840s; in 1846 people from the interior came to the coastal towns in search of food.[15]

Town, village and tribe

The long history of close, but not always friendly, relations between the sedentary and migratory groups had shaped local culture in inland Syria. Well into the nineteenth century, a long belt, stretching from north to south, constituted a transitional zone in which cultivation, sometimes abruptly, gave way to natural pastures and steppes. The Sultanic road, the main caravan track connecting Anatolia with the holy cities of the Hijaz, ran through this fringe of sedentary Syria. From north to south, the main areas in which settled farming and migratory herding coexisted, were the plains of Aleppo and of Hama and Homs, and, passing the great oasis of Damascus, the plains and hills of the Hawran and the Balqa.

In this zone close relations existed between the urban and rural sedentary populations and migratory pastoralists. In the view of the sedentary and certainly the urban Syrians the migratory *ᶜarab* tribesmen formed the antipode of the *ḥaḍar*, the civilized world of the townsmen and villagers. As to the *ᶜarab*, they themselves felt equally distinct, especially from the peasants whose work they held in contempt. The antagonism between the sedentary and migratory populations reflected dissimilar and competing attitudes towards resources of the inland plains. Sedentary communities depended on considerable investments in both time and money for the maintenance of the arable fields, gardens and orchards, and of small and large irrigation works. The processing of

[13] Marcus, *Middle East*, pp. 128, 132; Munayyir, *Durr*, pp. 104–05

[14] Shihâb, *Lubnân*, pp. 784–88

[15] On plague in the 1840s, see FO, 195/170, 25 June 1841 (in Hama); 195/274, 1 May 1847. On the 1846 famine, see AE, Beyrouth, Carton 37, 11 April 1846

the crops, transport and market facilities required additional high investments. The world of the sedentary was reproduced by the human hand and had to be protected.

Nomadic pastoralism required comparatively little investment and the nomads hardly interfered with the habitat of the territories, which they frequented with their animals. Nonetheless, the world of the nomads was more fragile, depending as they did on the scarcer resources of the steppe and desert. The Syrian desert consisted largely of marginal land, and water resources were scattered. The rains were unevenly distributed over both time and locality. The nomads, therefore, depended strongly on intelligence and on the mobility of their socially strong group in order to make optimal use of vast desert space.[16] The *ᶜarab* constituted two main groups: the People the Sheep and the People of the Camel. The first reared sheep and goats and travelled over short distances, remaining close to villages for most of the year. Normally, family households possessed one or two camels or other pack animals for the transport of their belongings. The camel and horse breeders, the beduin proper, traversed the desert. Their migratory cycles linked far-away places deep in the desert to the skirts of the inland plains where they camped in summer. These highly mobile and armed beduin tribes constituted a force to be reckoned with. They were able to offer protection in return for payments to villagers, travellers, traders, but also to the People of the Sheep, who normally depended on locally dominant beduin tribes.

The popular antithesis between the sedentary and nomad could not hide their mutual dependence. A strong reciprocity existed between the two and, in particular, the inland cities depended strongly on trade with *ᶜarab* and trade through areas under their control. A high demand existed for the produce of the *ᶜarab* (animals for transport, meat, wool, skins, dairy products and alkali ashes) as well as for their services. They tended flocks and herds of well-to-do townsmen, transported merchandise, and offered protection and escort to traders and pilgrims along the desert tracks. The authorities, too, made use of these services, albeit not without some hesitation.[17] The *ᶜarab* largely produced for the sedentary population and exchanged their products and services for

[16] See, on the relation between nomadic and sedentary populations, Spooner, *Desert*; Nelson, *Desert*; Chaudhuri, *Asia*, pp. 263–65, 288–91; N. Lewis, *Nomads*, pp. 3–12; Doumani, *Rediscovering*, pp. 201–05; Ze'ev, *Ottoman Century* pp. 87–114.

[17] The first time the Ottomans hired *ᶜarab*, or, perhaps in their eyes were

foodstuffs, notably wheat, clothing, weaponry and household utilities. The towns harboured specialized marketplaces, which were frequented by *ᶜarab*. The more affluent tribesmen often owned houses in Damascus, Hama, or Aleppo.

The most important service the tribesmen could provide for villagers was protection in return for a yearly payment. This often happened through a locally dominant group of sheep rearing *ᶜarab*, who had acquired this right by paying their beduin overlords. Named *khuwwa*, 'brotherhood', this payment qualified the village for being a 'sister' of the receiving tribe and, subsequently, it became the object of the tribe's brotherly concerns. Although based on a clear inequality in the recourse to coercive means, this traditional contract between nomad and villager may well have been mutually beneficent in quiet times. The payment, however, was not a voluntary act and the degree of reciprocity varied. In times of tribal unrest the number of would-be brothers often increased; conversely, the position of the sister became less secure, now being claimed and protected by competing brothers. In times of tranquillity the *khuwwa* was, indeed, a payment in return for policing services. The sedentary clients were protected from harassment by other parties or even by individuals belonging to the receiving tribe. In times of tribal unrest the receiving tribe was often either unable or unwilling to provide protection, and competing parties could claim their share. Sometimes these claims contributed to the peasants' decision to evacuate a village. Other than through the chain of protection, villagers had few dealings with the beduin. This was because the cereal trade was dominated by the taxfarming officials, to whom the beduin came for their supplies of cereals. In the worst case scenario, the beduin appeared in a village as 'predatory horsemen'[18] during a lapse of order, be it tribal or provincial, or in years of severe weather conditions in the desert.

Villagers entertained close relations with the local sheep rearing *ᶜarab* and even though serious incidents involving *ᶜarab* and villagers are sometimes reported, the strong interdependence between the two favoured adjustments and reconciliation. Small *ᶜarab* encampments were to be found all over the area during the season. At harvest time, when the villagers were in need of farm hands, many *ᶜarab* pitched their tents near the villages or occupied vacant houses or nearby caves. After the

forced to buy them off, to safeguard the pilgrimage was in 1521, see Rafeq, *Administration*, p. 55

[18] Buckingham, *Travels*, p. 184

harvest had been gathered in, the sheep of the ᶜ*arab* grazed on the fields in exchange for a small fee. Often ᶜ*arab* tended the sheep, goats and cattle of villagers. The ᶜ*arab* who owned camels played a vital role in transporting the crop to the market. Some tribesmen lived in villages and were sometimes engaged in farming.

Most conflicts between sedentary and pastoralists concerned petty economic and social disputes, which reflected their close interaction. Not surprisingly, animals, either lost, stolen, sick, astray, or unpaid for, often played a role in these small local controversies. Typically, a villager would claim compensation for the damage done by a camel on the loose which had fed on his crop, or an ᶜ*arab* would claim compensation from a villager who had injured or even killed his camel by throwing stones at it or beating it in an effort to chase the animal away. ᶜ*Arab* specializing in local transport faced other risks. A lively trade existed in stolen pack animals. The purchase of a pack animal was anything but a secure investment and many lost their newly bought donkey, mule, horse or camel to thieves in the marketplace, to highwaymen, or to soldiers. Some faced lawsuits when people claimed the legal ownership of the animal before the court. Violent incidents in tranquil years were rare and usually connected to a controversy between individual tribesmen and villagers.[19]

Individual or small groups of ᶜ*arab* had the option to adopt a sedentary way of life in times when the prospects of farming were favourable; they returned to migratory herding when the economic situation in the villages deteriorated.[20] Peasants had a similar option and occasionally joined a tribe. In actual practice, the divide between sheep tenders and the peasants of villages on the edge of cultivation was far from sharp. People did cross the border, exchanging cereal cropping for sheep tending or the other way around, either seasonally or for longer periods. In times of invasions, war, and rebellion, a pastoral lifestyle often provided an alternative for the more vulnerable existence of the cereal-producing peasants.[21] A sequence of years with insufficient

[19] In a sample of sixty *diya* (blood money) cases dating from 1815 to 1890, only seven involved a village and ᶜ*arab* party, two of them relating to a feud between a family from the village of Baᶜrîn and the Turkî tribe. In all but one case it had been an ᶜ*arab* who had killed a villager and all the convicted ᶜ*arab* belonged to one of the more militant tribes.

[20] During the 1830s tribesmen repopulated some villages, but they deserted these villages in the early 1840s.

[21] See also Khoury, *State*, pp. 26 and 37

rainfall may have produced a similar move away from the dry farming of wheat and barley. Prolonged drought, however, occasionally forced nomadic tribesmen to feed their flocks and herds on village land. Tranquil years, of which there were more, induced some *ᶜarab* groups to take up farming, especially in areas to the south of Damascus and in the Jordan Valley.[22]

The conditions in the transitional zone must have confused outsiders, including non-local officials. Inhabited villages bordered to deserted ones, which offered seasonal sheltering for local *ᶜarab* tribes or for migrant Kurds and Turcomans, all of whom were often joined by the tent dwelling Gypsies in the northern parts.[23] Peasants regularly changed their homes for a vacant ancient house in a nearby deserted spot. Again other villagers pitched their tents near distant village land in order to guard the standing crop, often in the close vicinity of an old ruin. Small village communities were also engaged in a perpetual transhumance; with some regularity small groups left a village or hamlet and occupied a deserted settlement in the neighbourhood or elsewhere. Particularly in the stony Hawran to the south of Damascus ancient all-stone houses with solid walls and roofs were extant. After a few repairs, the dwellings served the limited needs of the wandering peasants. Given that most of the land was not held in private property, peasants had no strong bonds with the land.[24] Migratory farming, perhaps, enabled peasants optimal use of the scattered plots of fertile land in the stony and hilly terrain; they tilled the land for one or two years and moved on, allowing the plots to lie fallow. Typically, few orchards were found in this area. But some of the people involved were escaping from the authorities, burdened with tax arrears or other debts. Feuds with other villagers or violent encounters with *ᶜarab* may have forced others to take up this way of life, which offered survival at best. In some case people had to satisfy themselves with caves and caverns from which they tilled small patches of land and engaged in seasonal hunting and gathering. But for other village communities living in the vicinity of rich grazing land, pastoralism constituted an important or even primary source of income; villagers from the Nablus areas, for instance, descended with their livestock to the Jordan Valley.[25]

[22] Burckhardt, *Travels*, pp. 344–46
[23] Brown, *Travels*, pp. 202–03
[24] Burckhardt, *Travels*, pp. 221–22, Buckingham, *Travels*, pp. 168–69
[25] Doumani, *Rediscovering*, p. 30

In the north, less stone walls had survived. Ruins of castles, churches and other larger stone buildings were abundant, but the traditional walls of mud brick houses of the plains had eroded, forming numerous small elevations in the wide northern space. But again it was hard to tell the difference between wandering, tent dwelling peasants and a couple of ᶜ*arab* families camping in an old ruin. Moreover, the two regularly mixed. The first would probably have tended sheep and goats, whereas the latter often sowed some wheat for their own consumption. Kurdish and Turcoman tribesmen also found temporary residence in old ruins. Transhumance was also common in the few marsh areas of the north, like the Ghâb, where buffalo tending communities used portable huts. Others, in particular fishermen, lived in semi-permanent encampments near the marshes in the winter season, and escaped from the summer fevers to the adjacent mountains and hills.[26]

Syrian society was a mobile society, adjusted to travel and migrations for longer or shorter periods. This mobility found expression in the institute of the guesthouses, which were found in many places, offering lodging and food to every traveller. This public service enabled also the less privileged subjects of the sultan to look for (better) opportunities elsewhere, when needed.[27]

Policing the border

The need to maintain tranquillity along the major roads connecting Anatolia with Iraq, Syria and the Ottoman dominions beyond, as well as the protection of the cultivated areas bordering on the desert, played a crucial role in the administration of the Syrian provinces. The maintenance of security along the lines of communications through the deserts and borderland had always been problematic. The Ottomans, like their predecessors, followed two different, but complementary, sets of policies. On the one hand they encouraged the tribes to adopt a loyal attitude towards the state by giving them a stake in the orderly conduct of administration and trade. The dominant tribal factions were granted privileges, like the right to levy toll, and offered lucrative contracts for the provision of camels and horses and for the protection of caravans, convoys or even cultivated areas. Their sheikhs were treated with honour and received yearly payments. In return for these favours they

[26] Burckhardt, *Travels*, pp. 133–35
[27] *Ibid*, p. 160

policed the desert and the cultivated borderlands, and at times provided auxiliaries to support Ottoman military efforts.[28]

On the other hand, however, the maintenance of order was not, of course, entirely left to the tribal sheikhs and their para-military forces. In their efforts to come to an understanding with the powers of the *bâdiya* the authorities continued to use coercive methods as well. Along the major roads of communication imperial troops, the so-called *muḥâfiẓ*s, were stationed in fortified villages or traffic facilities, like caravansaries (*khân*) and water reservoirs. Local para-military forces from areas bordering on the steppe and desert were engaged in the protection of traffic and sedentary life in addition to the salaried soldiers. A more radical method to restrain the *ʿarab* tribes was the transfer of Turcoman tribes from Anatolia, settling and employing them as police force in strategic locations.

The functions of the various military or para-military groups included the restriction of tribal movements near or in the transitional zone. Deeper in the *bâdiya* the Ottomans had not been able to maintain garrisons or trading facilities and this deficiency constituted the principal source of the power and prosperity of the leading tribal confederation, the Mawâlî, which constituted a heterogeneous formation, comprising both sheep rearing pastoralists and horse and camel breeding nomads. They controlled an area stretching from Hama and Homs in the west to the oasis of Palmyra in the east and the Euphrates area in the north. The overland trade along the Silk Road leading from northern Iran to the important commercial centre of Aleppo, as well as the Baghdad-Damascus trade, passed through Mawâlî country.[29] The ruins of Salamiyya, situated in a well-watered valley some 40 kilometres to the southeast of Hama, served as one of their main strongholds. The Mawâlî domination of the desert and the adjacent areas dated back to the thirteenth century and their leading sheikh was traditionally titled *amîr al-bâdiya*, the Lord of the Desert. Prior to 1574 the Ottomans had shown considerable reluctance in acknowledging the privileged status of the Mawâlî and campaigned several times against them in order to gain

[28] See, for the Mawâlî and the history of the Syrian provinces in the sixteenth and seventeenth centuries; Abu Husayn, *Leaderships*; Bakhit, *Damascus*; Zakariyâ, *ʿAshâ'ir*, pp. 86–108; Lewis, *Nomads*, pp. 7–8; Masters, *Origins*, pp. 116–17

[29] The *amîr al-bâdiya* was entitled to make private arrangements with European factories for the protection of their goods, see Masters, *Origins*, p. 117

their full submission. They failed to do so and in 1574 the Ottoman authorities formally adopted the traditional policy of co-optation.

The arrangement between the Ottoman authorities and the Mawâlî chieftains was reasonably effective and certainly long-lived. The Mawâlî were occasionally involved in revolts or suspected of supporting unfriendly parties, but considering the some times confused political situation in the Syrian provinces, their endurance alone made them viable partners. In the early seventeenth century, when the Ottoman central authorities faced numerous revolts, the so-called *Celâli*, Syria witnessed the emergence of several rebellious groups, most notably the Kurdish Junbulâṭ clan of the Aleppo area. The Mawâlî chieftains appear to have kept a low profile during this period of upheaval, although internal struggles for power occasionally resulted in a violation of the agreement with the authorities.[30]

From the mid-seventeenth century onward the record of the Mawâlî as the police force of the desert became poorer and by the close of the century the old tribal order had collapsed. The precise causes of the erosion of Mawâlî power are unknown, but it is most likely to have been connected to changing patterns of tribal migrations and possibly to changing patterns in overland trade.[31]

Tribal shifts

The desert was divided into a number of tribal territories in which usually one tribal group dominated over others who were often its clients. Changes in the migratory patterns of the *ᶜarab* tribes of the deserts of Northern Arabia, Syria and Iraq went largely unnoticed as long as they did not result in tribal conflict. The gradual displacement of the *dâyira*, the annual cycle of migration of a given tribal group, would eventually be followed by conflict or agreement over the redistribution of the resources of a section of the *bâdiya*. In the course of the seventeenth century, or possibly earlier, sections of several tribes from northern Arabia expanded their migratory range to the north. These tribal shifts may have been generated by climatic changes or population pressure – the original causes are simply unknown – but in any case the 'nomadic' consideration that the herds needed the best possible grazing is most likely to have motivated the expansion. Tribesmen would

[30] Abu Husayn, *Leaderships*, pp. 52, 55, 121–22; Masters, *Origins*, p. 117

[31] See, for changing patterns of the overland trade, Masters, *Origins*, pp. 8–36.

normally not restrain their herds unless agreement or force compelled them to do so.[32] Undoubtedly, years of drought, but also of severe cold, did play a role in the tribal shifts. However, not only years of privation induced tribes to look for alternative pastures. Prosperity could also force a tribe to occupy additional pastures for their growing herds.[33]

The tribal groups from northern Arabia found no insurmountable resistance in the *bâdiya* of Syria and Iraq. By 1700 the Euphrates area was incorporated into the migratory cycle of some ᶜAnaza and Shammar tribes, the two main tribal groups of northern Arabia.[34] The pastures and water resources of the Syrian desert and steppe compared favourably with those of Arabia. Access to permanent rivers like the Euphrates, and later the ᶜÂṣî was certainly a great asset for any tribe.

The prospects of good grazing in the areas which had been dominated by the Mawâlî clans eventually generated more massive tribal shifts. Nearly all the large tribes of the ᶜAnaza confederation of northern Arabia were to change their migratory cycle. The inclusion of inland Syria into their migratory range coincided with a decline of agriculture in the transitional zone. The land under cultivation contracted and in several areas pastoralism increasingly competed with agriculture, sometimes replaced it. It is uncertain whether the tribal shifts constituted one of the original causes of the crisis of settled farming in the Syrian interior. Tribesmen were attracted to the transitional zone partly because land was going out of cultivation due to failing investments in agriculture and its protection. Moreover, a portion of the peasant population turned to pastoralism and associated with tribal groups.[35] However, once the tribal pressure in the desert increased and the position of the Mawâlî as the dominant group was violently questioned by newly arrived tribes, tribal warfare affected agriculture in the transitional zone. The Mawâlî were gradually pushed out of the heart of the desert to its outskirts and even

[32] See, for a general discussion on tribal migrations the works cited in note 6.

[33] In 1877, for example, the Ruwâla claimed pastures to the east of Hama for their flourishing herds at the expense of the Sibaᶜa, see Oppenheim, *Beduinen*, vol. 1, pp. 79–80

[34] See, Lewis, *Nomads*, p. 8; Masters, *Origins*, p. 118

[35] See, for example Seykali, *Land*, p. 406. Spooner (*Desert*, p. 247) argues that every peasant knows how to tend animals and that every pastoralist knows how to cultivate. This maybe an exaggeration, but it is true that individuals or groups can move back and forth between pastoralism and agriculture. The heterogeneous Mawâlî included groups which were largely stationary and occupied themselves with extensive agriculture as well as rearing sheep.

beyond. Thus, the desert expanded; agricultural land was increasingly used for pasturage.[36]

It is uncertain to what extent the arrival of ᶜAnaza groups accounted for the first period of tribal unrest in the late seventeenth and early eighteenth centuries, when several inland areas were severely affected. Sedentary groups participated in the widespread banditry and pillaging which plagued the areas of Damascus, Hama and Homs, and Aleppo. The situation in Syria was not dissimilar to the Celâli crisis of the early seventeenth century, except that the new crisis in Syria was more prolonged and that the Mawâlî fully participated, not even hesitating to ransack the marketplaces of Hama and Homs.

The disturbances and tribal pressure subsided in the course of the 1720s, but resurfaced in the second half of the eighteenth century. The tribal shifts acquired a more massive dimension, at times taking the form of tribal drifts, and profoundly changing the tribal map of the entire Fertile Crescent. The acceleration of the northward expansion of the ᶜAnaza was partly the result of natural calamities. The great drought of 1756, followed by extreme cold in winter, caused many tribes to look beyond their traditional pastures and may well have caused the acceleration of the tribal shift. Even the famed waterwheels of Hama came to a standstill due to the frost, a rare event.[37] Badly protected as they were against severe cold, many casualties occurred among the *ᶜarab*. Their flocks and herds were also badly affected.[38]

By the middle of the eighteenth century, it was most likely common knowledge in northern Arabia that the prospects for grazing in Syria were favourable. At any rate, it became a feasible option to drive the herds to the Syrian pastures in times of dearth. The sedentary population had been less aware of the shifting patterns of migration and was shocked by what was in their eyes a sudden arrival of thousands of ᶜAnaza tribesmen near their villages or towns in years of disaster. These massive flights were the most dramatic phenomenon of a long-stretched process.

Wahhâbî challenge

Changing political relations between the tribes of northern Arabia form another factor which is likely to have contributed to the migratory shifts.

[36] In this sense desert or *bâdiya* '. . . is economic rather than a geographical expression.' Lewis, *Nomads*, p. 24

[37] Budayrî, *Dimashq*, p. 193.

[38] Rafeq, *Province*, p. 215.

The formation of the Wahhâbî movement in the Najd in the mid-eighteenth century may have led to the political exclusion of several ᶜAnaza and other tribes. This puritan Islamic, Ḥanbalî, movement is named after its ideologue Muḥammad ibn ᶜAbd al-Wahhâb (1703–1792) who had engaged the support of an ᶜAnaza tribal group, lead by the Saᶜûd family of the desert town of Dirᶜiyya. From the late 1740s onwards this Wahhâbî-Saᶜûdî coalition slowly established its authority over the Najd and some adjacent areas. The movement showed a remarkable hostility against local religious traditions, in particular saint veneration, but through his political and military skills, Ibn Saᶜûd won over many tribes. The tribesmen were obliged to accept the Wahhâbî principles, but also shared in the spoils of war.

The Wahhâbî movement did not only challenge local tribal power and religious practice in the Najd. In the beginning of the nineteenth century, they openly challenged the ascendancy of the Ottoman sultan over the domains of Islam and, to the great embarrassment of the sultan, occupied the holy cities of Islam, Mecca and Medina, in 1803 and 1805 respectively. For nearly a decade the Ottoman sultan was unable to fulfil his sacred duty as Servant of the two Holy Shrines. Prior to this shocking event, Wahhâbî troops had brutally attacked the Shiite holy sites at Karbala in Iraq; they massacred many hundreds of inhabitants and pilgrims and carried off valuable booty from the shrines. According to a local chronicler, the booty enabled them to prepare for their assault on the Hijaz.[39] Syrian chronicles do not mention the massacre of Karbala, but the occupation of Mecca lead to a sudden awareness of the rebellious movement. For a decade the Wahhâbî presence determined provincial politics, including the tribal policies.

It is open to speculation whether there was a direct relation between the migration of several ᶜAnaza tribes and the rise of the Wahhâbî desert state. Most of these tribes were already in the process of expanding to the north and the rise of the Wahhâbî desert state may have quickened the expansion. There are no indications that the 'northern' ᶜAnaza tribes like the Wuld ᶜAlî, Ruwâla, Fadᶜân and ᶜAmârât (which migrated to Iraq) had been forced to leave their traditional pastures by political or military means. On the one hand, some may have felt increasingly uncomfortable with the strict rule of the Wahhâbîs and, at least partly, moved north in order to preserve

[39] Al-Basrî, *Mukhtaṣar*, p. 28

their independence.[40] On the other hand, ᶜAnaza tribes in the Najd played a dominant role in the Wahhâbî movement; the leading family of the movement, Saᶜûd, belonged to an ᶜAnaza faction, which was closely related to some of the tribes which moved north, like the Wuld ᶜAlî and the Ḥasana. What seems certain is that many tribes that were beyond the reach of Wahhâbî forces, were nonetheless strongly affected by the movement. They adopted, at least partly and temporarily, a number of its principles, like paying *zakâ* – the yearly tribute to the Wahhâbî chief Ibn Saᶜûd, performing regular prayers, and, at least among the sheikhs, abstaining from smoking.[41] Most of the northern ᶜAnaza tribes appear to have associated themselves voluntarily with the Wahhâbî movement, but they rarely joined Wahhâbî expeditions. However, they did offer logistical support for the largest Wahhâbî raids on the Damascus area in 1809 and 1810 '. . . and led Ibn Saoud to the most wealthy villages.'[42]

The arrival of ᶜAnaza tribes

The first ᶜAnaza tribe to arrive in the northern plains was the Ḥasana.[43] They made their presence felt in the course of the 1770s when they regularly clashed with the Mawâlî. The Mawâlî lost part of their traditional pastures and were driven with their animals to more marginal pastures or to partly cultivated areas, especially to the north of Hama, the Aᶜlâ and Zâwiya hills. In 1786 the Mawâlî revolted and attacked scores of villages all over the area, including the foothills of the Nuṣayrî Mountains. Untypically, they not only pillaged but also killed a large number of local strongmen and village sheikhs. In a counter-offensive, provincial troops slaughtered the Mawâlî.[44] The Mawâlî had irrevocably lost their prominent position in the *bâdiya* of Hama and Homs. The Ḥasana acquired the right to levy toll from caravans passing through the Palmyra area.

From the mid-1780s onwards the Ḥasana constituted the most powerful tribal group in the area to the east of Hama and Homs. Their leading

[40] The ᶜAnaza Sibaᶜa appear to have left for Syria in order to avoid the paying of excessive tribute to the Wahhâbîs, see Burckhardt, *Notes*, vol. 2, pp. 5–6

[41] *Ibid.*, pp. 58–61

[42] Burckhardt, *Ibid*, vol. 1, p. 4

[43] Zakariyâ *ᶜAshâ'ir*, p. 108. He believes that they first arrived in 1757. If so, this would have been after the severe winter of 1756/57.

[44] Kurd ᶜAlî, *Khiṭaṭ*, vol. 3, pp. 5–6

sheikh, Muḥannâ al-Fâḍil, acquired a nearly legendary status for his bravery. Some of the smaller tribes which had frequented the area for centuries became their clients. The Ḥasana collected protection money from these tribes, as well as from the villages which were situated in or close to their summer pastures, a time-honoured privilege, which, however, was rarely sanctioned by law. The authorities conceded to this practice with reluctance.[45] During some years the Ḥasana even collected *khuwwa* in villages along the road leading from Aleppo and to Latakia.[46]

The control of the Ḥasana over the Hama and Homs area was never complete[47] and was certainly short-lived compared to that of their Mawâlî predecessors. During the second decade of the nineteenth century they were confronted with the expansion of the ᶜAnaza tribe of the Fadᶜân and their dependants, the Sibaᶜa. The Fadᶜân was one of the two large ᶜAnaza tribes sections of which had extended their migratory range to the Syrian interior during the second half of the eighteenth century, the other being the Ruwâla. The latter were in the process of claiming the desert between Damascus and Palmyra as their summer pasture, while the Fadᶜân had moved further to north, to the plain of Aleppo.[48] Exactly when Fadᶜân tribesmen first arrived in or near the Hama area is not known, and the same is true for the Sibaᶜa. Burckhardt, when travelling from Hama to Palmyra in 1810, noticed that Bishr ᶜAnaza occupied all watering places.[49] In the spring of 1814 many more arrived from their traditional winter pastures in the Najd. Their massive arrival in the area to the east of the ᶜÂṣî river alarmed the locals and the authorities, who believed that the Wahhâbîs had expelled the tribes. When the authorities ordered the tribes to evacuate the area and return to the Najd, they refused to comply, claiming that they had suffered from a lack of grazing land.[50]

[45] A later court case reflects the ambivalent attitude of the authorities towards the raising of *khuwwa*. A man from the Ḥasana had gone to the village of Tallsikkîn in order to collect the *khuwwa* due to him and was killed by an officer while doing so. His uncle appealed to the court and, being the sole heir, received a compensation for the death of his cousin, see SMH 43, p. 53, 1 Dhû al-Ḥijja 1238

[46] Ghazzî, *Kitâb*, vol. 3, p. 250

[47] The Ḥasana were *sharqiyya* and in winter they took their herds far into the Syrian desert, possibly as far as northern Arabia

[48] Lewis, *Nomads*, pp. 8–12

[49] Burckhardt, *Notes*, vol. 1, p. 5

[50] Shihâb, *Lubnân*, pp. 607–8. Shihâb estimated that the Fadᶜân and Sibaᶜa

The ᶜAnaza tribes of the Ḥasana and Ruwâla, too, considered the arrival of the Fadᶜân on the northern plains a major menace to the fragile tribal relations in the wider area. They combined their forces with provincial and local troops in an attempt to relieve the area from the new arrivals. The effort was largely ineffective. The Fadᶜân retreated, only to return later and retaliate against their ᶜAnaza opponents, especially against the Ḥasana.[51]

The conflict of 1814 was linked to a division among the ᶜAnaza tribes. The Fadᶜân was a leading tribe of the Bishr ᶜAnaza, which included the Sibaᶜa, whereas both the Ruwâla and the Ḥasana belonged to the Muslim ᶜAnaza. A divide along kinship lines was, and still is, a common feature of tribal ideology in which good, or bad, qualities correlate with lineage, rather than with wealth, occupation, rite or locality. This dialectic ideology sanctioned rivalry and hostilities, but often fails to explain tribal animosity. In 1814 the Fadᶜân and Sibaᶜa may have been confirmed in their belief that the Ḥasana and Ruwâla were indeed cursed by descent, but only three years later Muslim and Bishr tribes combined their forces and attacked the local tribes of Hama. The attack followed the occupation by Egyptian troops of the Wahhâbî stronghold of Dirᶜiyya in the Najd, but the two events were not necessarily connected. Severe cold may have induced the ᶜAnaza tribes to occupy the pastures and to appropriate the flocks of the local tribes in order to satisfy their needs. Such tribal coalitions constituted a great menace to tribes which had been excluded. In 1817 the local tribes of Hama lost thousands of sheep to the raiders.[52] Tribal coalitions of this kind – the small, but militant local Turkî tribe also participated in the raids – were short-lived, but in given circumstances even the most hostile tribal groups could join forces.[53]

The pragmatism on the part of the tribes, which in a sense runs contrary to the tribal ideology, explains why the authorities, and others, were often confused about tribal alliances and hence did not always distinguish between the separate tribal groups and factions in their

who gathered in the area to the southeast of Hama, included 20,000 combatants, many of them on horseback. His estimates, however, are often highly inflated when describing dramatic events.

[51] *Ibid*

[52] Shihâb (*Lubnân*, pp. 636–38) writes that the combined ᶜAnaza forces carried off 45,000 sheep

[53] As, for instance, in the case of the attack on a Christian village in 1860. See n. 68, p. 36.

reports. This implies that reliable documentation about tribal structures and relations is scarce. Collective action by ᶜ*arab* tribes, be it in raids or invasions such as described above, suggested a greater sense of unity and concord than was actually the case. Burckhardt's comment on the Bishr ᶜAnaza illustrates the importance of these small, self-reliant groups: 'To detail all their minor branches or towayef [*tawâyif*], would be to give an index of all their families, every large family and their relations constituting a small tribe in itself.'[54]

The patterns of association in the *bâdiya* were not easily discernible and, consequently, the perception of the tribal shifts at the time was, and still is, confused. What is certain is that in the early decades of the nineteenth century a new tribal division of Syria became apparent, a division which was not to change radically for about a century. In the central and southern areas the Ruwâla and Wuld ᶜAlî established their domination over the other tribes, as well as over some cultivated areas bordering the desert, in particular the Hawran. In the north the Fadᶜân played a similar role and their clients, the Sibaᶜa, manifested themselves in the Hama area. The position of the Sibaᶜa was relatively insecure due to the nearness of the area dominated by the Ḥasana and Ruwâla.

The function of the ᶜAnaza tribes differed from that of their predecessors, the Mawâlî. Unlike the Mawâlî, the ᶜAnaza tribes constituted relatively homogeneous groups comprising mainly camel- and horse-breeding nomads, who travelled over great distances. Their high mobility was one of their assets, but it also implied that groups headed, almost in their totality, for the distant winter pastures in autumn and only returned in late spring, leaving the area to others for the months in between. The Fadᶜân, and even more so the Ruwâla and Wuld ᶜAlî, constituted a formidable force, but they did not control the desert fringe, as the much more complex tribal entity of the Mawâlî had once done. But it was not only the formation of the tribes and their migratory patterns which influenced the nature and degree of their control, but also their relation with the local tribes, the sedentary population and, of course, with the Ottoman administration.

The local tribes of Hama

In the early decades of the nineteenth century some 25 tribes were formally tied to the district of Hama, in the sense that they paid their taxes there. These tribes were known as the ᶜ*ashâyir al-dâyira*, the tribes

[54] Burckhardt (on the Bishr ᶜAnaza), *Notes*, vol. 1, p. 5

of the local migratory cycle. Their migratory cycles comprised the districts of Maᶜarra, Hama and Homs, as well as the Palmyra and Hamad desert region.[55] As a rule the local tribes, or rather sections of the tribes, pitched their tents in or near the cultivated areas in late spring and moved, often in the company of other tribes, eastward in autumn to spend the winter in the *bâdiya*. Some small *ᶜarab* units remained in or near the cultivated areas all year long. The local tribes comprised both predominantly sheep- and camel-rearing tribes, but the distinction between the two categories was not always clear-cut, because the first usually tended camels as well, and the latter sheep and goats. The sheep rearers, referred to as *raᶜiyya* or *shawâyâ*, did not move much further than the Jabal, an area some 70 kilometres to the southeast of Hama. The others may have taken their herds of camels as far as Palmyra and the Hamad.

Not all local tribes constituted independent units. Over half of the tribes were actually subsections of one of the larger tribes.[56] They often, but not always, moved jointly during the *mashâriq* and the *maghârib*, the migration to the east or to the west respectively, but dispersed themselves over the winter and summer pastures in smaller encampments. Some larger tribes had a number of client tribal units, which were either small tribes or sections of other tribes.

During the sixteenth and seventeenth centuries most, if not all, tribes of the *dâyira* of Hama either belonged to the Mawâlî or were subjected to the authority of this large federation. The Mawâlî comprised a large number of tribes, ranging from small semi-nomadic pastoralists to predominantly camel- and horse-breeders who followed extended migratory cycles. However, none of these tribes appear to have migrated over distances comparable to those covered by the tribes of northern

[55] See, for a list of the tribes, annex 1. Although these tribes were considered local, most of them were related to tribes that frequented other parts of Syria or much more remote areas, like Iraq, the Najd and even eastern Arabia.

[56] In the records of the Hama court no clear distinction in terminology is made between a tribe and a tribal subsection. Both are usually referred to as *ᶜashîra* or simply as *ᶜarab*. Sometimes the relation between the tribal units is given as follows: *ᶜarab* Abû Kamâl of the Ḥadîdiyyîn or *ᶜarab* al-ᶜUqaydât al-Daghâmisha. Occasional reference is made to *jamâᶜ*as, the following of a tribal sheikh. The more precise tribal designations like the *ᶜarab* al-Qamṣa belonging to the *ᶜashîrat* al-Sibaᶜa of the *jamâᶜat* Ibn Murshid (SMH 53, p. 257, 2 Shaᶜbân 1268), are rare.

Arabia, at least not during Ottoman times. The Mawâlî had been locals for centuries in the northern half of Syria.

By the late eighteenth century the Mawâlî had lost much of their former strength, but they still constituted the most powerful local tribal group. The Mawâlî tribes who frequented the Hama area belonged mostly to the Shamâlî, the Northern Mawâlî, which, as a result of earlier migratory shifts occupied pastures to the south of the Qiblî faction, the Southernners.[57] The core of the Shamâlî was formed by the Mashârifa, Banî ᶜIzz, and the Ṭûqân. The sheikh, or *amîr*, of the Mashârifa acted as *serkerder ᶜurbân* Hama, chief of the *ᶜarab* of Hama. In this capacity he received a yearly payment from the local government.[58] These payments were made in return for police duties, especially the protection of villages against tribal incursions. However, the Mawâlî had ceased to be a reliable police force and the continuation of the payments to their *amîr* until at least 1830, appears to have been rooted in tradition rather than efficiency.[59]

The other larger local tribes included the Banî Khâlid, the Nuᶜaym, and Bashâkim. The Banî Khâlid derived its name from the Muslim conqueror of Syria, Khâlid ibn al-Walîd, and claimed to have descended from tribes, which campaigned under his command. The leading family of the Banî Khâlid, Dandan, had a right to a share of the revenues of the extended properties of the Khâlid ibn al-Walîd shrine and mosque in Homs.[60] The number of tents of the Banî Khâlid may have exceeded 500 in the early nineteenth century, about half of which belonged to the Banî Khâlid proper and the remainder to various related tribes.[61] The Nuᶜaym, which included apart from the Nuᶜaym proper, five or six

[57] None of the Qiblî Mawâlî tribes fell under the authority of the Hama administration, but the leading Jamâjima tribe as well as the Khuṭabâ' were no strangers to Hama and the villages of the plain.

[58] It concerns a payment called *mâl muwassaṭa* SMH 43, p. 183, 7 Rabîᶜ I 1233; SMH 49, p. 329, 23 Rabîᶜ I 1245; Burckhardt, *Notes*, vol. 1, p. 10

[59] The governor of Aleppo also made payments to the *amîr* of the Mawâlî, see Burckhardt, *Notes*, p. 10. Burckhardt remarks that the *amîr* of the Mawâlî commanded a police force of 400 horsemen, but that they were '. . . reckoned treacherous and faithless.'

[60] Zakariyâ, *ᶜAshâ'ir*, p. 444; Oppenheim, *Beduinen*, vol. 1, p. 324. This claim to an honourable descent was refuted by the medieval geographer al-Qalqashandî. However, the Banî Khâlid do consider themselves to be Quraysh, *ibid*.

[61] Burckhardt (*Notes*, vol. 1, p. 13) estimated that the Banî Khâlid proper

associated tribes, may have constituted the largest tribe of the area.[62] The Bashâkim formed the largest client tribe of the Mawâlî.[63]

Most tribes mentioned above are known to have frequented the Hama area in the early Ottoman period or before.[64] Several tribes which were of importance around 1800 had moved to the area during approximately the previous half a century, notably the Ḥadîdiyyîn and the Turkî, whereas one other important tribe, the Fawâᶜira, was of recent local formation. The Ḥadîdiyyîn, or rather part of them, had been expulsed by the northward migration of the Fadᶜân from their traditional pastures in the Aleppo area. Little is certain about the history of the Ḥadîdiyyîn and the Turkî, except that after they had established themselves in the Hama area they belonged to the more militant tribes.[65] They were regularly involved in tribal clashes, especially after the Fadᶜân and Sibaᶜa had extended their migratory range to the Hama area. Both the Turkî and the Ḥadîdiyyîn entertained unfriendly relations with the Mawâlî. The Fawâᶜira comprised several breakaway factions of the Mawâlî and their clients.[66] The Fawâᶜira also figured among the more valiant tribes, but, unlike the Turkî and Ḥadîdiyyîn, they formally belonged to the category of local tribes and paid their taxes to the governor of Hama.

As a rule, the militancy of a tribe correlated with their mobility and the more militant tribes, or their leading sections, were predominantly camel- and horse-breeders. Occasionally the Ḥadîdiyyîn, Fawâᶜira and Mawâlî challenged the superiority of the Fadᶜân and Sibaᶜa, but conflicts among themselves were much more numerous. The reason for the relative high frequency of tribal incidents is most likely related to the

had 200 to 300 tents. Together with their subsections they paid almost a quarter of the total amount of the taxes resting upon the local tribes.

[62] They were assessed at more than 25 per cent of the fixed cash taxes payable by the *ᶜarab* tribes of Hama. It is unclear whether the Nuᶜaym of the adjacent Homs area, where they constituted the largest formation, were included in the assessment.

[63] Zakariyâ, *ᶜAshâ'ir*, p. 503; Oppenheim, *Beduinen*, vol. 1, 322–3

[64] Yûsuf, *Rîf*, p. 102

[65] Zakariyâ (*ᶜAshâ'ir*, p. 501–3), according to informant of the tribe, connects the small tribe of the Turkî to the ᶜAnaza tribesmen of the ᶜAmârât who migrated to the Euphrates area. Burckhardt (*Notes*, p. 11) believes that the Turkî are of Mawâlî extraction. He estimated the number of Ḥadîdiyyîn horsemen in the Hama area at 400, *ibid.*

[66] Several accounts of the origin of this tribe exist, but the Mawâlî and related tribes play a principal role in all of these, see Zakariyâ, *ᶜAshâ'ir*, p. 449

establishment of the primacy of the ᶜAnaza and the general insecurity which accompanied that process. The migratory cycles and grazing rights of most, if not all tribes were affected and new pastures and water rights had to be established and defended. The animosity between the Bishr ᶜAnaza (Fadᶜân and Sibaᶜa) and the Muslim ᶜAnaza (Wuld ᶜAlî, Ruwâla and Ḥasana) influenced the relations between the local tribes to some extent. The area in which the Ruwâla held sway was not far from the Hama area. The Ruwâla acted as the patron of the one tribe with which most, but not all, local tribes were regularly on bad terms, the Ḥasana. Tension between the Mawâlî and the Ḥasana remained high after their wars over the pastures of Hama and Homs in the late eighteenth century. The Fawâᶜira and the Turkî, too, entertained for a while hostile relations with the Ḥasana. The Mawâlî, Turkî and Fawâᶜira all enjoyed friendly relations with Bishr ᶜAnaza. A few other tribes, however, were usually on friendly terms with the Ḥasana, notably the Banî Khâlid and the Ḥadîdiyyîn and they were closer to the Muslim ᶜAnaza. It should be kept in mind, however, that numerous conflicts between the local tribes failed to be congruent with this tribal divide.[67]

The tribes and the local economy

The local tribes were well integrated into the local economy. Especially the villagers entertained close relations with the local *ᶜarab*, even though serious incidents involving *ᶜarab* and villagers are reported as late as the 1870s; in 1860, for example, in the wake of the massacre of Christians in Damascus, in which *ᶜarab* participated, the Christian village of Squlaybiyya to the west of Hama was attacked by a number of local tribes.[68] But violent incidents in more tranquil years were rare and usually related to a controversy between individual tribesmen and villagers.[69] The strong interdependence between the two favoured adjustments and reconciliation. Small *ᶜarab* encampments were to be found all over the Hama area during the season. In spring both *ᶜarab* and peasants flocked with their herds, horses and mules to the diminishing lake of Tarîmsa,

[67] The Fawâᶜira were for instance, renowned for their militancy and hostility against the Ḥasana and their allies. During the nineteenth century they were engaged in tribal wars against the Ruwâla, Ḥadîdiyyîn and Banî Khâlid, but also against the Mawâlî, Fadᶜân and Turkî, see Zakariyâ, *ᶜAshâ'ir*, p. 449.

[68] SMH 57, p. 15, 7 Rabîᶜ 1277

[69] See, n. 19, p. 23

which boasted the richest pasture.[70] At harvest time, when the villagers were in need of farm hands, many *ᶜarab* pitched their tents near the villages or occupied vacant houses or nearby caves. After the harvest had been gathered in, the sheep of the *ᶜarab* grazed on the fields in exchange for a small fee. Often *ᶜarab* tended the sheep, goats and cattle of villagers. The *ᶜarab* who owned camels played a vital role in transporting the crop to Hama or elsewhere. Individual tribesmen lived in villages and were sometimes engaged in farming. In the course of the nineteenth century the number of settled tribesmen increased sharply, but this process was only to gain, momentum during the second half of the century. Prior to that time individual or small groups of *ᶜarab* only adopted a sedentary way of life when the prospects of farming were favourable, which was hardly the case during the period under study, and they returned to the pastoral life when the economic situation in the villages deteriorated.

As in all the towns of the Syrian interior a number of *ᶜarab* lived in Hama, the main market for the produce of the local tribes. Out of the forty approximately crafts of the town, about a quarter depended on supplies of the tribes. Meat, wool and skins were traded on the Hama market and the locally produced *abâya*, a thick woollen cloak for which Hama was famous, may serve to exemplify the close-knit relations between the tribes and the town. Well-to-do locals owned considerable flocks of sheep that were taken care of by *ᶜarab*, as partners or otherwise, a practice referred to as *ghunûmiyya*. *ᶜArab* and inhabitants of the town were also frequently partners in transport, owning pack animals jointly. Contrary to peasant indebtedness, the magnitude of *ᶜarab* indebtedness to local moneylenders, or to the local treasury, appears to have been small.[71]

The relations between the ᶜAnaza and the sedentary were of a different nature. Contrary to the local tribes the ᶜAnaza, with the exception of the Ḥasana, entertained no close economic relations with the villages. The ᶜAnaza marketed their camels, horses, leather, and alkali ashes largely in town and depended for their demands of wheat, clothing,

[70] Burckhardt, *Travels*, p. 142

[71] Compared to the period after 1830 the court registers contain relatively few data on loans and debts involving a rural party, and nearly all of these concern indebted peasants. Some large debts were recorded for villages in areas which suffered far less from village desertion than others. After 1830 the magnitude of *ᶜarab* indebtedness remained small, whereas the peasants' indebtedness increased dramatically.

weaponry and utensils on the urban market.[72] The small community of the Sawâkhina, people originating from the oasis of Sukhna to the north of Palmyra, played an important role in the trade with the ᶜAnaza tribes. Hardly any details on the economic relations between the ᶜAnaza and the town are to be found in the court records of Hama.[73] This does not imply, of course, that no disputes arose, but rather that when disputes were settled, this happened outside the court.

The ᶜAnaza tribes and the administration

Whereas the local tribes made considerable contributions to the local treasury, the ᶜAnaza tribes usually did not pay taxes except, maybe, the smaller charges resting on the produce they sold on the urban markets. By the early nineteenth century the leading Mawâlî tribes, too, paid their taxes. The ᶜAnaza tribes received more or less regular payments in the form of *khuwwa* from villages and local tribes, but toll levies and governmental payments constituted superior sources of income for most of these tribes. Although their military strength and high mobility enabled the ᶜAnaza tribes to evade the authorities or even challenge them, they regularly entered into relations with the Ottoman authorities in order to acquire privileges and permissions. The Wuld ᶜAlî were the most privileged of all, receiving yearly payments, both from central and provincial government, for the safe passage of the pilgrimage convoy to Mecca and Medina. They also supplied huge numbers of camels to the governor of Damascus. The dominant sheikh of the Wuld ᶜAlî in the first decades of the nineteenth century, Dûḥî ibn Sâmir, was so closely associated with the governors of Damascus that he remained all year round within reach of Damascus. The less privileged Ruwâla depended on his mediation in order to receive permission to purchase cereals in the Damascus area. The Fadᶜân, Sibaᶜa and Ḥasana all imposed passage money on the caravan trade between Syria and Iraq.[74]

The attitude of the authorities towards the ᶜAnaza tribes varied, but,

[72] Occasionally ᶜAnaza tribesmen purchased some wheat in the villages, see SMH 49, p. 267, [Rabîᶜ II] 1245. Later in the century a part of the market in the Ḥâḍir quarter of Hama was called Bâzâr ᶜAnaza, see SMH 56, p. 514, 5 Dhû al-Qaᶜda 1277

[73] A description of the trade of the ᶜAnaza tribes with the towns is given by al-Ṣâyigh, *Muqtarab*, f. 9–10. He gives an example of a trader from Hama who made a large profit by barter trade with the tribes.

[74] Burckhardt, *Notes*, vol. 1, pp. 3–5

by and large, they failed to establish more balanced relations between the ᶜAnaza tribes and the sedentary groups. On the one hand, the authorities sought to appease the tribes by entering into negotiations with them, by offering them lucrative contracts for the supply of camels and horses or simply by paying them off. At times they tried to mobilize their support in subduing other tribes or unruly military groups.[75] On the other hand, they regularly confronted them militarily and tried to provoke controversies between rival factions within the tribes. Most important, however, was the refusal to grant their leadership an authority similar to that of the Mawâlî *amîr*s. No tribal leader of the Fadᶜân or Sibaᶜa ever acted as *amîr al-bâdiya*, Lord of the Desert, nor did they perform police tasks on a regular basis, as the Mawâlî had done and were still supposed to do. The highest honour that could befall a sheikh of the Fadᶜân was to be invested by the authorities with the position of 'Chief of the ᶜAnaza'.[76] This title was exclusively honorific and is unlikely to have impressed the Ruwâla and Wuld ᶜAlî. The most senior sheikh of the latter, al-Tayyâr, was called Abû al-ᶜAnaza, the Father of the ᶜAnaza. This customary title did not reflect the actual balance of power among the various sections of the Wuld ᶜAlî. Nonetheless, reciprocity in the relations between the tribes and the authorities was vital. In 1810 the Ruwâla, who had been less successful in claiming privileges, guided Wahhâbî warriors to the Hawran. This spectacular raid ended the career of a once promising governor.[77] Shortly thereafter the relations between the authorities and the Mawâlî suffered a heavy setback when the governor of Aleppo, with the help of some ᶜAnaza, had a Mawâlî chief killed.[78]

There are several reasons why the authorities hesitated between a policy of reconciliation and one of confrontation during the first decades of the nineteenth century. Firstly, the mood in the imperial centre, Istanbul, had changed. The central policy was increasingly directed against the, often self-proclaimed, privileges of local and provincial power groups, including tribal groups. Armed confrontations with the tribes could be motivated by this policy, but at times also by the bare

[75] See, for example, the conflict of 1815, p. 117–8. In 1811 the governor of Aleppo attempted to mobilize the support of the Fadᶜân in his conflicts with the Aleppine Janissaries who had entered into an alliance with the Mawâlî, see Bodman, *Factions*, pp. 11–12

[76] Lewis, *Nomads*, p. 26

[77] See p. 100–101

[78] Shihâb, *Lubnân*, p. 584

need to relieve an area from sudden and massive tribal invasions. The main handicap of the provincial authorities in the pursuit of the policy of confrontation was the inadequacy of the military. A second important reason that helps explain the inconsistency of the tribal policies of the time was the insecurity which prevailed in the *bâdiya*. A new tribal division was only becoming apparent and a new tribal order was in the making but not yet established. The authorities lacked sufficient intelligence on the relations between the different tribes or factions within a tribe and could easily offend one tribal group by entering into negotiations with, or bestowing some favours on another. Finally, traditional attitudes from the side of the authorities prevented the drafting of a more effective tribal policy. In the northern part of the *bâdiya*, the authorities in Aleppo and Hama continued to honour the old contract with the, now politically marginal, Mawâlî chief. In the Hawran similar time-honoured, but now outdated, policies remained of some importance; the chiefs of the once more formidable tribes of the Sardiyya and Fuḥayl were still contracted to assist in the collection of taxes and the protection of the area. However, not unlike the Mawâlî these two tribes no longer had the capacity to do so.[79]

It was only in the course of the 1830s that ᶜAnaza tribes were successfully contained by military force. In 1832 all of Syria was occupied by the armies of the governor of Egypt, the famed Muḥammad ᶜAlî Pasha, who had rebelled against his master, the sultan. The Egyptian administration even made an end to the collection of *khuwwa*. The containment of the ᶜAnaza tribes during the 1830s, however, was not the result of indigenous developments in the Syrian interior and depended to a great extent on continuous and massive, and therefore expensive, employment of regular troops. As soon as the Egyptian troops were withdrawn, the tribal pressure on the cultivated areas increased sharply. ᶜAnaza and other tribesmen recovered lost pastures and liberties. Instances of robbery increased swiftly.[80] In disregard of pledges by their sheikhs to the contrary, they started to collect *khuwwa* again.[81] Instances of tribal skirmishes over land close to the villages and towns recurred; in the late spring of 1842 ᶜAnaza and Ḥadîdiyyîn factions warred over the

[79] Burckhardt, *Notes*, vol. 1, pp. 9–10

[80] For instance, Fadᶜân and Sibaᶜa tribesmen carried off animals, as well as a boy, from the village of Mûrik to the north of Hama, SMH 51, pp. 408 and 413, 17 Rabîᶜ II 1257

[81] SMH 51, p. 413, 3 Jumâdâ I 1257

control of pastures near Hama and carried off the crops of numerous villages. It was believed that over 200 women and children drowned in the ᶜÂṣî river when they tried to escape from the tribesmen, suggesting that this was one of the larger tragedies which occurred in the long stretched process of tribal shifts.[82] In the winter of 1843–1844 ᶜAnaza raids forced large numbers of villagers to seek refuge in the province of Aleppo.[83] During much of 1844 and 1845 the ᶜAnaza virtually controlled the countryside of Hama and Homs. Only in the autumn of 1845 did Ottoman troops succeed in restoring order to a certain degree. Throughout the late 1840s and 1850s the impact of the shift continued to be felt in the Syrian interior. Only from the early 1860s onward did conditions become much more settled, a new order coming about in what had been the fringes of cultivation for many centuries. At a remarkable pace ancient farmland was brought under cultivation and new agricultural settlements mushroomed by the end of the century.[84]

[82] FO, 195/196, n. 48, Damascus, 25 June 1842

[83] F.O. 195/207, n. 1, Damascus, 13 January 1844.

[84] See, on this process, Lewis, *Nomads*

2. The office-households of the province

Occasional lapses of order are part of the history of the Syrian interior. In Ottoman times, order was equated with the reign of justice. The sultan and his servile, predominantly military, *askeri* class were to render justice and good governance in cooperation and close consultation with religious specialists, in particular, but not exclusively, of Sunni Islam.[1] The reign of justice was severely challenged around 1700 when disturbances were recorded over large areas. Social and political order was under severe pressure. The restoration of the Circle of Justice had become more problematic because the main traditional instrument for its maintenance, the military, seemingly failed to adhere to earlier standards and was unable to meet new military needs of an empire that was no longer expanding. The main military formations competed for privilege and economic gain, and regularly clashed with each other. As a result, disturbances spread to the cities as well, and Damascus especially became the scene of intense and, at times, violent competition among local and imperial janissaries for the decades to come.[2] Popular discontent about local and provincial officers and officials was widespread. Their inability to protect the sedentary population against the tribes was certainly not the sole cause for complaint. The permanence of intimidation and profiteering appeared to have undermined the foundations of local and provincial administration. Oppressive rule added much to the general misery around 1700. In the words of Muḥammad al-Makkî, a contemporary religious sheikh from the twin town of Hama, Homs: 'The people suffer from dearth, inconvenience and hardship, partly because of the *ʿarab*, partly because of the (local) rulers and the high prices.'[3]

[1] Ulema who served the Ottomans, in particular in the judicial services, were normally part of the *askeri* class.

[2] Barbir, *Ottoman*, pp. 89–97; Rafeq, *Province*, pp. 24–42

[3] Makkî, *Târîkh*, pp. 296–97; See also Nâbulsî, *Ḥaqîqa*, p. 46

The rise of the ᶜAẓm alliance

The effects of the widespread disturbances in the Syrian interior in the early decades of the eighteenth century were most worrying to the central authorities. Firstly, the *ḥajj*, the yearly pilgrimage to the holy shrines of Mecca and Medina, had become difficult to organize and to protect, and this undertaking was at the heart of the religious prestige of the sultan.[4] Secondly, the contraction of settled farming in some areas bordering on the Syrian Desert resulted in a decline of revenue. The analogous depopulation of villages along the major roads of communications, most notably the Sultanic Road, discouraged trade, because these villages normally furnished vital facilities such as lodging and provisioning. Confronted with the instability the Ottoman authorities sought to check nomadic groups by restricting their migratory movements and by stimulating or enforcing settlement along the major roads. By offering the more powerful tribes contracts for the protection of trade and traffic and the provisioning of the pilgrimage, or by buying them off, the authorities sought their cooperation in provincial affairs.

From the point of view of the state, another more important strategy to restore order was to encourage the formation of promising local and provincial military alliances. The area of Maᶜarra, Hama and Homs played a crucial role in the emergence of a particularly powerful alliance headed by members of the ᶜAẓm family.[5] The origin and early careers of members of the family have remained obscure. The stronghold of the ᶜAẓms was Maᶜarra, a small town situated on the Sultanic Road within a day's travel north of Hama. It is believed that the first member of the family to have a remarkable career, Ismâᶜîl Aghâ, was the son of a professional soldier, possibly a janissary. Apparently, janissaries or other military took advantage of the confused political situation in the Syrian provinces and took up residence in small and troubled places, aspiring to a local career.[6] In the chronicle of Muḥammad al-Makkî of Homs, which abounds in desperate comments on the state of insecurity in the larger area, Ismâᶜîl Aghâ, or Ibn al-ᶜAḍm as he was called,[7] suddenly

[4] In the period 1691–1724, the *ḥajj* convoy was attacked at least twelve times, see Barbir, *Ottoman*, pp. 200–01

[5] The history of this family has been dealt with in detail by Rafeq (*Province*). See also Shamir, *ᶜAzm*; Barbir, *Ottoman*; ᶜAẓm, *Usra*; Schatkowski Schilcher, *Families*

[6] Rafeq *Province*, pp. 90–92

[7] In the local vernacular the consonant Ẓ is usually pronounced as Ḍ. Chroniclers and scribes often followed the local vernacular in their writing.

appears in a setting of seemingly incessant raids, robberies, brutalities and clashes involving Mawâlî, Turcomans and *aghawât*, the local military. He is first mentioned in connection with the sending of wheat and barley to Homs in 1717. This was just after the town of Hama had been relieved from *ᶜarab* by the cavalry of the fortress village of Ḥasya, situated to the south of Homs. The *aghawât* of Ḥasya constituted the dominant military faction in the Homs area and their commanders often served as governors of the district.[8]

Aghawât based in unappealing places like Maᶜarra and Ḥasya played a major role in the slow pacification of the area in between Aleppo and Damascus. Pocock, passing through the area in the late 1730's, described Ḥasya as '. . . a miserable place, there being only the governor's house, a mosque and two or three houses enclosed within a wall adjoining to the khan and a few other houses built on hollow ground.' He found '. . . only some bad water in a pond.'[9] Most of the occupants of this and similar fortified villages were probably *muḥâfiẓ*s and their families, janissaries who occupied fortresses along the major lines of communication. Like Maᶜarra, Ḥasya was situated along the Sultanic Road, in an area which had suffered from village desertion. Such places were extremely vulnerable to tribal attacks, but apparently also served the military as the proper locations for entering into negotiations and alliances with tribal factions or, when necessary, to campaign against them. In some cases, the rural setting may have enabled commanders to control the marketing of cereals, in particular wheat and barley. Much of the crop was collected as taxes in kind by local troops and stored in granaries. These supplies were vital in times of crisis and constituted a great asset to career aspiring soldiers.

An alliance of some kind between the military of Maᶜarra in the north and those of Ḥasya to the south, appears to have existed. The latter also campaigned on several occasions in the Hama area against the Mawâlî. Support from Haṣya helps to explain the accomplishments of Ismâᶜîl Aghâ al-ᶜAẓm of Maᶜarra, who was appointed to the governorship of the districts of Maᶜarra, Hama and Homs in March 1719.[10] He was quick to

[8] Makkî, *Târîkh*, from p. 343 onwards

[9] Pococke, *Description*, vol. 2, pp. 139–40

[10] The victory of Ibrâhîm Aghâ, the commander of Homs over *ᶜarab* near Hama in 1717 appears to have paved the way for Ismâᶜîl Aghâ al-ᶜAẓm to proceed to the south. Ibrâhîm Aghâ served under Sulaymân Aghâ of Ḥasya, then governor of Homs. Some time later a certain ᶜAbdallâh Aghâ was sent from Homs to help protect Hama against the *ᶜarab*, see Makkî, *Târîkh*, pp. 343–56

establish a reputation as a resolute but just and even generous ruler, at least in the eyes of the chronicler. Muḥammad al-Makkî prayed for the well-being of a governor: 'May God give him strength and make him stand firm and prolong his rule and deliver him and his troops from his enemies, amen, amen, amen.'[11]

Ismâʿîl Aghâ al-ʿAẓm was appointed for a term of seven years to the governorship of Maʿarra, Hama and Homs on the condition that he would repopulate villages and restore public order. Soon after his appointment to Maʿarra, Hama and Homs Ismâʿîl sent wheat and barley to Damascus which was running short of food. In late 1719 he was ordered to settle the Turcomans.[12] He had only served about two years when he was promoted to Tripoli. The province of Tripoli occupied a marginal position in the provincial configuration of the wider region at the time. In the decades prior to the appointment of Ismâʿîl Aghâ in 1721 the *wâlî*, governor-general, of Tripoli appears to have exercised little authority over the Homs and Hama districts. On one occasion the governor of Tripoli told the dignitaries of Homs, who visited him in order to inform him about the desperate situation, that had not taken control of Homs, because he had understood that *ʿarab* he had ruined it, together with Hama.[13] Not all governors of Tripoli showed so little eagerness to intervene, but the handling of affairs in the area was largely left to the local military and to the governors of the two large inland cities: Aleppo and Damascus.

The remarkable career of a petty local officer like Ismâʿîl Aghâ al-ʿAẓm is, of course, not to be attributed solely to local alliances and to his personal qualifications, however remarkable these may have been. He received support from the governor of Aleppo, to which Maʿarra belonged, and after he had manifested himself as an able officer he received further backing.[14] Through the good offices of this influential pasha, Ismâʿîl Aghâ gained recognition in the capital. Imperial troops were sent to help him subject the insurgent tribes, both Mawâlî and Turcoman, and he and his family were granted privileges which ensured them sufficient funds. Thus Ismâʿîl Aghâ and his following were able to render services the Porte valued most: the protection of trade and traffic, including the convoys of pilgrims, the provisioning of the towns, the

[11] Makkî, *Târîkh*, p. 283

[12] *Ibid.*, pp. 371–77

[13] *Ibid.*, p. 334

[14] Occasionally Ibrâhîm Aghâ of Ḥasya was supported by the governor of Aleppo as well; see *Ibid.*, p. 126

protection of cultivated areas and the settlement of Turcoman tribes.[15] After having given proof of his abilities in the Hama-Homs area, he became an obvious candidate for higher office. When Ismâ^cîl Pasha al-^cAẓm was named governor of the province of Damascus in 1725, he was entrusted with the pacification of the entire Syrian interior, from Ma^carra in the north to the land east of the river Jordan in the south. His brother Sulaymân succeeded him in Tripoli and a son of his was entrusted with the administration of the district of Hama.

ᶜAẓm pre-eminence

Ismâᶜîl Aghâ had laid the foundation of what would be the strongest family-based power group of eighteenth-century Syria. His heirs were able guardians of his legacy and obtained numerous governorships. The first two generations of ᶜAẓm governors exerted a great influence over the affairs of the Syrian provinces of which Damascus was the most prominent. A large area was brought under a relatively effective provincial administration. Especially their success in the handling of the yearly pilgrimage to the holy shrines of Mecca and Medina in their capacity as commander of the pilgrimage (*amîr al-ḥajj*) contributed to their prestige as well as their wealth. Given its great religious relevance, the pilgrimage constituted the centrepiece of provincial administration in the region. Long-distance trade, in which the pilgrimage played an important role, was patronized by the ᶜAẓm governors.

The tribal policies of the ᶜAẓms are to be understood in the light of the all-important pilgrimage. They involved the large tribes of the area to the south of Damascus in the provisioning and protection of the pilgrimage. Some received sizeable payments, known as *ṣurra*, or *ṣarr*, in order to facilitate the passage of the convoy of pilgrims. Prior to the migration of the ᶜAnaza to southern Syria, the Sardiyya and Banî Ṣakhr tribes received these payments. The Sardiyya and Banî Ṣakhr dominated the steppes of southern Syria. When the ᶜAnaza Wuld ᶜAlî

[15] Ismâᶜîl Aghâ al-ᶜAẓm was appointed for a term of seven years to the governorship of Maᶜarra, Hama and Homs under the condition that he would repopulate villages and restore public order. Soon after his appointment to Maᶜarra, Hama and Homs Ismâᶜîl sent wheat and barley to Damascus which was running short of food. Late 1719 he was ordered to settle the Turcomans, see Makkî, *Târîkh*, pp. 371–37. He had only served about two years when he was promoted to Tripoli; see also Ibn Kannân, *Yawmiyyât*, 360–67

extended their range of migration to southern Syria they received payments as well, eventually at the expense of the Sardiyya.[16]

When established as governors, the ᶜAẓm family moved its country resort from Maᶜarra to Hama. The district of Hama had been granted as a *malikane*, a leasehold for life, to Ismâᶜîl al-ᶜAẓm prior to his appointment to Damascus; a privilege which remained for a long time in the family. Nominally part of the province of Tripoli, the Hama and Homs districts were integrated into the province of Damascus.[17] It was not unusual that the *malikane* of a district was given to high officials other than the governor of the province of which the district was part. A *malikane* did not always remain in the hands of an official for his lifetime. In practice it was often attached to certain offices and earmarked for the covering of specific expenditures. The *malikane* of Hama was increasingly given to the governors of Damascus in their capacity as commanders of the pilgrimage. Members of the ᶜAẓm family nearly monopolized the combined office of governor-general and *amîr al-ḥajj* between 1725 and 1757. The *mutasallim*, district governor, of Hama, Homs and Maᶜarra was normally recruited from the family or from their entourage. The fate of much of the Syrian interior had become entangled in that of the ᶜAẓm family and their clients.

Tribal pressure on the cultivated fringes diminished during the rule of the ᶜAẓms. The ᶜAẓms had been keen to protect the villages because the local wheat and barley production constituted a vital policy instrument. Their ability to provide the urban populations with wheat figured high among their qualifications for the office of provincial governor. For the Damascene population supplies of wheat from Hama became vital in times of shortage.[18] The area under cultivation in the district of Hama is most likely to have increased during the heyday of the ᶜAẓms, partly as a result of the settlement of several Turcoman tribes in fertile but, by then, largely deserted area to the south of the town of Hama. Some Turcoman tribes had resisted this policy of forced settlement, but others occupied villages that had not been assigned to them, chasing away the

[16] See Rafeq, pp. 70–71, 198 and 214–15; Oppenheim, *Beduinen*, vol. 1, 379–84; Zakariyâ, *ᶜAshâ'ir*, p. 417; Barbir (*Rule*, p. 143) erroneously includes the Banî Ṣakhr and Sardiyya into the ᶜAnaza confederation.

[17] The bond with Tripoli remained preserved in some regulations, for instance in the assessment and collection of the *jizya*, the capitation tax payable by Christians and Jews. It is uncertain whether the Hama district became formally attached to Damascus before 1832.

[18] See, for example, Budayrî, *Ḥawâdith*, pp. 74 and 157.

original inhabitants. Only by 1840 were these tribesmen resettled by Asʿad Bey al-ʿAẓm, then governor of Hama.[19] Pocock, who visited Hama in the late 1730s, described the town of Hama as flourishing because it was the only town in the wider area to which the *ʿarab* came for supplies. According to Pocock, the tribes had committed themselves to refrain from harassing caravans which headed for Hama.[20]

The coming to prominence of the ʿAẓm family has been interpreted in various ways; some considered it as a manifestation of localism, and subsequently as a sign of the waning power of the imperial centre, but more recently it has been argued that the ʿAẓms were instrumental to the policy makers in Istanbul.[21] The origin of the family is uncertain, as are their early careers; the military were highly mobile especially in unruly years. What is certain is that they succeeded in creating, with the support of superior authorities, a local base, militarily, politically and economically. Once the family was firmly established in Hama and Damascus, their interests became closely connected to these localities. However, it is also evident that the family's orientation remained 'Ottoman'. The ʿAẓms may have believed that they had acquired the right to the governorship of Damascus and the neighbouring provinces of Sidon and Tripoli, and they were certainly able to accumulate great wealth, but they considered themselves part of the Ottoman establishment. They were loyal servants of the sultan and refrained from defying his authority. Their dependence on the imperial centre became especially manifest in cases of a change of personnel in the small ruling elite of Istanbul. For instance, the ʿAẓm governors were dismissed and imprisoned collectively in 1730, after a *coup d'état* in Istanbul. They were pardoned and reinstalled in 1731. In 1757 the high financial needs of the new sultan, Mustafa, played a dominant role in the decision to execute the most successful of all ʿAẓm governors, Asʿad Pasha, who had served for an uninterrupted period of 14 years as governor of Damascus.[22] Whatever the exact motives were, the execution shocked

[19] Barbir, *Ottoman*, pp. 168–9. Already in the sixteenth century some of these villages had been populated by Turcomans, see Yûsuf, *Rîf*

[20] Pocock, *Description*, vol. 2, pp. 143–44

[21] See for an evaluation of the literature on the ʿAẓm family, Barbir, *Ottoman*, pp. 56–64. Barbir takes a 'centralist' position. See, for a critique on Barbir, Philipp, *Syrians*, pp. 6–7, who argues that the ʿAẓms were strongly inclined to local autonomy.

[22] Rafeq, *Province*, p. 221; see also on containment of provincial households, Göçek, *Rise*, pp. 60–65

the public at the time. It also helped to pave the way for the formation of an alternative centre of power.

The shift of provincial power

After the death of Asᶜad Pasha, the ᶜAẓms failed to preserve their nearly exclusive position as governors of Damascus and the provinces of Tripoli and Sidon. Damascus was losing its traditional dominant position in the region to Acre, capital of the province of Sidon. Several developments contributed to this provincial shift of power, in which a small and partly ruined port on the Mediterranean coast was to succeed a large inland city as the region's political centre. The ᶜAẓms and their main allies and clients were strongly rooted in the Syrian interior, but had difficulty in wielding their authority in coastal Syria and their hold was tenuous at best. They never succeeded to curb the power of a number of local strongmen in parts of Palestine and Lebanon. Although the members of the family or their associates usually occupied the governorship of the coastal provinces, the ᶜAẓms considered these to be secondary to the Syrian interior.[23] Local power groups made use of this, at times, indifferent attitude towards the western periphery of inner Syria. A veteran warlord of the Galilee, Ẓâhir al-ᶜUmar (d. 1775), even openly contested the authority of the ᶜAẓm governors, and succeeded in maintaining a firm hold on northern Palestine, including Acre. In recognition of his local pre-eminence, the central authorities granted him the governorship of Sidon, shortly after the death of Asᶜad Pasha.

The shift in provincial power from the interior to the coastal area was a complex process. The Ottoman context was one of an empire which found difficulty to adopt to the changing relations with European powers. A series of defeats in the late seventeenth century made an end to centuries of territorial expansion and with it the acquisition of war spoils

[23] That Tripoli had become a satellite province of Damascus is reflected by the function of its governor, who was of the rank of *mirmiran* and served as *başbuğ al-jarda*, the commander of the troops which brought provisions to the *ḥajj* convoy on their return from Mecca and Medina. The governor of Damascus was of the higher rank of *wâlî* and was, in his capacity as *amîr al-ḥajj* superior to the *başbuğ al-jarda*. During the tenure of Asᶜad Pasha, his younger brother Saᶜd al-Dîn usually served as *mirmiran* in Tripoli, see Budayrî, *Ḥawâdith*, p. 108. Later, during the reign of Muḥammad Pasha al-ᶜAẓm in Damascus (1771–72 and 1773–83) his sons Yûsuf Pasha and ᶜAbdallâh Pasha acted in this capacity, see *Rafeq*, p. 317

and the seizure of land, the inhabitants and their production of which could be taxed. Loss of revenue, combined with the impotence of the Ottoman armies was accompanied by internal tensions. However wounded the empire was, it not merely survived the crisis, but recovered to an extent. But disaster struck again; from the late 1760s onwards the Ottomans suffered heavy defeats against the Russians, followed by a new round of internal challenges to the power of the sultan. Apart from events in the Balkans, which due to the vicinity to the capital urged a more immediate response, developments in Egypt and the Hijaz were about to alarm the central authorities. During much of the Ottoman period the political history of Syria and that of Egypt had largely followed separate courses, but from the early 1770s an at times strong interrelation came about.[24] Two Egyptian rebellions impacted heavily on the Syrian provinces; first, in 1771 the Egyptian governor ʿAlî Bey sent his armies to Palestine and Damascus. The enterprise proved to be suicidal, but it paved the way for the most influential office-household in the Syrian provinces in the late eighteenth and early nineteenth centuries: that of Aḥmad Pasha, better known as Jazzâr Pasha. A far more dangerous challenge to the authority of the sultan, and even the continuation of Ottoman dynastic rule, followed half a century later when the famed governor of Egypt, Muḥammad ʿAlî Pasha's armies occupied Syria and much of Anatolia. Two other invasions contributed to the insecurity of life and property in the decades in between. In 1798 French forces invaded Egypt and, in 1799, Palestine. Napoleon's move had serious repercussions for the Syrian provinces, if only because of the massive employment of Ottoman troops that passed through Syria. Five years later the Ottomans were, again, taken by surprise; now by Wahhâbî forces that occupied the holy city of Mecca and, soon after, the city of the Prophet, Medina. The empire had become accustomed to challenges against its hold of territories in Europe, but the challenge against Ottoman sultanic authority over the Sacred Cities, al-Ḥaramayn, implied rejection to the legitimacy of sultanic rule from within the realm of Islam. As a result of the occupation of the Hijaz by Wahhâbîs, the pilgrimage became very problematic and was even suspended for a couple of years. Because the economy of Damascus was tied to the pilgrimage and because the prestige and income of its governor were derived from the provision and protection of the convoy of pilgrims, the

[24] See, on the Egyptian interference with Palestine, Crecelius, *Roots*, pp. 64–103 and *Egypt's*

situation in the city deteriorated. Damascene authorities were incapable of dealing with this severe threat to Ottoman prestige. The central authorities came to depend increasingly on the services of the governor of Egypt, Muḥammad ʿAlî Pasha, in their efforts to regain their hold on the Hijaz. In 1813 Egyptian troops restored Ottoman authority over the Holy Cities. The emergence of Egypt as a regional power under the governorship of Muḥammad ʿAlî Pasha had serious repercussions on the position of the Syrian provinces within the empire.

Changes in economic relations and the distribution of resources accompanied the shift of provincial power. The rise of Acre is often linked to the expansion of the European capitalist economies. The basic idea is that the economies of the region became more susceptible to fluctuations on the international market and that as a result of changing demands and trade patterns some areas, like the hinterland of Acre, witnessed crop specialization and became suppliers of raw material for the European, in this case mainly French, industries. This incorporation of cotton-growing territories into what is called the world economy, or the complex of economic relations dominated by the expanding European capitalist economies, facilitated the rise of local lords like Ẓâhir al-ʿUmar, who indeed profited greatly from the cotton trade.[25]

Whether the increase in cotton production in the hinterland of Acre was a decisive factor in the rise of Acre as a political centre, however, is questionable. It is true that cotton exports facilitated the rise of Ẓâhir al-ʿUmar, but, notwithstanding his endurance, he was not the man who made Acre the political point of gravity of Syrian provinces. The area and markets under his control did not compare to those controlled by the ʿAẓms. It was only in the 1770s, after the invasion by the troops of ʿAlî Bey of Egypt, that a non-local officer, the later Jazzâr Pasha, made Acre his stronghold; he changed the political geography of Syria. Jazzâr Pasha may have build on the economic achievements of Ẓâhir al-ʿUmar, but he established his domination in a period in which trade with Europe fell to an all time low. The major effect of the changes in trade

[25] See, for example, Philipp, *Syrians*, pp. 9–10; Barbir, *Ottoman*, p. 180. See on the theoretical approaches, Wallerstein, *World-system*, Wallerstein et al., *Incorporation*, and Kasaba, *Ottoman*. Note that a difference exists between the concepts of *the* world economy and *a* world economy. The first usually refers to the modern universal capitalist economy which is conceived as constituting a single market. A world economy refers to an economically autonomous geographical region which forms an organic unity, for instance the Ottoman empire, see Braudel, *Civilisation*, and Chaudhuri, *Asia*, pp. 382–87

and demand patterns on the Syrian provinces in the second half of the eighteenth century was the decline of its export-oriented trade. The foreign trade conducted in Aleppo, the grand old entrepot of the Silk Road, had been on the decline for some time, but decreased dramatically after 1750, the year in which the last caravan from Iran entered the town.[26] French trade with the coastal areas of Syria had shown a remarkable increase during the mid-eighteenth century, at the time when Ẓâhir al-ʿUmar reached the zenith of his long career. But in the course of the second half of the century, in particular after the Egyptian invasion and partly as a result of the policies of Jazzâr Pasha, who expelled the small French merchant community, a sharp decline of exports shipped from the Syrian ports occurred.[27] Trade had been dominated by French merchants and at the close of the century European trade with the coast came to a virtual standstill following Napoleon's invasion of Egypt and Palestine, and with it a period of nearly two centuries of relatively intensive commercial contacts between the coast and Europe came to a close. European trade with the Ottoman empire had shifted to the Aegean provinces. The economy of Damascus appears to have been less susceptible to fluctuations in demand and trade patterns, because its economy was tied to the pilgrimage.[28]

Acre figured as the political centre of Syria from the mid-1770s to the early 1830s, a period which coincided with a prolonged recession of trade with Europe. It was only from the 1830s onwards that trade relations between the Syrian coast and Europe intensified, mainly as a result of growing local demand for manufactured goods from Europe. The vessels calling at the Syrian ports were often unable to find return cargo, which indicates that the production of cash crops, such as cotton, was limited. The volume of the Syrian exports did increase from the 1830s onwards, but this did not necessarily reflect an increase in local output. Exports of cotton and wheat appear to have been largely diverted from the local to the European market before the mid-eighteenth century. Moreover, the purchases of Syrian wheat did not always relate to a growing European demand for the commodity as such, but to the need for ballast for the returning ships.[29]

Fluctuations in the local and regional trade may have been of greater importance for the shift of provincial power, but this trade is poorly

[26] Masters, *Origins*, pp. 30–33

[27] Owen, *Introduction*, p. 151

[28] Rafeq, *Province*, pp. 314–16 and Rafeq, *Qâfilat.*

[29] Owen, *Middle East*, p. 91; Schatkowski Schilcher, *Families*, pp. 36–7

documented.[30] However, both in quantity and value, trade with Europe compared bleakly with local and regional trade. The volume of this trade fluctuated considerably because it depended to a large extent on the irregular appearance of shortages in one area or the other following failing harvest or other calamities. War could create a sudden rise of demand. The French invasion of Egypt in 1798 was a case in point. Napoleon was forced to purchase provisions for his troops locally because the British fleet blockaded his lines of communication with France.

It is difficult to assess the effects of the tribal shifts of the second half of the eighteenth century on the balance of provincial power. Conditions in the countryside of Damascus, Aleppo, Hama and other towns of the interior had become problematic. Village desertion showed an increase in several areas of the interior, but tribal pressure was not the only cause of the agricultural crisis. The material base of the peasantry had been weakened by heavy taxation and they often lacked the means to make the necessary investments in seeds, ploughing animals and transport. Also in several areas which did not border on the desert the land under cultivation contracted, including some coastal areas, like parts of Palestine and the plain of Latakia.[31]

Peasants flocked to the larger cities, where it was easier to gain a livelihood. No large investments in time and money were needed to find an odd job in the urban fabric. Although the cities were the seat of the government, it was easier to evade the demands of the authorities in large urban centres like Aleppo or Damascus than in the villages. Rephrasing the words of the traveller William Brown: the authorities tax that what is most apparent, and most difficult to remove, and contrary to property in the countryside, property in the cities is often veiled from the eyes of the government.[32] The agricultural crisis undoubtedly affected the urban economy, but an increase in the trade with the tribes may have offered a compensation for the decrease in trade with the villages. Regional trade suffered from insecurity along the trade routes to

[30] There are no reasonably reliable figures at hand for the regional trade conducted in Damascus prior to the 1830s, i.e. prior to the Egyptian occupation of Syria. The economic policies of the Egyptian government stimulated European, mainly French and British, economic activity in Syria, see Reilly, *Merchants*, pp. 4–7

[31] Land desertion also occurred in the Acre area during the late eighteenth century, see Rafeq, *Province*, p. 314 and Philipp, *Social*, p. 101

[32] Brown, *Travels*, p. 399; see also Bodman, *Political*, p. 16

Baghdad and the Hijaz, but until the occupation of Mecca and Medina by the Wahhâbîs, the pilgrimage was conducted successfully, with the painful exceptions of the years 1757 and 1784 when beduin attacked and pillaged the convoy. Both instances resulted in disorder in Damascus. In general, the governors of Damascus serving in the second half of the eighteenth century were quick to adapt to the changing tribal division in the desert and steppeland to the south of their city and acknowledged the prominent position of the Wuld ᶜAlî of the ᶜAnaza.

Jazzâr Pasha and the province of Damascus

In the second half of the eighteenth century the imperial centre had difficulty containing provincial power groups. The Ottomans had irrevocably lost the initiative in Europe. As a result of the confusion in Istanbul following the military setbacks, power groups in several parts of the empire gained prominence, among them the *mamlûk* military of Egypt.[33] In the early 1770s the then governor of Egypt, ᶜAlî Bey, challenged Ottoman suzerainty and pursued expansionist policies. His troops invaded Palestine in 1771, as he allied himself with Ẓâhir al-ᶜUmar and even with the Russians. The *mamlûk* troops even captured the city of Damascus, but abandoned this conquest after ten days. The central authorities were only able to restore a degree of control over Egypt and Palestine by relying upon *mamlûk* officers who were reluctant to openly confront the Sultan.

The situation in the coastal areas of southern Syria remained unsettled until the late 1770s when a former *mamlûk* officer of ᶜAlî Bey, Aḥmad Pasha, a Bosnian nicknamed al-Jazzâr, the Butcher, for his blatant lack of compassion, restored order and started to impose his rigid rule.[34] From 1775 until his death in 1804, Jazzâr Pasha reshaped the political landscape of the Syrian provinces Sidon, Damascus and Tripoli. Jazzâr Pasha and his *mamlûk* household followed a policy of exclusion and appropriation. He excluded traditional intermediary groups in the administration of the taxes, raised tax rates and imposed extended monopolies on trade. Any show of discontent met with strong coercive action. He invested heavily in the military and turned Acre into the strongest fortified town of the Eastern Mediterranean. In 1799 Jazzâr Pasha became the hero of the day after Napoleon had occupied

[33] The term *mamlûk* refers to white male slave-soldiers of non-Arab extraction who were recruited by military commanders, as well as their descendants.

[34] See, on Jazzâr Pasha in Acre, Cohen, *Palestine*; Baytâr, *Ḥilyat*, pp. 127–32

Egypt and invaded Palestine, by withstanding the French assault on Acre, although the pasha's forces suffered heavy losses.[35]

In the years in which Jazzâr Pasha was establishing his rule firmly in the province of Sidon, the governorship of Damascus was in the hands of Muḥammad Pasha al-ᶜAẓm. During his long rule (1771–72 and 1773–83) Damascus witnessed tranquillity and relative prosperity, and Muḥammad Pasha was to be remembered as a just ruler and a charitable man. Muḥammad Pasha occupied himself with reconstruction works in Damascus and, of course, with the pilgrimage. Contrary to most of his predecessors, he was reluctant to interfere in the affairs of the Lebanon and northern Palestine and thus evaded a confrontation with Jazzâr Pasha, although relations between the two pashas were not friendly.[36]

After the death of Muḥammad Pasha al-ᶜAẓm, Jazzâr Pasha prepared himself for the governorship of Damascus. However, suspicious of his self-reliant position the Porte tried to limit the power of Jazzâr Pasha by refusing him a permanent hold on the province of Damascus, which was still considered the most prestigious governorship of the region. Jazzâr Pasha served four times as governor of Damascus, but being well aware of the reservations against him in the imperial centre, he continued to reside in his fortified town of Acre. The ᶜAẓm family profited from this containment policy, in the sense that the leading member of the family, ᶜAbdallâh Pasha, the son of Muḥammad Pasha, remained a candidate for the governorship of Damascus. ᶜAbdallâh Pasha al-ᶜAẓm served three times as governor of Damascus in the late eighteenth and early nineteenth centuries, but he was the last of the family to be granted this governorship. The province of Tripoli disintegrated and became a dependency of Acre. From the late 1790s to 1833 Tripoli was intermittently ruled, often to the dismay of the Porte, by Muṣṭafâ Aghâ Barbar, a protégé of Jazzâr Pasha and his heirs.[37]

The containment policy of the Porte implied that the governorship of Damascus started to change hands much more frequently after 1783. Until 1812 provincial rivals often alternated with each other and as a consequence provincial factionalism thrived.[38] The swift rotation of

[35] See, for an edict celebrating the event, SMH 46, p. 276, [Dhû al-Qaᶜda] 1213, see also Mannâᶜ, *Sijill.*

[36] Cohen, *Palestine*, pp. 64–66; Rafeq, *Province*, pp. 310–13. Prior to Damascus, Muḥammad Pasha served in Aleppo and left a favourable impression there as well, see Bodman, *Political*, pp. 103–04

[37] See Khûrî, *Barbar*

[38] See chapter 4

governors of Damascus persisted, but from 1812 onwards only non-locals were appointed.[39] This was a remarkable change of policy, since the governorship of Damascus had been dominated for nearly a century by locals, or by non-locals who had made their career in the province in the service of the ʿAẓms and, from the mid-1780s, by Jazzâr Pasha and his heir Sulaymân Pasha. This policy contrasted sharply with the attitude towards the province of Sidon which remained in the hands of the heirs of Jazzâr Pasha, first Sulaymân Pasha and then ʿAbdallâh Pasha, both former *mamlûk*s. The successful appointment of central candidates in the Syrian interior indicates that the power of local military households had eroded. To a lesser extent this was also true in the case of the *mamlûk* household of Acre which was denied access to the resources of the Syrian interior.

Early reform in the provinces

After the military disasters in Europe and the proliferation of power groups in the empire during the late eighteenth century, the need to reform some of the empire's main institutions became apparent, at least to some segments of the ruling Ottoman elite. Naturally, the function of the army became a point of dispute after the poor showing on the battlefields. Military reforms were initiated by Sultan Selim III, but two principal problems obstructed his policy of reform. Firstly, the opposition to fundamental changes of the military structures was strong, not only within the janissary corps. The second principal problem was the lack of adequate funding. Sultan Selim III and his supporters sought to increase the income of the central state by establishing a stricter control over the provincial resources and the allocation of the revenue. Even though the sultan succeeded in increasing the income of the central treasury, he largely depended on traditional measures to do so, like raising tax rates, confiscation and debasement of the currency. The more radical military reforms came to an end in 1807 when the traditional military, the janissaries, and other conservative forces, especially from the religious establishment, joined forces against Selim III and had him replaced by his cousin Mustafa II.[40]

[39] In that year Sulaymân Pasha Silahdar was appointed; he was a native of Hama, but made his career in Istanbul.

[40] Shaw, *Between*; Shaw, *History*, vol. 1, pp. 260–77; Findley, *Bureaucratic*, pp. 113–15; Zürcher, *Turkey*, pp. 23–31

The *coup d'état* did not meet with widespread approval in the provinces. A number of provincial governors even tried to intervene in favour of the reformers. In several parts of the empire, governors had built a strong base for their own personal rule and they hoped to achieve a more secure status. Governors who served in the European provinces had some reason to support military reforms, because they were within reach of enemy forces, but they hesitated to support Sultan Selim III, whose reforms were also directed against their self-reliant positions.[41]

A strong drive to alter the provincial administration came from some governors, who had been successful in exploiting the traditional system, for instance Jazzâr Pasha of Acre and Muḥammad ʿAlî Pasha of Egypt. They sought to monopolize the appropriation of the provincial surplus and to control prices. Their main targets were contending provincial factions, which were either subjected or eliminated. Jazzâr Pasha relied primarily on the enforcement of strict monopolies and the exclusion of middlemen in the fiscal system. Even though he was able to a considerable extent to enforce his will by use and threat of force, he failed to impose himself on various local societies for long; the hinterland of Acre, in particular the Nablus area and Mount Lebanon, remained difficult to control. Muḥammad ʿAlî Pasha was a more of a reformer when compared to Jazzâr Pasha who relied on the austere use of traditional instruments only. After Muḥammad ʿAlî Pasha had crushed the *mamlûk* factions in 1811, he radically changed the provincial administration by abolishing many of the privileges of officials and officers. In the rural areas tax farming was supplanted by a unified fiscal regime, and a direct link between the provincial state and the producers was established. In order to be able to implement the reforms and to discipline the population to cooperate, the proficiency of the bureaucracy and the armed forces had to be improved. The functions and attributions of officials and administrative bodies were carefully defined. Both the bureaucracy and the army were enlarged to the extent that the resources of the provinces were hardly adequate. In particular the investments in the building of the new standing (*niẓâm*) army constituted a heavy drain on the resources.

The economic policies of Muḥammad ʿAlî Pasha were largely motivated by the excessive needs of his armies and bureaucracy. It was especially in its economic policies that the new Egyptian regime differed

[41] Shaw, *History*, vol. 2, pp. 1–3

from other reformers in the empire. New crops, techniques and industries were introduced on a relatively large scale and to the direct benefit of the treasury or the army. Economic growth and military control constituted the basic principles of the administration of Muḥammad ʿAlî Pasha.[42]

The efforts of Muḥammad ʿAlî Pasha, in particular those in the military field, made a very strong impression on the sultan of the time, Mahmud II and those in his entourage who favoured reform.[43] They were apprehensive of the growing power of the governor of Egypt, but until the early 1830s Muḥammad ʿAlî Pasha did not openly challenge the authority of the sultan. On several occasions his military services to the sultan were most vital to preserve the prestige of the empire, notably in the containment of the Wahhâbî movement in the Hijaz and of the Greek revolt. Disputes about a proper compensation for these services, and the losses involved, eventually engendered an open confrontation between the sultan and his powerful servant. In November of 1831 Muḥammad ʿAlî Pasha directed his forces into Syria and his troops advanced far into Anatolia.

By that time Mahmud II had adopted some of the measures taken earlier by Muḥammad ʿAlî Pasha in his military reforms – the janissary corps was abolished in 1826 – and he was making preparations for the financial reorganization of the provinces. The occupation of Syria and parts of Anatolia by the armies of Muḥammad ʿAlî Pasha served as a strong impetus for the central authorities to formulate new policies, partly in order to mobilize foreign support for their cause. After he had annexed Syria to his realm, the position of Muḥammad ʿAlî Pasha radically changed. While his authority was confined to Egypt and the Hijaz, he had been relatively secure, although he was obsessed by possible moves against him on the part of the central authorities. In 1831, however, he not only challenged the supremacy of the sultan, but also alarmed the European powers who feared that Muḥammad ʿAlî Pasha's moves could lead to a swift disintegration of the empire and, subsequently, to the disturbance of the balance of power in Europe. When the sultan called in the assistance of the Russians to protect

[42] See, on Muḥammad ʿAlî Pasha, Fahmy, *All*; al-Sayyid Marsot, *Egypt*; Hunter, *Egypt*, pp. 9–32; Holt, *Egypt*, pp. 176–92; Lawson, *Social*

[43] See, on the reign of Mahmud II, E.I.2, vol. 6, pp. 58–61; Lewis, *Emergence*, pp. 74–103; Shaw, *Ottoman*, vol. 2, pp. 8–34; Zürcher, *Turkey*, pp.32–51

Istanbul from a possible Egyptian attack, Great Britain started to exert strong pressure on the contending parties to find a solution through negotiations. In the treaty of Kutahya of March 1833 the Syrian governorships were conceded to Muḥammad ʿAlî Pasha. The Ottoman sultan regarded this as a temporary concession to a rebel governor and the Egyptian hold on the area remained insecure. Contention between Cairo and Istanbul endured and Sultan Mahmud II was preparing for war for most of the time, feeling reassured by a growing concern for the future of the empire on the part of the British government. It was left to a new sultan, Abdülmecid (1839–1861), or rather to the Ottoman statesman Mustafa Reşid Pasha, and to the British, to settle the affair with Muḥammad ʿAlî Pasha. He and his family were offered the permanent governorship of Egypt. The pasha was reluctant to accept this, in his eyes, greatly unsatisfactory offer, but British naval forces finally forced the evacuation of the Egyptian army from Syria in 1841.

It is difficult to underestimate the magnitude of the changes which Muḥammad ʿAlî Pasha's regime brought about in Egypt. The pasha might have treasured the Ottoman character of his rule, but in fact Egyptianized the administration and conscripted the Egyptian peasantry in his armies. He thus laid the foundation of a nation state. Nominally, Egypt remained part of the Ottoman empire, but it continued to follow a separate course. The effects of Muḥammad ʿAlî Pasha's policies on the Syrian provinces and the empire at large are less clearly evident, except that they, unintentionally, speeded up the process of reform, as well as the incorporation of the empire into the new capitalist world order. The Egyptian regime encouraged production for its armies and for export, but its expansionist policies created conflict with the dominant capitalist power, Great Britain. The British government traded political support for the sultan for a free trade treaty with the entire Ottoman empire. Free trade had not been a favourite of Muḥammad ʿAli Pasha, who sought to protect Egypt's state-sponsored industries and to establish central state control over all the resources of his domain.

With the evacuation of the Egyptian troops in 1840 and 1841, the Syrian provinces witnessed the resurgence of some traditional practices and even formations, but they were not to last for long. The provincial and local mechanisms of power that had emerged in the eighteenth century did not survive the combined effects of reform and economic change. This did not imply that local participants in the administration and trade had difficulty to adapt to changing circumstances. A large number of families which had careers in the eighteenth and early nineteenth centuries succeeded in finding a new niche in the reforming state.

3. Local participation in the administration

The eighteenth century is known as the era of the ascendancy of local power groups in provincial administration. In the Syrian interior, as well as in the coastal areas, indigenous men and their families came to play a dominant role in the various branches of provincial administration. Locals had never been absent in provincial rule, but the extent of their participation and the seniority of some of the offices they occupied clearly differentiated this era from others. Two important qualifications, however, should be made. The first concerns the problematic delineation of 'being a local'. The military functions, which numbered many in the administration, were often performed by people of extra-local origins. A portion of them, including people occupying the most senior posts, created a strong local base and thus became part of local society. Military having a non-local background who failed to acquire a local rooting or made a career elsewhere may well have outnumbered those who 'went native'. Therefore, it seems appropriate to distinguish between at least three categories of participants in administration: innate locals, non-innate locals and non-locals. A second qualification concerns the uneven distribution of these three categories over the military and religious offices. In contrast with the military offices for which people from all three categories competed, the offices which required religious, legal and scribal training were primarily occupied by innate ulema and Christian and Jewish scribes and book-keepers. The military were more mobile and yielded greater powers, but they were also more vulnerable to changes in the political structures of the empire.

The *aᶜyân* and local administration

Already in the course of the seventeenth century local elements had gained access to the *askeri*, the imperial military ruling class. In Damascus the recruitment of locals for the janissary force gave rise to formation of the *yerli*, the local janissary corps juxtaposed to and often in competition with the imperial janissaries. The latter corps was known locally as *qabîqûl* or simply as *qûl*, and was sometimes referred to as *dawlat al-qalᶜa*, the 'state of citadel' as opposed to the *dawlat* Dimashq, the 'state of Damascus', an alternative designation for their local counterparts.[1] The participation of locals in the administration reached its height in the eighteenth century when they occupied leading positions, such as provincial and district governorships.

This strong local representation in the administration was embodied by the so-called *aᶜyân*. In its broadest definition the *aᶜyân* comprised the most prominent men of local society and they are often referred to as notables. During the eighteenth century the term acquired a more precise meaning, namely those among the notable members of local society who '. . . exercised political influence and were accorded official status.'[2] This restriction is of some importance because it excludes a large number of locals who may have been distinguished socially but who did not play any role of significance in local administration and politics. The nature of the relations with the administration is crucial in defining the composition of the *aᶜyân*. In the Balkans and western Anatolian provinces people could be formally appointed *aᶜyân* by gaining access to the local *dîwân*, or council.[3] This practice appears to have been applied in Damascus as well: 'As custom goes, the Pasha then installed the *aᶜyân* and the office-holders'.[4] Contrary to the Balkans and western Anatolia no *dîwân*s seem to have been established in the district (*sanjaq*) capitals of the Syrian provinces prior to the 1830s. In the provincial (vilayet) capitals like Aleppo and Damascus, however, the *dîwân* constituted an important consultative body.

The term *aᶜyân* occurs often in Syrian literary sources, but much less frequently in official documents. In both the literary and documentary sources the term is normally, but not always, used in its broad definition.[5] The ambiguity may partly explain the confusion about the

[1] *Qabîqûl* is a corruption of *kapikulu*. See Rafeq, *Forces*.

[2] E.I.2, vol. 1, p. 778.

[3] It concerns the position of *ayanlık*, which was formally abolished by imperial decree in 1786, but the degree was largely ignored in the provinces. Note that the term *aᶜyân* is also used as a singular. *Ibid*.; Inalcik, *Centralization*.

[4] Al-ᶜAbd, *Târîkh*, p. 82, see also pp. 36 and 48

[5] In the Hama records the word occurs frequently in the opening lines of edicts, but mostly in the term of address of the district governor. The word occurs with some regularity in combination with its near equivalent *wujûh*. In most edicts the addressees were first the district governor, or the judge, followed

composition and the function of the *aᶜyân* in some studies.[6] According to the strict definition of *aᶜyân* the Syrian provinces had only a small number of *aᶜyân* and, due to the absence of a *dîwân*, a district such as Hama none, but the habitual form of address to its *mutasallim* of a district (governor of *sanjaq*) was *zayd al-amâjid wa-l-aᶜyân*, the Cream of the Most Glorious and of the *Aᶜyân*. He was usually recruited from locally prominent military and the use of the term *aᶜyân* fits well into the general pattern.[7]

It is useful to broaden the concept of *aᶜyân* to a locally distinguished class which participated in the provincial government. Wealth may have constituted the prime criterion for inclusion in this class,[8] but this wealth was not necessarily inherited wealth, although part of it often was. The *aᶜyân* depended to a large degree on income derived from governmental sources or from sources to which access was gained through participation in the administration.[9] But the status of the *aᶜyân* did not merely depend on their wealth. The special nature of the relationship between *aᶜyân* and the state was acknowledged by the authorities and by local society, or at least part of it.

The differentiation within the class of *aᶜyân* depended on the degree of their dependence on power delegated to them by the state, on their dependency on local political resources, as well as on their ability to transfer their power and wealth to their heirs. The military-administrative class, here referred to as the (leading) *aghawât*, constituted the dominant segment of *aᶜyân* in much of Syria, including

by the religious dignitaries and the *baqiyat wujûh al-balda wa-aᶜyânuhâ*, the other dignitaries of the town and its *aᶜyân*. See for example, SMH 49, p. 15, 4 Rabîᶜ I 1240

[6] Barbir (*Ottoman*, pp. 65–89), for example, speaks of 'notables' and implicitly includes petty local ulema and religious students into this category, see also Marcus, *Middle East*, p. 351, note 2. Schatkowski Schilcher (*Families*) is unique in her use of the definition of estates (German *Stande*). Like Barbir she includes people who differed markedly in wealth, status and influence into one single category. However, she recognizes the limitations which she imposes upon our understanding of local society by dividing it into seven estates; she states that the political activities by leading members of the separate estates '. . . were only minimally based upon their position within their respective estates.'(p. 131)

[7] See, for example, SMH 43, p. 55, 13 Jumâdâ II 1220

[8] Inalcik, *Centralization*, pp. 40–41

[9] In the court records of Aleppo the use of the term *aᶜyân* was restricted, significantly, to tax farmers, see Marcus, *Middle East*, p. 349, note 78

Damascus and Hama. The second clearly discernible segment of *aʿyân* in the Syrian provinces comprises the religious-administrative class, the leading ulema. A third segment comprised merchants and bankers. The latter were often members of the urban Christian and Jewish communities. Merchants seem to have played a less prominent role in the Syrian provinces, in particular in the Hama area, when compared to the Balkans.[10] Most military and religious *aʿyân* were, however, deeply involved in trade and finance. It has been argued that the military, too, were far stronger in the Balkans during the late eighteenth century than their counterparts in Damascus and Aleppo.[11] However, in the case of Damascus there are clear indications, as will be shown later, that the leading local *aghawât* constituted the dominant political factor during most of the eighteenth and early nineteenth centuries.[12] Local political traditions or specific social or economic circumstances influenced the composition of the small privileged group of *aʿyân*, but with the exception of Aleppo *aghawât* had attained ascendancy. In Aleppo, the so-called *ashrâf*, a class claiming descent from the prophet Muḥammad and with this certain privileges, had acquired a structure which resembled to a certain degree that of the *yerliyya* of Damascus: both constituted a large and highly differentiated group, which lived in residential areas; they were involved in tax farming, trade and local industries; and their militia protected and promoted their interests.[13]

The sword: *aghawât* and beys of Hama

The *aghawât* constituted the backbone of the local administration in the Syrian interior. They included the officers of military or para-military formations, as well as people from a military background, but who occupied not strictly military administrative positions. The title of *aghâ*

[10] Merchants and bankers are defined by Hourani (*Ottoman*, p. 49) as the 'secular notables' and by Inalcik (*Centralization*, p. 37) as 'bourgeoisie', see also Göçek, *Rise*, pp. 60–65.

[11] Barbir, *Ottoman*, p. 71

[12] The prominence of the *aghawât* during the early nineteenth century is demonstrated by Shihâb (*Lubnân*, p. 667), who, when referring to the *akâbir*, grandees, of Damascus, mentions three individuals, all of them *aghawât*, namely ʿAnbar Aghâ al-Qazzâr, Darwîsh Aghâ ibn Jaʿfar Aghâ (see pp. 102, 105–108) and ʿAbd al-Ghanî Aghâ al-Shâmlî (see pp. 105, 123, 199)

[13] On the situation in Aleppo see Bodman, *Political*, pp. 79–102; Marcus, *Middle East*, pp. 61–62

was hereditary and did not necessarily refer to a person's occupation. An *aghâ* could be promoted to bey when called to higher office. Occasionally, the title of bey also became hereditary. This was, for example, the case with the ᶜAẓm family, all male members of which were referred to as bey in the early nineteenth century. The ability of the leading *aghawât* to maintain or mobilize armed, often irregular, units constituted their main asset. The *aghawât* were involved in administrating the locality predominantly as police and security officers, tax farmers and collectors. The governors of the provinces normally had a military background and the same was true of the district governors.

Around 1700 most or at least the more influential *aghawât* in the Hama and Homs area occupied the fortress villages of Ḥasya and Maᶜarra, but in the course of the eighteenth century a change in residence occurred. Following the example of the ᶜAẓms they increasingly took up residence in the town of Hama and, albeit less frequently, in Homs. A number of households of *aghawât* remained rurally based, the main fortress villages being Ḥiṣn al-Akrâd along the road to Tripoli and Khân Shaykhûn and Tallbîsa on the Sultanic Road.

The differentiation within the body of *aghawât* of the area was pronounced and it is difficult to see them as a single social formation. The differentiation largely followed the magnitude of the wealth and political capital generated by office holding as well as the degree of success in transferring this professionally generated capital to one's heirs. The more prominent households of *aghawât* in the Hama area were formed around particular families. There was no tradition of *mamlûk* households. The leading *aghawât* of these families recruited soldiers and officers, *atbâᶜ*, from various areas and occasionally acquired an adolescent *mamlûk* who received his training in the family household. In order to preserve or bolster the family's position, young male members of the family, either sons, teenaged brothers, nephews or cousins were prepared for office.

Notwithstanding the difficulties they faced on the provincial level from the mid-eighteenth century onward, the ᶜAẓm family remained the leading *aghawât* household of Hama for many decades to come. No other household compared to theirs in terms of wealth and status. The ᶜAẓms were the only local family which included a fair number of pashas. The governor of the district of Hama was, until the early 1820s, mostly, but not always, recruited from the family or from their associates. Foremost among the latter was the Jundî family from Maᶜarra, the original stronghold of the ᶜAẓm family. The careers of *aghawât* of the

Jundî family were closely related to the rise of the ʿAẓms to provincial prominence. They acquired a strong foothold in the neighbouring district of Homs. Three *aghawât* of the Jundî family acted as governor of Hama around 1800, one of which a former commander of the fortress village of Tallbîsa. The Jundîs ceased to play a role of significance in Hama after the 1810s, but retained their position as dominant *aghawât* of Maʿarra and Homs for much of the nineteenth century.[14]

Not all *aghawât* had acquired strong local roots; a number of them settled in the district permanently around 1800, but at times the governor (*wâlî*) of Damascus appointed *aghawât* from Damascus or elsewhere to serve in the Hama district, mostly for shorter periods. The area also served as a place of refuge for dissatisfied officers and their following, who were sometimes able to establish themselves as military households. The most important household of such a strongman in the Hama area was that of Mullâ Ismâʿîl, who resided in or near Hama for about twenty years.[15]

Apart from the ʿAẓm family, the *aghawât* families of Hama comprised the Jijaklî, Barâzî, Turkumânî and Ṭayfûr families, most of whom gained prominence during the first decades of the nineteenth century. They had first arrived in the area in the closing decades of the eighteenth century. Little is known about the early careers of these *aghawât*, but their arrival coincided with the decline of the power of the ʿAẓms on the provincial level, although some of them may have started off as their clients.

The majority of *aghawât*, especially those residing in villages and those in the service of the leading *aghawât*, lacked a family name, which makes it difficult to trace their origin and career patterns.[16] Apart from the fortress villages, rural *aghawât* mainly lived in the Turcoman villages to the south of Hama, reflecting the originally military function of the settled Turcoman tribes. The *aghawât* of the tribally organized sedentary Turcoman were headed by the *bey-i büyük*.[17]

[14] See, for the Jundî family and their relation with the ʿAẓms and Hama; Jundî, *Târîkh*, vol. 2, pp. 334–39.

[15] Military strongmen were generally referred to as *ḥukkâm* (sing. *ḥâkim*), which was not a formal title. On Mullâ Ismâʿîl, see p. 115–9

[16] The lists of *muḥâfiẓ*s (janissaries manning the fortresses of the area) are typical in this respect; only few *aghawât*, let alone soldiers, were recorded with what may be considered a family name, SMH 46, pp. 193–97, [Rajab] 1208

[17] SMH 46, p. 202, 1 Rajab 1209

Evidently, only few of the *aghawât* families of Hama could be considered *awlâd al-ᶜarab*, of Arab ancestry. This was true for both the rural *aghawât* and their more distinguished urban counterparts. The origin of the ᶜAẓms was, and still is, disputed.[18] Some believe that they belonged to *awlâd al-ᶜarab*, but others deduct from (weak) evidence that the second *aghâ* of this family to become governor of the province of Damascus did not speak Arabic.[19] The origins of the families are of interest because they shed light on recruitment and career patterns of officers in the Syrian provinces, many of whom originated from Anatolia. The ᶜAẓm family may have originated from the Konya area, the Jijaklîs were of Turkish origin, whereas both the Barâzîs and Ṭayfûrs were Kurds. Within two or three generations they were considered to be locals. Most eventually adopted Arabic as their language, but rural *aghawât* belonging to Turcoman or Kurdish tribes often preserved, like their kin, their mother tongue. The adoption of a family name by Turkish and Kurdish *aghawât* may be considered a sign of integration into the predominantly Arabic local culture as well. The more renowned urban *aghawât* often married into prominent local families of undisputed Arab ancestry.

The only segment of people of Arab ancestry with a distinct military tradition were the *ᶜarab*. Service in one of the military formations often attracted tribesmen to the towns,[20] but none of the more prominent *aghawât* families of the town of Hama seem to have been of *ᶜarab* ancestry. Some sheikhs of the Mawâlî, and possibly of a few other tribes, however, were referred to as *aghâ*. These *ᶜarab aghawât* may have belonged to retinue of the *serkerder*, the leading Mawâlî sheikh. Muḥammad al-Khurfân was the most distinguished Mawâlî commander of the time. One of the leading *aghawât* families of Damascus, the Shâmlî family, was of *ᶜarab* extraction. Two members of this family served as governor of Hama in the late 1820s and early 1830s.[21] In the course of the second half of the nineteenth century it also became a policy to bestow on many *ᶜarab* sheikhs, also from the lesser tribes, honorary titles, such as bey, and even pasha.

[18] See, for a discussion of the origins of the ᶜAẓm family Rafeq, *Province*, pp. 85–91 and Barbir, *Ottoman*, pp. 56–64

[19] Shamir, 'ᶜAẓm', p. 71, n. 2

[20] The same was true for Kurds and Turcomans, see Masters, *Origins*, p. 46.

[21] Namely ᶜAbd al-Ghanî Aghâ and Rashîd Aghâ al-Shâmlî (also spelled Shûmlî). See also Schatkowski Schilcher, *Families*, p. 146

The ranks of *aghawât* were largely closed to non-Muslims. Non-Muslim, or rather non-Sunnite, private para-military forces did exist in the Nuṣayrî Mountains and Lebanon. Their commanders were local strongmen, who often acted as tax farmers. In the Nuṣayrî mountains these strongmen were referred to as *mîr*, in the case of the Ismailis, and *muqaddam*, in the case of the Nuṣayrîs. Some Nuṣayrî *muqaddams* could mobilize quite formidable forces and the leading *muqaddam* of the Matâwira, the dominant Nuṣayrî kinship group of Jabal Kalbiyya, claimed the title of bey.[22]

The pen; ulema and *muᶜallims* of Hama

Most offices in the district of Hama which required religious learning and scribal training were occupied by local people. The Kaylânî family had a near monopoly of the major judiciary and religious offices. The family traced its origin to ᶜAbd al-Qâdir al-Jîlânî, the celebrated late medieval mystic, whose followers organized themselves in the Qâdiriyya order. The first Kaylânîs arrived in Hama in the fourteenth century from Baghdad. This family of mystics and ulema, both Shâfiᶜî and Ḥanafî schools of law, was highly regarded.[23] In the late eighteenth and early nineteenth century the *qâḍî* (judge), the chief *muftî* (jurisconsult), the *naqîb al-ashrâf* (head of the local descendants of the prophet), as well as the *shaykh al-sajjâda al-Qâdiriyya* (head of the Qâdiriyya order) was nearly always selected from this family. The family headquarters, the Kaylâniyya, built on the bank of the ᶜÂṣî river, contained a mosque and a convent. Apart from their ancestor ᶜAbd al-Qâdir, some members of the family had also acquired sainthood and their shrines were frequented by locals.

The other highly esteemed learned family of Hama was the ᶜAlwânî family, descendants of the locally much venerated mystic and scholar

[22] It concerns ᶜUthmân Khayr Bey who, by the late 1820s had extended his influence over much of the southern part of the ᶜAlawî Chain, including part of the *muqâṭaᶜa* of Ḥiṣn al-Akrâd, see SMH 49, p. 570, 5 Dhû al-Ḥijja 1249 (In a rare exercise of Islamic discipline the scribe of the court spelled his name as ᶜUṣmân, but he apparently had no objection to the use of the title bey by the Nuṣayrî chief). His son Ismâᶜîl and grandson Hawâsh played important role in the politics of the area in the mid nineteenth century.

[23] Nâbulsî, *Ḥaqîqa*, pp. 49–50; Pocock, *Description*, vol. 2, p. 144

sheikh ᶜAlwân ibn ᶜÂṭiya (d.1527).[24] Their ancestor occupied the seat of *muftî*, but the ᶜAlwânîs, mostly adhering to the Shâfiᶜî rite, were later excluded from the main offices. They derived their strength mainly from a genuine Islamic institution; the *waqf*, public or private holdings in mortmain, usually referred to as religious or family foundations. The ᶜAlwânîs were a family of *waqf* holders and *mutawallî*s, administrators of *waqf* properties. The *waqf* properties of the family included shops, land and mills.[25] Like the Kaylânî family, the ᶜAlwânîs were considered *ashrâf*, descendants of the Prophet.

Apart from Kaylânîs and ᶜAlwânîs, the Ḥarîrî family may be counted among the local ulema families of importance, although some sheikhs of this family only established themselves later in the nineteenth century as leading ulema and started to compete with the Kaylânîs for the major religious offices. In the early nineteenth century, the sheikhs of a given family administered the *waqf*s that were attached to the shrines of their ancestors.[26] Like other cities, Hama numbered numerous, often crumbling, shrines, mosques and meeting places of various mystical orders, and consequently many petty sheikhs, not all of whom necessarily belonged to sheikh families.[27]

The 'secular' scribes were largely recruited from the Greek-orthodox community of Hama or nearby Homs, among them the Baḥrî family, members of which made careers in several provinces, including Egypt.[28] Like the ulema they belonged to the traditional literati and they were referred to as *muᶜallim*. The prominent role Christians played in the money market also figured among their qualifications. Both the office of *kâtib sancak*, the scribe of the district, and the *kâtib khazîna*, the scribe of the treasury, appear to have been secure offices, sometimes held for life.[29] The scribe of the treasury was assisted, at least in the early 1830s,

[24] Ṣâbûnî, *Târîkh*, pp. 135–37; see for his *fatâwâ* (legal opinions) and his works on mysticism, Brockelmann, *Geschichte*, vol. 1, p. 196; see, for a description of his shrine Gaulmier, *Pelerinages*, 143–45.

[25] They also held an entire but, towards the end of the eighteenth century deserted, village (al-Bûẓliyya) as *waqf*: SMH 46, p. 204, 1 Rajab 1209

[26] SMH 43, p. 141, 9 Jumâdâ II 1217

[27] See, for the shrines which survived into the twentieth century, Gaulmier, *Pelerinages*

[28] See on the Baḥrî family, Philipp, *Syrians*

[29] Al-muᶜallim Mûsâ Walad Ḥannâ, for instance, was appointed *kâtib sancak* for his lifetime: SMH 43, pp. 125, 27 Shawwâl 1216

by the *ṣarrâf*, cashier of the treasury.[30] Not all scribal offices were held by Christians. The books of the local granary were kept by an *aghâ*, the (*anbârjî*), and the same was true for the provisioning stations and guesthouses, the *manzilkhâna*.[31]

The ᶜAẓms and Kaylânîs of Hama

Two families of *aᶜyân* stand out for their high degree of participation in the government and dependence on income derived from governmental resources or from sources to which access was gained through office-holding: the ᶜAẓms, representing the military-administrative class, and the Kaylânîs, representing the religious-judiciary class. The ᶜAlwânî family, which rarely held major offices, but which depended to a large extent on income derived from the administration of *waqf* properties, may be included in this small elite as well. None of the members of the other families mentioned thus far could be considered local *aᶜyân* prior to the 1820s, with the possible exception of the Mawâlî chiefs of the Khurfân family.[32]

A clear indication of the distinguished position of the ᶜAẓms, Kaylânîs and ᶜAlwânîs within local society and their special relation with the government is the addition of the prestigious Ottoman suffix *zade* to their surname.[33] With the exception of non-local officials, the use of honorific titles was restricted to members of these three families, the title of *efendi* being reserved for the learned, the Kaylânîs and ᶜAlwânîs. All three families showed a remarkable ability to transfer their status and wealth to their heirs, although the ᶜAẓms failed to preserve their eminent position on the provincial level.

The ᶜAẓm and Kaylânî families possessed great wealth, albeit unevenly distributed over the various branches of the families. In a later chapter, some particulars of the finances and properties of two members of the ᶜAẓm family are given.[34] Here, an abstract of a

[30] SMH 49, p. 570, 5 Dhû al-Ḥijja 1249

[31] SMH 49, p. 114, 11 Jumâdâ I 1241

[32] The Mawâlî chiefs were, however, not tied to the district of Hama; they were not locals in the strict sense. Also in the province of Aleppo they exerted considerable influence and received payments from the governor general of that province.

[33] *Zade* denotes 'son of', but in local usage it was frequently used in addition to the Arabic equivalent *ibn* or to the more prestigious *najl*.

[34] See p. 124

waqfiyya, charter of a *waqf*, of ᶜAbd al-Qâdir Efendi ibn Ibrâhîm Efendi Kaylânîzâde, the *naqîb* for most of the 1820s may serve as an indication of the magnitude of the wealth concentrated in the hands of one of the *aᶜyân*. The document also gives us an idea of what may be called the geography of wealth. The newly established *waqf* comprised the following:

- a bakery in the Bârûdiyya quarter opposite the house of the heirs of Ismâᶜîl Aghâ al-Zaᶜîm;
- a shop in the Sûq al-Ṭawîl next to the shop belonging to the *waqf* of Banî Malik;
- a shop in the Ḥâḍir quarter next to the coffee house belonging to the *waqf* of Yâsîn Efendi al-Kaylânî and the shop belonging to the heirs of the late Khâlid Efendi al-Kaylânî;
- an irrigated field (*zûr*) near the village Qumḥâna, held jointly with the heirs of the late ᶜAlî Efendi al-Kaylânî and with the brother of the *wâqif* (founder of the *waqf*) ᶜAbdallâh Efendi (all properties mentioned below are held jointly with this brother, apart from those in the Homs district);
- an irrigated field near the village of Khaṭṭâb, next to the field of Aḥmad Bey al-ᶜAẓm, son of the late ᶜAbdallâh Pasha;
- nine shops in the Ḥâḍir quarter, next to the shop belonging to the *waqf* of the Arbaᶜîn Mosque;
- seven shops in the Ḥâḍir quarter, next to the nine mentioned above;
- a water mill near the village Murîj al-Durr, on the ᶜÂṣî River, held jointly with the heirs of ᶜAbd al-Razzâq Efendi al-Kaylânî;
- a shop in the Sûq al-Shajara quarter next to the shop belonging to the shrine of Sheikh ᶜAlwân, May God sanctify his secret;
- a shop in the Jawra quarter, next to the shop belonging to the heirs of al-Ḥâjj Zayn;
- an oil press next to the courtyard belonging to the *waqf* of the late Asᶜad Pasha al-ᶜAẓm;
- a shop in the *sûq*, market, of the saddle makers, next to the square belonging to the *waqf* of Asᶜad Pasha al-ᶜAẓm;
- two shops in the *sûq* of the skinners next to the shop belonging to the *waqf* of Asᶜad Pasha;
- half of a water mill near the village al-Sadda in the Homs district, the other half belonging to the *waqf* of the Khâlid ibn al-Walîd Mosque of Homs;

- a *khân*, including shops and depots, in Homs, next to the coffee house owed by Aḥmad Bey al-ᶜAẓm;
- four shops built next to the *khân* mentioned above;
- three shops in Homs, next to the *khân* belonging to the *waqf* of Asᶜad Pasha al-ᶜAẓm;
- four shops in the Bâb ᶜUmar quarter in Homs, next to the shop and the depot belonging to the *waqf* of Asᶜad Pasha al-ᶜAẓm, and next to the shop of the Christian Jurjus Ghandûr;
- four fields (*arḍ*) near Hama.

Out of the yields, rents, of this *waqf* some modest charity payments were to be made yearly: 80 q. to the great mosque of Medina, 50 q. to the main mosque in Hama, the Nûrî, and 72 q. to four local reciters of the Koran.[35]

Despite the fact that their properties were located next to each other, a clear distinction was maintained between *umarâ'*, commanders, and the ulema, the learned.[36] The ᶜAẓms and Kaylânîs may have competed at times for influence, but normally respected their respective privileges and did not compete for the same offices before the mid-nineteenth century.

The ᶜAẓm family distinguished itself from the Kaylânîs and ᶜAlwânîs by their tradition of high office-holding. They had acquired cosmopolitan traits. Branches of the family had established themselves in Damascus, Aleppo and Cairo in the wake of the exceptional political career of the family during the eighteenth century.[37] They married into several influential families in these centres of administration and commerce. The ᶜAẓms of Damascus were particularly influential and belonged to the leading families of the inner city.

The Kaylânîs were more parochial, notwithstanding their illustrious ancestry. The connection with their namesakes in Baghdad may have

[35] SMH 49, pp. 131–141, 29 Rajab 1241

[36] The form of address of the leading members of the families varied; in the case of the ᶜAẓms, *Iftikhâr al-umarâ' al-kirâm* (The Pride of the Noble Commanders) was the most common, and in the case of the Kaylânîs and ᶜAlwânîs, *Zayd al-faḍâ'il wa ᶜumdat al-ᶜulamâ'* (The Cream of the Illustrious and Pillar of the Learned).

[37] In Hama, Burckhardt (*Travels*, p. 147) met the army commander, Nâṣîf Pasha al-ᶜAẓm (who is also known as Nuṣûḥ Pasha) and remarks that he is well-known for his travels in Europe and Barbary and for his brave defence of Cairo (against the French).

remained of some importance, as well as the ties with the Gaylânî family of Cairo, which like themselves claimed descent from ʿAbd al-Qâdir al-Jîlânî.[38] The establishment of the Damascene branch of the Kaylânî family was connected with the rise of the ʿAẓms to provincial power and even though several members of the family held positions of influence in that city, they were not regarded as genuine Damascenes, contrary to the Damascene ʿAẓms.[39] They remained first and foremost locals and clients of the Damascene ʿAẓms. The ʿAlwânî family was a genuine local family which held a reputation of great piety, also beyond Hama.In the late 1820s, members of the Jijaklî family manifested themselves as *aʿyân*, when they attached the suffix *zade* to their name. The family had acquired strong interests in tax farming, but found difficulty in preserving their prominent position after 1841. Some of the other *aghawât* families which had also relatively recently settled in the area, most notably Ṭayfûr and Barâzî, joined the ranks of local *aʿyân* in the 1830s and 1840s. By then, however, the function of the *aʿyân* was in a process of transformation due to the strengthening of central control. Unmentioned thus far is one group which did exert political influence but seemingly fails to conform to the qualifications of *aʿyân*, the merchants of Hama. It is true that many of the *aghawât* and ulema were deeply involved in trade, but some merchant families without special military or religious credentials, like the Ḥâjj Zayn family, belonged to the wealthiest locals. In their relation with the government they appear to have depended strongly on established 'political' families, primarily on the Kaylânîs. The *tujjâr* constituted a local interest group and their interests were apparently best served by the main, truly local, family. An indication that the *tujjâr* were far from constituting a corporate and politically viable group, is the frequent omission of the *tujjâr* as addressees in opening lines of the edicts which were read out in the courts.

The governor and the *aghawât*

The *sarâyâ* and the *maḥkama*, the court constituted the main institutions of local administration. The *sarâyâ* was not a formal institution as such, but comprised rather the building or buildings in which the

[38] Symbolically, the *muftî* Muḥammad Saʿdî Efendi al-Azharî al-Kaylânî, for example, had studied in Cairo and died in Baghdad, SMH 49, p. 147, 9 Shaʿban 1241 (letter from the *dîwân* of Damascus informing the *mutasallim* that the *muftî* had died). See also Jundî, *Aʿlâm* vol. 2, pp. 36–37

[39] Schatkowski Schilcher, *Families*, pp.194–96

mutasallim of the *sancak*, the district governor of Hama and his staff held office. He represented the *wâlî*, the governor of the province of Damascus, on the district level and was answerable to him. His main tasks consisted of the collection of taxes, the safeguarding of public security and the preservation of the villages.[40] He had to contribute to war efforts by sending provisions and to see to the supply of food and fodder of troops engaged in regional campaigns. Occasionally he himself participated in these campaigns. In order to perform these tasks in an effective manner, considerable powers were delegated to him.

The retinue of the governor of Hama included the *tüfenkçi başı*, the *mirahur*, and the *wakîl al-kharj*, the commander of the musketeers, the commander of the stables and the superintendent of expenditures respectively. The most senior officer in his service, however, was the *garib yiğit ağası*, officer of janissary cavalry. *Garib yiğit* forces first appear in the late seventeenth century in the Arab provinces, but little is known about the composition and activities of these cavalry units in these provinces.[41] They seem to have been recruited mostly from irregular forces. In Egypt they appear to have been attached either to janissary units or to private armies of provincial governors.[42] The remainder of the retinue of the governor consisted of envoys, guards and ceremonial attendants.[43] Apart from his private guard, the governor then had, in principle, direct control over a mounted force as well as the musketeers, who acted as the urban police force. The *aghawât* mentioned above were entitled to fees, called *ᶜawâyid*, collected from the population in lieu of or in addition to a salary.[44]

[40] Nearly all letters of appointment mention these three duties

[41] *Garib yiğit* forces, or rather the *gureba-i yemin* and the *gureba-i yesâr* constituted two janissary regiments in the central provinces, see Sertoğlu, *Osmanlı*, pp. 166–67

[42] Winter, *Egyptian*, p. 56. Neither Rafeq (*Local*) nor Ḥamûd (*ᶜAskar*) mentions these troops in their description of the local and provincial forces in the Syrian provinces. They seem to have served in Damascus during the rule of Asᶜad Pasha al-ᶜAẓm. On one occasion the latter expelled them after the local population, as well as the janissaries, had turned against a Kurdish *garib yiğit* commander, see Budayrî, *Ḥawâdith*, pp. 201–03. Piterberg, *Formation*, pp. 278–79

[43] Respectively a number of *çavuş*, *qawwâṣ* and the *qahwajî* (preparing coffee) and *tütünçi* (preparing waterpipes), see for example SMH 43, p. 187, 7 Rabîᶜ I 1233

[44] Also the *qassâmiyya* were entitled to collect these fees, see p. 131

The privilege of collecting fees distinguished these officers from other *aghawât*. The relation between the governor and some of these latter officers like the *delibaşı* and the *odabaşı* is unclear. The *delibaşı* commanded the *deli*s, a force which was called *dalâtiyya* in the Syrian provinces. Originally cavalry units in the service of provincial governors, by the eighteenth century they increasingly acted as auxiliary troops in the service of any patron who would hire them. The mounted *deli*s were usually hired to police the countryside, but unemployed *deli*s constituted a threat to public security in northern Syria.[45] The *odabaşı*, commander of the hall or barracks, belonged to the janissaries. Janissary forces played an important role in the economy and politics in both Damascus and Aleppo, but little is known about their counterparts in Hama. Their pay was organized differently from that of other local troops.[46] In the countryside, janissaries, referred to as *muḥâfiẓ*s (watchmen), manned a number of fortresses, each under the command of a *dizdar*. In the late eighteenth century the number of *muḥâfiẓ*s varied between 30 and 60 troops per fortress.[47] In the early nineteenth century some of the fortresses were, at least temporarily, abandoned, like Salamiyya, or occupied by rebels, as was the case with Qalᶜat al-Madîq.[48]

Some of the aghawât, like the *delibaşı*, who were not permitted to collect fees, may have acted in other capacities which did entitle them to do so. The officers and their troops who were in charge of the collection of proportional tax on agricultural produce (*qism*), mainly cereals, were entitled to collect a fee. The *qassâmiyya* were headed by the *qassâm aghâ* who served directly under the district governor.[49] The wheat and barley were stored in the local granaries which were administered by the *anbârjî*. The proper collection and storage of wheat and barley was a constant matter of concern for the higher authorities, because of the high economic and political value of the cereals. Barley was essential for the military and transport, whereas the ability to supply wheat to Damascus or other cities in times of scarcity contributed much to the

[45] Bodman, *Political*, p. 13

[46] An amount, referred to as *mal-i ocaqlık*, the money for the corps, was reserved for them, see SMH 49, p. 232, 24 Rajab 1242

[47] For a list of fortresses and the names of the *dizdar*s and *muḥâfiẓ*s, see SMH 46, pp. 193–97, [Rajab] 1208

[48] Salamiyya was the easternmost fortress, situated well into the *bâdiya*. It appears that the fortress was reoccupied in the late 1820s; see SMH 49, 9 Rabîᶜ I 1245. See, for Qalᶜat al-Madîq p. 117–8

[49] Note that the divider of inheritances was also called *qassâm*.

reputation of any district or provincial governor. The stocks of wheat also enabled them to manipulate the market and often provided them with a handsome additional income.

The actual number of *aghawât* in the Hama district is unknown, but it must have been considerable. Not only were the officials and commanders of the various units referred to as *aghâ*, but their senior aids and adult sons as well. Prominent locals employed *aghawât* in their households and these men were known as *atbâ*ᶜ, clients or following. This was not only true for the ᶜAẓms, but also for members of the Kaylânî family.[50] Many of the *aghawât* who served in the district are only referred to by their given name, which makes it very difficult to trace the career patterns, in particular of the middle and lower strata of the military. Of the *aghawât* households which established themselves firmly in the upper echelons of local administration and society in the course of the first three decades of the nineteenth century only the later stages in their careers are relatively well documented. For instance, *aghawât* of the Jijaklî and Barâzî families acted as *garib yiğit ağası* and *delibaşı*, respectively. The Jijaklîs were active as tax farmers in the western parts of the district, whereas the Barâzîs maintained strong relations with the tribes. The Turkumân family of *aghawât* established itself in the area to the north of the district and later extended their range of activities, including tax farming, to Hama. The Ṭayfûr family appears to have made a late, but quick career in the 1830s. The hereditary chiefs of the Mawâlî, the Khurfân family, as well as of the sedentary Turcoman tribes belonged to the more prominent *aghawât* families of the district as well.

The origin and early careers of a number of *aghawât* who failed to transmit their power to a next generation is obscure. The increased use of family names during the mid-nineteenth century is of great help in reconstructing the lineage of several families, but those families or individual *aghawât* who left few traces remain enigmatic. Among them, of course, were non-local individuals who had made a career elsewhere before they were appointed to office in Hama or were contracted by local authorities. Unfortunately, the origin and early career of one of the most important *aghawât* in the Hama district from the mid 1820s onwards, Faraj Aghâ, is obscure.[51]

50 See for example SMH 49, p. 289, [Rabîᶜ I 1244]

51 Given his close relations with the ᶜ*arab* tribes, he may have been of ᶜ*arab* extraction. See on Faraj Aghâ p. 122–4

The executive and the judiciary

Both judiciary and executive functions were combined in the office of *mutasallim*. As *ḥâkim al-ᶜurf*, the mutasallim decided on most criminal and fiscal cases. In principle, however, he could not overrule the judgements of the *ḥâkim al-sharᶜ* or *qâḍî* who presided over the *maḥkama sharᶜiyya* or *majlis al-sharᶜ*, the religious court. The qâḍî's executive powers were limited and he often depended on the district governor for the implementation of his rulings. Contrary to the *qâḍî*, the district governor was not tied to an extensive and detailed corpus of laws. He largely relied upon imperial orders and upon his personal judgement of a case. He hardly even kept record of his rulings. He had, of course, to comply with the directives emanating from the provincial and imperial centres, but these were generally stated in very broad terms, except in matters of taxation and market regulations.

The *qâḍî* may have had limited executive powers, but he exercised great responsibility. He considered a wide range of law suits and his judgement was in principle final. The large majority of the cases brought before the *qâḍî* concerned either matters of family law, or disputes in the spheres of property and commerce, such as legal ownership, partnership, loans, sales and lease contracts. The *maḥkama* was more than just a law court. Besides settling disputes, the *qâḍî* acted as notary public and auditor of the finances of *waqf*s, religious or family foundations.[52]

The functioning of the *maḥkama* was not strictly demarcated by religious law. Local realities were taken into account, but the reputation of the Muslims of Hama as devout, if not strict followers of the holy prescriptions, was reflected by court procedures. For instance, the word *fâ'iḍ*, interest, aroused indignation in the court.[53] In Aleppo courts, for instance, the *qâḍî* took a lenient attitude towards the charging of interest, following the normal practice and sultanic law.[54] Formal deviations from the *sharᶜ* occurred rarely in the Hama court. Local custom (*ᶜâda*) was of some importance, for example in

[52] See on the function of the *maḥkama*, especially, Jennings, *Kadi*, and *Limitations*; E.I. 2, vol. 6, pp. 3–6; Marcus, *Middle East*, pp. 101–20

[53] SMH 56, p. 521, 12 Dhû al-Qaᶜda 1277

[54] Marcus, *Middle East*, pp. 184–5. In the Damascus court the charging of interest was sometimes disguised by the inclusion of exceptionally large quantities of soap in a loan contract, see Rafeq, *Economic*, pp. 674–5 and *City*, pp. 323–24

the case of labour regulations.[55] However, many cases were settled without reference to legal principles, except that both parties had come to an understanding, which made a legal ruling. But, with some regularity, the *qâḍî* violated *sharᶜî* principles, particularly when one, or two, of the contending parties adhered to the Alawî faith. Alawîs, then known as Nuṣayrîs, constituted the second largest confessional community in the area. Like the Druzes, they enjoyed legal rights, a practice that ran contrary to the *sharᶜ*, which defined them as apostates. Occasionally, the *qâḍî* disallowed a testimony by a Alawî witness against a Muslim party, but normally an Alawî testimony against Muslims was – in contradiction to religious law – considered valid.[56]

The range of functions of the *qâḍî* was not restricted to the domains of religious law and local custom. The Hama court was also involved in the general administration of the district. Edicts emanating from both the imperial and provincial authorities were read out in court and entered into the records. At the introduction of a change of regulations or reforms, the *qâḍî* was involved in implementation. The involvement of the *qâḍî* confirmed the legitimacy of reforms and other actions, because the higher authorities of the state were keen not to separate imperial from religious law. In times of popular dissatisfaction they used the court as an instrument to emphasize that they were seriously concerned with the local affairs and poised to restore confidence in the *ᶜadl*, the rule of justice.

Perhaps of greater practical consequence was the use of the court as a check on the dealings of the district governor. By denying him the exclusive right to deal with taxation, public security, market regulations and other matters which were defined by imperial rather than religious law, the higher authorities sought to counterbalance his power. Frequently, the *qâḍî* received orders to conduct an investigation into the, mainly financial, dealings of high ranking *aghawât*, including the district governor.[57] The latter was often present or represented during litigations of serious interest, reflecting the need or ambition of this official to exert some control over the dealings of the court.

[55] The *qâḍî* justified such rulings with the phrase *ḥasab al-ᶜâda* (as the custom goes).

[56] See, on the legal position of the ᶜAlawîs/Nuṣayrîs, Douwes, *Knowledge*, pp. 163–65

[57] See p. 63–4

In principle the *qâḍî* was neither answerable to the *mutasallim* nor to the *wâlî*, but served directly under the imperial *dîwân*. Complaints about his dealings were to be directed to the latter body. In the circumstances of the time, this was not always practical because of distances and the *dîwân*'s inadequate control over local affairs. It had delegated part of its powers to the provincial governors and their *dîwân*s. Petitioning higher authorities was very common, which indicates that filing formal complaints could be effective. The dismissal of at least one of Hama followed a petition addressed to the *wâlî*.[58] However, it seems that petitioning the provincial, let alone the imperial *dîwân*, produced an effect only when the petition was supported by influential locals, preferably *aᶜyân*, including the *muftî*, who was considered the spokesman of the local community. Given that the Kaylânî family not only dominated the offices of the *qâḍî* and *muftî*, but also other religious-administrative offices they were difficult to ignore.

The court and local society

In large cities such as Damascus and Aleppo, the chief judge was nearly always a non-local, who served for a limited period. His deputy judges often exerted more political influence because of their prolonged tenure and because they represented local families and factions. The influence of the *qâḍî* was also limited by the *iftâ'*, the jurisconsultancy. *Muftî*s of the various Sunnite rites played an important role in the local juridical system in the Syrian provinces, both inside and outside the court. The jurisconsultancy constituted to some extent an alternative for the *qaḍâ'*, the judgement of a case by the *qâḍî*. People had the option of asking for a *fatwâ*, legal opinion on a given issue in order to settle a dispute. The frequency of this type of settlement, that is, without the formal involvement of the court, is unknown. People often consulted a *muftî* prior to opening litigation in court. Such a litigation was not a mere formality, even though the *qâḍî* normally backed the *fatwâ*. The reason that people frequently referred the case to the *qâḍî* after they had consulted a *muftî* was that the *ḥujja* produced by the court formally settled the case. Contrary to a *ḥujja*, a *fatwâ* contained a hypothetical version of the issue in the form of a question and the identity of the litigants remained concealed. The question was often answered by a simple confirmation or refutation, without any argumentation. Apart from the identity of the litigants, a *ḥujja* contained a clear verdict.

[58] SMH 49, p. 278, 27 Muḥarram 1244

The function of the *muftî* was rather casual, except for the Ḥanafî *muftî*s appointed by the *shaykh al-islâm*, the supreme *muftî* of the Ottoman state. In the Syrian provinces these Ḥanafî *muftî*s were, as elsewhere, recruited from local ulema families and the appointment was, in principle, for life, but was reconfirmed yearly. In Damascus the candidates for the office of Ḥanafî *muftî*, as well as the *naqîb*, were not selected from one single family. In the late eighteenth and early nineteenth centuries the Murâdî family, which maintained close relations with some of the ᶜAẓms, dominated the office of *muftî*, but they faced competition from ulema of the ᶜAjlânî, Maḥâsinî and Bakrî families. The office of Ḥanafî *muftî* of Damascus, and other large cities, constituted the highest and most prestigious office occupied by a member of the local religious elite and the Damascene *muftî* acted, albeit informally, as the principal representative of the local community. He often voiced the complaints of various interest groups or those of the population at large.[59]

In smaller towns like Hama, the *qâḍî* was nearly always a local, and like the Ḥanafî *muftî*, he normally was recruited from the Kaylânî family. The *muftî* was assisted, and often represented, by his aide, the *amîn al-fatâwâ*.[60] The political function of the Ḥanafî *muftî* in Hama differed from that of his counterpart in Damascus, because his position vis-à-vis the *qâḍî*, and the administration at large, depended strongly on the relations within the Kaylânî family. The *muftî* was not necessarily the leading member of the family. Muḥammad Saᶜdî Efendi al-Kaylânî, for instance, who served both as *muftî* and *shaykh al-sijâda* until his death in 1825, was a man of learning and piety, and appears not to have been deeply involved in local politics. He was succeeded by his son Muḥammad Najîb Efendi, who served relatively briefly and of whom little is known. But his successor, Muḥammad ᶜAlî Efendi, who was from another branch of the family, became one of the main actors in local politics. From the late 1820s until his dismissal in 1845, he headed the family.[61]

[59] See, on the function of *iftâ'* in the Ottoman Empire in general, E.I.2, vol. 2, pp. 866–7. See, on the Damascene *muftî*s and the Murâdî family, Schatkowski Schilcher, *Families*, pp. 117–22 and pp. 160–165. Her list of *muftî*s is incomplete. See, on the *muftî* Asᶜad Efendi al-Ṣiddîqî (al-Bakrî) and his brother Khalîl Efendi, the *naqîb*, *Al-ᶜAbd*, p. 89 and pp. 137–38

[60] This subordinate, but still prestigious position was reserved for most of the period under discussion for sheikh Muḥammad al-Dabbâgh. See, on this sheikh, Mardam Bey, *Aᶜyân*, pp. 169–70

[61] He was dismissed and exiled after charges of corruption had been filed

The *maḥkama* and the *iftâ'*, constituted the local institutions *par excellence*. The court functioned as a meeting place for the locally influential and was generally open to the public. Members of the ʿAẓm family or their envoys, as well as of other prominent families like the ʿAlwânî and Jijaklî, frequented court sessions. They, or their representatives, often acted as *shuhûd al-ḥâl*, witnesses who assented the handling of a court case. The *qâḍî* hardly ever decided on a case without consultation with either religious experts, such as the *muftî* or sheikhs of the ʿAlwânî family, or with people whose expertise was in a specific field, like the market or tax regulations, or who had an intimate knowledge of the quarters, villages and the tribes. Village sheikhs, for example, were often present at court sessions.

The presence of experts and interested parties compensated for the shortage of staff of the *qâḍî*, which merely consisted of a scribe and a couple of court ushers. The court was a place for negotiating and bargaining. It combined the diverse local interests with the principles of religious, imperial and local laws and traditions. The *qâḍî* presided over a local institution where the *muslims*,[62] the local public, discussed and settled their disputes. The *qâḍî* often acted as arbitrator and sanctioned the negotiated settlement by issuing a *ḥujja*. Occasionally, people who had earlier brought their case to the notice of the *mutasallim* in his capacity as *ḥâkim al-ʿurf*, applied to the *qâḍî* to have the governor's ruling confirmed.[63] When attending a case, his presence was stated in the opening line of a deed, which expresses his eminence, but he never acted as *shâhid al-ḥâl*, indicating the distinction between his office and that of the *qâḍî*.

against him, but he returned to office for a short period afterwards. Apart from *muftî* he acted as *naqîb*. See, on some Kaylânî *muftî*s, Jundî, *Aʿlâm*, vol. 2, pp. 35–38. Numerous references to the *muftî*s are to be found in the court records, where they appear either in connection with a *fatwâ*, or as litigants. See, on the death of Muḥammad Saʿdî Efendi, SMH 49, p. 147, 9 Shaʿbân 1241. See, on the charges of corruption against Muḥammad ʿAlî Efendi: SMH 52, p. 261, 21 Muḥarram 1264 and F.O. 78/959, Damascus 25 February 1853

62 The phrase: '. . . the parties argued and quarrelled and then *muslims* interfered and mediated between them, and they agreed upon a compromise . . .', often occurs in court deeds. The word *muslims* refers to the public, which may include Christians.

63 See SMH 48, p. 133, 5 Jumâdâ II, 1235; SMH 49, p. 269, 6 Rabîʿ II 1245. No case was found in which the *qâḍî* overruled the *mutasallim*. Only later in the century did this happen, albeit very rarely.

Variations in the position of *a*ᶜ*yân*

The question whether the composition of the group of *a*ᶜ*yân* in Hama and their relation with other segments of local society was typical for the Syrian interior can not be answered with any certainty, due to the large variation in local circumstances[64] and the scarcity of detailed studies on other places. From the little we know of the *a*ᶜ*yân* of nearby Homs, it appears that the situation in this town did not differ markedly from that in Hama except that aᶜyân from Hama constituted a more dominant group having a far larger geographical reach. In Homs, the *aghawât* of the Jundî family dominated military-administrative domain. Like the ᶜAẓms, who were by the first decades of the nineteenth century their former patrons, the Jundî family were confronted with increased competition, in particular from the rural *aghawât* Tall Kalakh area, situated halfway to Tripoli. Not unlike the Kaylânî family, Atâsî, the leading religious family of Homs, demonstrated a remarkable endurance throughout the eighteenth and nineteenth centuries. A similar pattern seems to have existed in the provincial centres, Damascus and Aleppo. Of course, the configuration was much more complex in these cities due to the size of their populations and administrations. But here as well the *aghawât* were more vulnerable to change than the learned. The reliance on power delegated to the military-administrative class, combined with the heavy reliance on provincial coalitions, made this group vulnerable to changes in the political order of the province and the empire at large. The religious-judiciary offices were less vulnerable to political shifts on the provincial level. Apart from co-optation by the state, the religious *a*ᶜ*yân* depended much more on local political resources. Their status as learned custodians of the Islamic tradition endowed them with moral authority and prestige which the *aghawât* lacked.

64 The *a*ᶜ*yân* of Nablus, for instance, entertained very different political and economic relations. See, Doumani, *Rediscovering*

4. Provincial alliances and factions

Among the key words in the chronicles and court records of the late eighteenth and early nineteenth centuries is 'injustice' (*ẓulm*). Acts of injustice (*maẓâlim*) encompassed all sorts of abuse of power, like intimidation, exaction, outright extortion, and profiteering by governors, officers and other officials. The word was very frequently used in all sorts of directives and letters of appointment emanating from the centres of higher authority. Accusations of oppressive acts legitimized punitive action against the servants of the state and were the most common ground for the filing of complaints. Ottoman political culture was not unique in this respect; as in other traditional states it was balancing between what was deemed to be necessary and ideal, and that which proved to be feasible. The state lacked the means to enforce the ideal state of justice and, in order to cope with all sorts of problems, adopted methods which were defined as oppressive by its own laws.[1]

The hard times

In the late eighteenth and early nineteenth centuries, both central and provincial authorities faced a variety of problems with which they found great difficulty to cope. First and foremost, the Ottoman state suffered heavy losses of life and land in Europe. While trying to organize its defences, its hold over the south-eastern Mediterranean provinces of Egypt and Palestine became problematic, in particular in the closing years of the eighteenth century following the French invasion. The loss of the Holy Cities of Islam to Wahhâbî forces constituted another blow to the sultan. Apart from what was clearly and painfully visible, like war, revolt, famine, and plague, slower and more hidden transformations altered circumstances. The effects of changes in trade patterns were felt in many places and lead to the search of alternative markets and produce. The nomadic pressure on cultivated land increased and peasants migrated to towns or villages which seemed to have better

[1] See, for the Late-Roman empire, Cameron, *Mediterranean*, pp. 91–92

prospects, thus violating one of the ideals embedded in Ottoman fiscal thinking: that of the thriving village, producing its full share of revenues.[2]

The officials who had to cope with the problematic situation in the Syrian provinces regularly fell back on 'oppressive' measures. The spread of exaction and other forms of harassment that spread in an earlier episode are often attributed to changes in the military organization of the provinces in the late sixteenth century, especially the maintenance of private armies by provincial governors and strongmen.[3] Afterwards the central authorities had tried to curb the power of their servants in the provinces and to mitigate excessive abuse of power in provinces by assigning part of the revenue collection in the provinces to officials other than the governor and by introducing the swift rotation of senior provincial officials.[4] The measures had some effect, but were accompanied by the emergence of local elements in the administration. The ascendancy of the *aᶜyân* in the administration of the provinces in the eighteenth century often went hand in hand with strong competition and sometimes ensued long and devastating feuds.[5] Several parts of the Syrian interior witnessed outbreaks of violence as a result of competition for political and economic resources, tribal expansion and mobilization for war in the years between 1786 and 1804 and to a lesser extent from 1805 to 1818.

The interior and Acre factions and the governorship of Damascus

In the province of Damascus the policy of the swift rotation of provincial governors was abandoned in the 1720s, albeit not wholeheartedly, when a local military faction, the ᶜAẓm *aghawât*, had been allowed greater access to revenue sources by being granted tax farms which were not part of the province, including the district of Hama. They were allowed prolonged tenures. The change of policy was motivated by the

[2] See, for instance, the analysis of an earlier rural crisis by Aziz Efendi quoted in Darling, *Revenue-raising*, p. 289

[3] Barkey, *Bandits*; Kunt, *Sultan's*, pp. 90–93; Inalcik, *Centralization*, pp. 27–28; Rafeq, *Changes*, p. 59

[4] These measures were also motivated by the shortage of cash for the payment of pensions and the increasing number of candidates for provincial offices, see Inalcik, *Centralization*, pp. 29–30

[5] Ibid., p. 49.

general lack of security at the time when the management of the all-important pilgrimage to Mecca and Medina had become seriously endangered. Although the ᶜAẓms were highly successful in the handling of the pilgrimage and in curbing tribal unrest, the central authorities showed their reluctance to support dynastic governors, but they looked for alternative candidates in their retinues. In 1757, Asᶜad Pasha al-ᶜAẓm was replaced by one of his former officers in 1757. Eventually, a former *mamlûk* of Asᶜad Pasha was made governor in 1760, after three others had failed to bring the province under control after the *ᶜarab* attack on the convoy of pilgrims shortly after Asᶜad Pasha's departure.[6] The new governor, ᶜUthmân Pasha al-Kurjî, served for nearly twelve years. His successor was again recruited from the ᶜAẓm family, Muḥammad Pasha, the last *wâlî* of Damascus who was allowed a long tenure, from 1772 until his natural death in 1783.[7] In the three years following his death Damascus witnessed a swift rotation of provincial governors, amongst them Jazzâr Pasha of Acre who held his first and shortest tenure in Damascus.

The policy of the central authorities towards the province of Damascus in the late eighteenth and early nineteenth centuries was largely motivated by the desire to contain Jazzâr Pasha and his *mamlûk* household of Acre.[8] The refusal to grant Jazzâr Pasha a permanent hold on Damascus may not have mitigated the ambitions of the pasha, but he was pinned down in his fortified coastal town, where he continued to reside during the years he served as governor of Damascus. Jazzâr Pasha turned Acre into a fortification, not so much to defend the part of the empire under his control against the encroachments of foreign hostile parties, but to protect himself against the enemy from within.

Appeasement was part of the containment policy of the central authorities towards Jazzâr Pasha. He was not excluded from what remained the most prestigious governorship in Syria, Damascus. Four times Jazzâr Pasha was granted the governorship of Damascus, serving for about nine years in total. Three other candidates were used to counterbalance the strongman of Acre, at first Ibrâhîm Deli Pasha, and afterwards ᶜAbdallâh Pasha al-ᶜAẓm and Ibrâhîm Pasha al-Ḥalabî. These

[6] Apart from the *ḥajj* disaster, the province suffered from famine in 1758 and was struck by a heavy earthquake in 1759, followed by plague.

[7] After he had been in office for less than a year, he was replaced by a non-local governor, Muṣṭafâ Pasha, but Muḥammad Pasha returned to office after some months.

[8] See pp. 56–58

three pashas represented, for lack of a better designation, the interior factions, which consisted largely of the disintegrating ʿAẓm faction and their associates.

After the death of Jazzâr Pasha in 1804, his heir Sulaymân Pasha saw himself placed in a position similar to that of his former master; his hold on Acre was secure, but he was only one among other candidates for the governorship of Damascus. To the relief of many, Sulaymân Pasha proved to be a man of far less ambition. The factions of the interior profited to a limited degree from the milder disposition of the heir of Jazzâr Pasha. Ibrâhîm Pasha al-Ḥalabî and ʿAbdallâh Pasha al-ʿAẓm both served another term. In 1806, when it had become apparent that he was unable to cope with the Wahhâbî occupation of the Hijaz, the latter was replaced by his senior aide, Kunj Yûsuf Pasha, as the exponent of the interior.[9] Kunj Yûsuf Pasha was allowed more time, but following Wahhâbî raids on the Hawran to the south of Damascus his career ended as he fled to Egypt. Only after this dramatic departure was Sulaymân Pasha appointed governor of Damascus, a position which he occupied for less than two years.

By rotating the leaders or exponents of hostile factions – the Acre faction on the one hand and the factions of the interior on the other – as governors of Damascus in the period of 1885–1812, the central authorities kindled provincial factionalism. Combined with the effects of the French invasion, the Wahhâbî occupation of the Hijaz, and instances of the tribal warfare in the inland plains, politics in Syria assumed a very coercive character. In this setting, acts of severe 'oppression' became common and, at times, extreme violence disturbed the towns and villages. In 1812 the central authorities ceased to recruit the governors of Damascus from the ranks of what were by then exhausted rival provincial parties.

The revolts of the late 1780s

The closing years of the 1780s were characterized by a rebellion against Jazzâr Pasha by some of his troops, violence in Damascus and a revolt of the Mawâlî in the Hama and Homs area which sparked off other revolts in the Syrian interior, especially in the northern parts.[10] Jazzâr Pasha

[9] See, for a biography, Baytâr, *Ḥilyat*, pp. 1596–1602

[10] The following is based on Al-ʿAbd, *Târîkh*, p. 11–19; Dimashqî *Ḥawâdith*, p. 15–16; Kurd ʿAlî, *Khiṭaṭ*, vol. 3, p. 5–6; Munayyir, *Durr*, p. 80–83; Shaṭṭî, *Rawḍ*, pp. 25–26; Koury, *Province*, pp. 57–64

was appointed to Damascus for the first time in 1785.[11] After having served for nearly one and a half years as governor, Jazzâr Pasha was dismissed. He returned to Acre, but faced severe difficulties when some of his leading *mamlûks* took up arms against him. He had a narrow escape, but managed to regain control and executed or imprisoned his opponents and everyone who he believed had been in favour of them. Suspicious of any possible source of opposition to his rule, he also expelled the French merchants. The revolt against Jazzâr had an impact on his relations with the factions of the interior, because quite a number of people fled the areas under his control and sought refuge in Damascus or elsewhere in the interior.

Inland Syria received its share of violence starting in Damascus. In 1788, Ibrâhîm Deli Pasha, also known as Ibrâhîm Pasha al-Dalâtî, a Kurd who had made a career as a professional soldier in the service of ᶜAẓms – hence his name – was appointed to Damascus.[12] Prior to Damascus he served as governor of Tripoli, but Jazzâr Pasha had him removed in favour of one of his own candidates. Soon after Ibrâhîm Deli Pasha returned from his first pilgrimage, he was forced to flee Damascus, following a revolt of the janissaries of the citadel and *aghawât* of the Maydân quarter. The governor first retreated to a village to the south of Damascus, where he was joined by some Damascene dignitaries, among them the *muftî*, Muḥammad Khalîl Efendi al-Murâdî, who had just returned from Istanbul.[13] The party then left for Hama in order to collect troops. Nearly three months later, Ibrâhîm Deli Pasha returned to Damascus after he had received a reply from the Porte to his report on the revolt. Apparently the central authorities had ordered him to take whatever measures necessary to re-establish order in Damascus. With the help of troops from Hama and Druze militia from the Lebanon the governor's mercenaries defeated the janissaries. He then besieged the citadel and, after the mediation of one of the leading ulema and the *delibaş*, the janissaries surrendered. Some of them were executed, but most were expelled or allowed to escape, among

[11] It is uncertain whether Jazzâr Pasha was the third or the fourth governor to serve after Muḥammad Pasha al-ᶜAẓm. In the list of governors produced in Munajjid's *Wulât*, which is based on a mid-nineteenth-century Ottoman almanac, he is the third. In the chronicle of Dimashqî (*Ḥawâdith*, p. 11) he acts as the fourth.

[12] See for a short biography Shaṭṭî, *Aᶜyân*, 25–26

[13] He had probably gone to Istanbul in connection with the petition which led to Jazzâr Pasha's dismissal. See p. 91.

them their commander, Aḥmad Aghâ al-Zaᶜfaranjî. The *delibaşı* was Mullâ Ismâᶜîl, a highly influential officer who was later to play a less conciliatory role in the district of Hama.

The Mawâlî *ᶜarab* under the leadership of their *amîr* Muḥammad Khurfân took the opportunity to rise in revolt after the mobilization of troops from the Hama area to suppress the rebellion in Damascus. The grievances of the Mawâlî concerned the growing strength of the Ḥasana of the ᶜAnaza confederation who had taken control over part of their pastures.[14] The Mawâlî attacked scores of villages all over the area, including the foothills of the ᶜAlawî Mountains. Contrary to the tradition of trying to avoid bloodshed as much as possible, the Mawâlî killed a large number of people, especially village elders and local *aghawât*.

The counter-offensive against the tribesmen was directed from Aleppo and Hama. The Mawâlî were dealt a severe blow; hundreds of them were killed. At the same time Ottoman troops advanced from Antakia to the areas north of Hama to which the revolt had spread as well. The troops caused widespread destruction in the villages of the northern Zâwiya and, what is more, carried the plague with them. The epidemic spread and northern Syria was hit by an extremely serious plague in the following year.

The close of the decade, then, was catastrophic. The spread of violence revealed the collapse of the political structures in the interior as they had developed during the ᶜAẓm period. The course of events, however, was not totally untypical. The Damascene *qabîqûl*, the imperial janissaries who manned the citadel, as well as the *aghawât* from the Maydân, the stronghold of the *yerli* or local janissaries, had a history of revolts. Since the mid-seventeenth century the containment of the military factions in Damascus had been problematic. Ibrâhîm Deli Pasha was not the first governor who had been forced to retreat following a military revolt. Also the ᶜAẓm governors had had some major difficulties in restraining the Damascene military, but they had been relatively successful compared to others.[15] The Maydân quarter had stood up to severe punitive actions before, most recently in 1758.[16] The expulsion of military forces from Damascus had occurred earlier in the

[14] See p. 28–9

[15] In the 1730s the two *wâlî*s of Damascus, who served in between the first and second term in office of Sulaymân Pasha al-ᶜAẓm, had been ousted by the military. See Rafeq, *Province*, pp. 112–43

[16] One of the *wâlî*s who tried to bring Damascus under control after the pillaging of the *ḥajj* convoy in 1857, ravaged the Maydân quarter. Asᶜad Pasha

century as well. Only during the prolonged rule of Muḥammad Pasha al-ᶜAẓm (1772/3–1783) had Damascus not witnessed open military dissension.

Opposition and support for Jazzâr Pasha and the ᶜAẓms in Damascus

It is unclear whether Jazzâr Pasha's policies during his first term in office in Damascus had contributed to the political instability in Damascus. Strict monopoly policies and the imposition of forced loans had made him enemies among the local elite, but it seems that he tried to link up with the most prominent family, the Damascus branch of the ᶜAẓms, by marrying a daughter of the late Muḥammad Pasha.[17] Jazzâr Pasha was to become most unpopular among the Damascenes during the 1790s, but at this early stage he may have had some support because he had the reputation of having '. . . restored justice and security' in the coastal areas prior to his first appointment to Damascus.[18] Jazzâr Pasha is most likely to have been upset by his early dismissal as governor of Damascus in 1786, but there is no indication that he had a hand in the janissary revolt.[19] He was dismissed after Damascenes under the leadership of the *muftî* Muḥammad Khalîl Efendi al-Murâdî had complained to the Porte about his attempts to impose a monopoly on the cereal trade. Given the strong reliance of merchants and *aghawât* of the Maydân on the cereal trade, it seems probable that they were among the petitioners.[20] During his later terms in office in Damascus however, Jazzâr Pasha's main local allies, came from the Maydân, among them some of the *mutasallims* who represented him in the districts.

al-ᶜAẓm, too, had resorted to drastic action against the Maydânîs, see Burayk, *Târîkh*, pp. 62–63 and Rafeq, *Province*, p. 166

[17] The marriage did not endure. See Koury, *Province*, p. 58

[18] See Burayk, *Târîkh*, p. 121

[19] Jazzâr Pasha had expected to be appointed to Damascus after Muḥammad Pasha al-ᶜAẓm had died in 1783 and again after the latter's successor, a son of ᶜUthmân Pasha al-Kurjî, had died within a month's time. However, another son of ᶜUthmân Pasha was appointed, Darwîsh Pasha. On both occasions Jazzâr Pasha had been confident about the promotion to Damascus, to the extent that he received congratulations and made preparation for his departure from Acre. See Rafeq, *Province*, pp. 318–19; Cohen, *Palestine*, p. 66

[20] Dimashqî, (*Ḥawâdith*, pp. 14–15) writes that 'the people of Damascus' directed a petition to the Porte. Schatkowski Schilcher deduces from this that Jazzâr Pasha faced massive opposition (*Families*, p. 37). Petitions, however, were

During the janissary revolt, a number of religious dignitaries[21] sided with Ibrâhîm Deli Pasha. The position of the ʿAẓms of Damascus in this conflict is unclear, but it may well be that the fact that the Pasha retreated to the Hama area to collect troops indicates support for his case from this grand family. The ʿAẓm family entertained strong relations with the notable families, primarily religious *aʿyân*, of the inner city of Damascus, like the learned Murâdî family. Damascene factionalism in the decades to come often followed the traditional antagonism between the inner city and the Maydân, although none of these two major parts of the city were organized in single, internally coherent factions. Also, the *aghawât* from the northern quarters, let alone the imperial janissaries, were certainly not without influence, but neither of these constituted a solid, united formation. Alliances could easily dissolve at a time when the higher authorities were reluctant to fully support any party.[22]

During his terms in office in the 1790s and especially during his last term in the early years of the nineteenth century, Jazzâr Pasha had a number of notables and *aghawât* executed, while others died of neglect in his prisons, among them three Ḥanafî *muftî*s. The fact that the Ḥanafî *muftî*s constituted a prime target of Jazzâr Pasha's repression reflects the central position of this particular office in Damascus. Since the *qâḍî* of Damascus was not recruited locally, the chief *muftî* was the most senior religious *aʿyân*.[23] The *muftî*s, and others who suffered persecution, may have been associated with the ʿAẓms in one way or another, but not all of them should be considered as their clients or as belonging to the ʿAẓm

usually signed by a number of the more noble citizens, who may or may not claim to represent the local population.

[21] Apart from the *muftî*, Shaṭṭî (*Rawḍ*, p. 25) refers to *wujûh*, a term which usually denotes non-military notables. Apart from the *muftî*, Al-ʿAbd, *Târîkh* (p. 14) refers to 'a number of *efendiyya*', religious dignitaries.

[22] Schatkowski Schilcher (*Families*) distinguishes between two camps only, the ʿAẓm faction and the Maydân faction, but also writes that the situation was confused (p. 40). However, it is highly doubtful that the Damascene ʿAẓms figured as the leading family of the inner city, in the sense that the other prominent families like the Maḥâsinîs, Bakrîs and Murâdîs always – or often – looked to the ʿAẓms for support and guidance. The confusion arises from the multitude of, often unstable, alliances in and between the inner city and the Maydân, as well as other quarters.

[23] Two of the *muftî*s belonged to the Murâdî family and one to the Maḥâsinî. See Shaṭṭî, *Rawḍ*, pp. 40–41; Al-ʿAbd, *Târîkh*, p. 81 and pp. 88–89 and Schatkowski-Schilcher, *Families*, p. 38

faction. It seems certain that the Murâdî family was indeed closely connected with the ᶜAẓm family at the time, not only through the bonds of marriage. Shortly after ᶜAbdallâh Pasha al-ᶜAẓm had been appointed to Damascus for the first time in 1795, Asᶜad Efendi al-Maḥâsinî was replaced by ᶜAbd al-Raḥmân Efendi al-Murâdî as *muftî*. Other instances of the near simultaneous changes of personnel suggest that the governor was able to influence the appointment of the *muftî*.[24] During the last and most repressive years of Jazzâr's rule, the position of the *muftî* became precarious because this functionary often voiced the general grievances of the Damascene population against Jazzâr Pasha's policies and the brutal conduct of his troops and local aides.[25]

The victims of the wrath of Jazzâr Pasha were not necessarily allies of the ᶜAẓms. The ill-fated career of Aḥmad Aghâ al-Zaᶜfaranjî may serve as an example of the changing relations between the various actors. In 1786 Aḥmad Aghâ, then commander of the imperial janissaries of the citadel, revolted against the newly appointed governor. He was expelled from Damascus after the pasha had crushed the revolt and negotiated surrender. He fled to the Mawâlî *ᶜarab* who had risen in revolt, but then sought refuge in Hama. Not much later he was employed by Ibrâhîm Deli Pasha as *mutasallim* of Jerusalem. Jazzâr Pasha appointed him to Hama in the early 1790s, but shortly afterwards he was killed by Muḥammad Aghâ, Jazzâr Pasha's deputy governor (*qâyimmaqâm*), possibly on the order of the pasha.[26]

[24] Al-ᶜAbd, *Târîkh*, p. 26–7 (ᶜAbdallâh Pasha al-ᶜAẓm and ᶜAbd al-Raḥmân Efendi al-Murâdî, later executed by Jazzâr Pasha) and pp. 137–38 (Kunj Yûsuf Pasha and Asᶜad Efendi al-Ṣiddîqî (al-Bakrî)). When Jazzâr Pasha was appointed in 1790, Muḥammad Khalîl Efendi al-Murâdî was exiled and replaced by Asᶜad Efendi al-Maḥâsinî, who, however, was later imprisoned by Jazzâr, and died of neglect.

[25] The authors of the *tarâjim* (biographical dictionaries) hardly make mention of the ᶜAẓms in connection with Jazzâr Pasha's policies in Damascus. They concentrated on the ulema who fell victim to the Pasha. Of course, the *tarâjim* mainly deal with the learned members of society, but some *aghawât* are mentioned in connection with Jazzâr's repression. See, for example, Shaṭṭî (*Rawḍ*, p. 38–43) who gives the *tarjama* of Jazzâr Pasha by Maḥmûd al-Hamzawî and by ᶜAbd al-Razzâq al-Bayṭâr.

[26] Al-ᶜAbd, *Târîkh*, p. 20–1; Dimashqî, *Ḥawâdith*, p. 19. Schatkowski Schilcher (*Families*, p. 38) writes that Aḥmad Aghâ belonged to the ᶜAẓm faction, but there is no indication that this was this case. He was killed before ᶜAbdallâh Pasha al-ᶜAẓm was first appointed to Damascus. Muḥammad Aghâ was one of the principal aides of Jazzâr Pasha and extremely unpopular in

The leading member of the ʿAẓm family at the time, ʿAbdallâh Pasha, had started his career under his father Muḥammad Pasha and had served as governor of Tripoli and commander of the troops bringing provisions to the returning convoy of pilgrims. In 1794 ʿAbdallâh Pasha was appointed to the governorship of Aleppo. A year later he was transferred to Damascus replacing Jazzâr Pasha. The family was popular among the Damascenes who cherished good memories of the tranquil rule of his father, who had established a reputation of righteousness and piety. News of ʿAbdallâh Pasha's appointment was received with joy. For the time being no eyes were cut out or noses cut off, to mention two of the penalties for minor offences which had become routine during Jazzâr Pasha's rule.[27]

ʿAbdallâh Pasha al-ʿAẓm failed to fulfil the high expectations and, unlike his father, he was not to be remembered as a just ruler, but as a rapacious one, although the more violent acts perpetrated during his later years in Damascus were ascribed to his senior aides, in particular to Darwîsh Aghâ ibn Jaʿfar Aghâ, rather than to the pasha himself.[28] ʿAbdallâh Pasha lacked the efficiency of his main contender, Jazzâr Pasha, as well as sufficient support from the central authorities who had decided that a quick rotation of the governorship of Damascus would better serve the interests of the state. For a decade, the appointment to the governorship of Damascus resembled musical chairs which, apart from ʿAbdallâh Pasha al-ʿAẓm and Jazzâr Pasha, a third candidate was to join, Ibrâhîm Pasha al-Ḥalabî, a strongman from Aleppo who had served under ʿAbdallâh Pasha in Aleppo and had succeeded him as governor when ʿAbdallâh Pasha was appointed to Damascus.[29] ʿAbdallâh Pasha was to serve three times as *wâlî* of Damascus, Ibrâhîm Pasha three times and Jazzâr Pasha another two times (he died while in office in 1804).

Jazzâr Pasha owed these appointments to his military resources.

Damascus. ʿAbdallâh Pasha had him strangled in 1802, see Al-ʿAbd, *Ḥawâdith*, p. 74. Dimashqî (*Ḥawâdith*, p. 21) writes that he had him killed during his first term in office (1795–98).

[27] Al-ʿAbd, *Târîkh*, pp. 25–28; Dimashqî, *Ḥawâdith*, p. 21

[28] Al-ʿAbd, *Târîkh*, pp. 82–84

[29] According to Bodman (*Factions*, p. 117–22) ʿAbdallâh Pasha had shown a lack of competence, while governor of Aleppo (1794), when he left the government to Ibrâhîm, then Aghâ. Ibrâhîm Aghâ had made his career in the household of a leading member of the Aleppine *ashrâf*. Among his qualities figured his ability to contain the *ʿarab* tribes. See, for a short biography, Shaṭṭî, *Rawḍ*, pp. 26–27

Whenever the situation in and around Damascus could not be controlled by one of the two other candidates, Jazzâr Pasha was, albeit with considerable reluctance from the part of the central authorities, engaged to restore order. At the turn of the century two incidents resulted in disturbances and political confusion: the French occupation of Egypt and coastal Palestine (1798–99) and the occupation of Mecca (1803) and Medina (1804) by the Wahhâbî-Saʿûdî coalition. The years following the French invasion were marked by fierce competition between the Acre and interior factions. In particular Jazzâr Pasha and ʿAbdallâh Pasha were locked in a nearly continuous state of provincial warfare. Only the arrival of the large armies from Anatolia, which headed for Egypt under the command of Yûsuf Pasha, the vizier, brought about a short cessation in the violent encounters between the two. The passage of the troops – which implied excessive demands of food and fodder and the occasional looting of villages – constituted a heavy drain on local resources and added to the general distress.

The occupation of Egypt had come as a shock and resulted in disturbances in Damascus and other places. Then governor ʿAbdallâh Pasha was replaced by Ibrâhîm Pasha by a military revolt, forcing him to leave left the city with his private troops; finally, Jazzâr Pasha's troops arrived and restored a degree of order.[30] When the vizier arrived he had several *aghawât* decapitated and their heads exhibited at the entrance of the citadel. Jazzâr Pasha hardly had the opportunity to visit Damascus during his shortest tenure; Yûsuf Pasha had him replaced by ʿAbdallâh Pasha seven months after his appointment.[31]

After the Wahhâbîs had occupied Mecca and, as a result, the pilgrimage under the command of ʿAbdallâh Pasha had experienced a humiliating reception in the sacred city, Jazzâr Pasha was again called to duty in Damascus. The Pasha stayed in Acre, but his troops took control of the city. This time ʿAbdallâh Pasha refused to accept his dismissal and proceeded with his troops from Hama, where he had campaigned against allies of Jazzâr Pasha (see below). Out of fear of his troops the inhabitants of the outer quarters of Damascus sought refuge in the inner city. However, the troops eventually turned against the pasha, because

---

[30] Jazzâr Pasha was normally appointed *wâlî* of Egypt as well. This latter appointment was at the expense of another member of the ʿAẓm family, Nuṣûḥ Pasha, who had been the commander of the troops that had defended Cairo unsuccessfully against the French assault.
[31] Al-ʿAbd, *Târîkh*, p. 36–60; Dimashqî, *Ḥawâdith*, pp. 22–25

they had not received their pay, and because they 'refused to fight the *dawla*', the military in Damascus.[32]

The military strength of Jazzâr Pasha was not always turned in favour of the central authorities. On the one hand, the pasha demonstrated the willingness to serve the sultan in troubled places. On the other hand he made sure that allies, among them the rebel Muṣṭafâ Aghâ Barbar of Tripoli, remained in place against the orders emanating from Istanbul. Armed conflicts over the control over Tripoli as well as over parts of Palestine and the Biqa valley constituted a major element in the competition between the Acre and interior factions. More often than not ᶜAbdallâh Pasha received official backing, but Jazzâr did not give in easily. One time he even obstructed the appointment of the Porte's (new) candidate to Damascus. It concerned Muḥammad ᶜAlî Pasha Abû Maraq, a protégé of Yûsuf Pasha who was in Yafa at the time of his appointment to Damascus. Jazzâr Pasha besieged Yafa, an act that caused great anger at the Porte. Abû Maraq escaped to Aleppo, but in the meantime ᶜAbdallâh Pasha had been re-appointed to Damascus.[33]

The relations between the ᶜAẓms and Jazzâr Pasha were hostile, not only because they were political rivals. A family feud had entered the relationship in the early 1790s. Jazzâr Pasha was accused of assassinating ᶜAlî Bey al-ᶜAẓm, a brother of ᶜAbdallâh Pasha. The *mutasallim* of Jazzâr Pasha had confiscated a large number of sheep from ᶜ*arab* with whom ᶜAlî Bey had contracted a partnership, making him the co-owner of the flocks. ᶜAlî Bey demanded the return of the sheep. The *mutasallim* asked Jazzâr Pasha, who resided in Acre, for advice in the matter. ᶜAlî Bey was poisoned shortly afterwards. It was believed that Jazzâr Pasha had ordered his local representative to kill ᶜAlî Bey secretly. The bey's mother decided to travel to Istanbul to bring the matter to the notice of the sultan, but she died before reaching the capital, some believed of grief, others saw the hand of Jazzâr Pasha in her death.[34]

[32] Al-ᶜAbd, *Târîkh*, p. 85–93; Shihâb, *Lubnân*, p. 405; An undated edict (SMH 43, p. 118) from Damascus to an unnamed *mutasallim* of Hama may well be related to the incident; it refers to the suffering of the population of Hama at the hands of troops which had just returned to Damascus.

[33] Shihâb, *Lubnân*, pp. 361–70; Munayyir, *Durr* , pp. 137–38

[34] Dimashqî, *Târîkh*, pp. 18–19

Violence and factionalism in Hama

After the French evacuation of Palestine, Jazzâr Pasha ordered his representative in Hama, ᶜAbdallâh Aghâ al-Maḥmûd, to organize festivities in that town in celebration of this God-given victory over the unbelievers. The town was decorated with colourful banners by the local dyers. The main event was the parade in which the guilds were the principal participants, but the military, peasants, gypsies and even ᶜAnaza *ᶜarab* had also been mobilized and joined the ranks of the paraders. According to the official report on the festivities, they paraded for more than three hours through the streets of Hama, '. . . without offending, fighting and quarrelling . . .' and also there had been '. . . no instances of immoral behaviour, deceit, coercion, iniquity or destruction.'[35] Apparently, such a show of harmony was rare and it was certainly not to last in the years to come.

With the erosion of support for the family in Istanbul after the mid-eighteenth century the ᶜAẓm family had to fall back on the exploitation of their rural and urban properties in the province, which included a number of large trading facilities. The demise of the family's power on the provincial level had serious repercussions on their position in their once secure abode of Hama. The area itself suffered from numerous tribal skirmishes, including the large Mawâlî revolt in the late 1770s. The *aghawât* of the area campaigned on several occasions against the Mawâlî. The leading member of the local ᶜAẓms, ᶜAbd al-Raḥmân Bey, was taken captive by the tribesmen, together with ᶜAbd al-Razzâq al-Jundî, commander of the fortress of Tallbîsa, who was executed by the Mawâlî.[36] ᶜAbd al-Raḥmân Bey was released, but the ᶜAẓms of Hama appear to have suffered a heavy blow in these years. They may have been involved in the suppression of the janissary rebellion of Damascus and undoubtedly contributed to the campaign against the Mawâlî insurgents, but they had lost, at least temporarily, the governorship of the district.[37] The Hama area became the scene of competition between the local ᶜAẓms and contending *aghawât*. These contenders were not necessarily tied to rival provincial factions, but they had the opportunity to ally themselves to these factions when such a move appeared convenient to strengthen their position. During the second term of

[35] SMH 46, p. 276, dated 1213

[36] Murâdî, *Silk*, vol. 3, pp. 11–20; Jundî, *Târîkh*, vol. 2, p. 336

[37] The identity of the *mutasallim* of the time, Yaᶜqûb Aghâ, is unknown, but he was not an ᶜAẓm.

Jazzâr Pasha in Damascus (1790–95) factionalism in Hama increased. In 1794 fighting between the men of the *garib yiğit ağası* and the *tüfenkçi başı* erupted, in the wake of which fire was opened on the Kaylâniyya, the headquarters of the Kaylânî family, the old associates of the ᶜAẓms.[38]

The 1795 appointment of ᶜAbdallâh Pasha al-ᶜAẓm, who belonged to the Damascene branch of the family, as *wâlî* was certainly welcomed by his relatives in Hama. His terms in office were interrupted, but he did manage to promote his family's interests. ᶜAbd al-Raḥmân Bey al-ᶜAẓm served as his *mutasallim* in Hama during his first tenure.[39] When Ibrâhîm Pasha al-Ḥalabî was installed as *wâlî* of Damascus ᶜUthmân Aghâ al-Jundî, the son of the aforementioned ᶜAbd al-Razzâq Aghâ, was appointed to Hama. ᶜUthmân Aghâ was twice replaced by ᶜAbdallâh Aghâ al-Maḥmûd, a member of the Dandashlî clan of the Homs area and one of the main allies of Jazzâr Pasha, but later ᶜUthmân Aghâ served both under Jazzâr Pasha and ᶜAbdallâh Pasha al-ᶜAẓm, indicating that this *aghâ* had established himself firmly in the area.[40]

The competition between ᶜAẓm and Jazzâr factions culminated in a bloody exchange between troops of the two pashas in the streets of Hama in 1803. ᶜAbdallâh Pasha had just been replaced by Jazzâr Pasha as governor of Damascus. ᶜAbdallâh Pasha heard the news of his dismissal while laying siege to Tripoli in order to arrest its Muṣṭafâ Aghâ Barbar, a client of Jazzâr Pasha. ᶜAbdallâh Pasha lifted the siege and directed his troops to Hama to relieve the town from the troops of ᶜAbdallâh Aghâ al-Maḥmûd, another of Jazzâr Pasha's associates, former governor of Hama and then governor of Homs. The *aghâ* had set off for Hama after his patron had received the letter of appointment. He may have proceeded to Hama in order to retaliate against the ᶜAẓms for the conduct of ᶜAbdallâh Pasha's troops prior to the siege of Tripoli. Along the way from Damascus to Tripoli the pasha's troops had looted some villages, and the road which connected the interior with coastal Tripoli ran through the area where ᶜAbdallâh Aghâ al-Maḥmûd and his Dandashlî clan held sway. During the fighting in Hama ᶜAbdallâh Aghâ

[38] SMH 46, 211, 1 Rajab 1209

[39] *Ibid*, p. 231, 7 Jumâdâ I 1210; p. 250, 25 Shawwâl 1211, and p. 230, 27 Ṣafar 1212

[40] *Ibid*, p. 352, 238 and 354, dated 15 Shawwâl and 15 Dhû al-Ḥijja 1213 and p. 309, 23 Rabîᶜ II 1214; SMH 43, p. 99, 7 Rabîᶜ I 1216 and p. 108, 27 Rajab 1216. ᶜAbdallâh Aghâ al-Maḥmûd served in 1799 both as *mutasallim* of Hama and *başbuğ* (commander) of the *jarda* under Jazzâr Pasha. A certain ᶜArâbî Aghâ served ᶜAbdallâh Pasha in the early nineteenth century as well.

al-Maḥmûd was killed, together with many of his and Jazzâr's soldiers who had joined the army of the strongman of Homs. The casualties among the inhabitants were high as well, but the troops of ᶜAbdallâh Pasha al-ᶜAẓm had dealt a heavy blow to his enemy. The remainder of Jazzâr's troops escaped, but were raided by *ᶜarab*. The ᶜAẓms seemed to have secured their old rural abode from a hostile takeover.

Jazzâr Pasha had no absolute control over his commanders and associates either. He may not have consented to the conduct of his troops and those of ᶜAbdallâh Aghâ al-Maḥmûd in Hama. A few years earlier, for example, he had informed ᶜAbdallâh Aghâ al-Maḥmûd, then *mutasallim* of Hama, that a number of horsemen and soldiers had departed for the north without his consent and that they were causing trouble along their way.[41] The last year Jazzâr Pasha served as *wâlî* of Damascus was characterized by indiscriminate violence, not only in Hama, but in Damascus as well. The pasha was old and suffered from failing health. Retired in his fortified retreat in Acre, he was losing his grip on the situation. His death in April of 1804 was greeted with great relief and outbursts of joy in most of Syria. Numerous verses were composed to commemorate his death, or rather the cruelties he perpetrated during the last decade.

> The people rejoiced and their grief passed away
> because of the perdition of he who is known for his injustice (*ẓulm*)
> he brought about wrongs (*maẓâlim*) in Damascus through his tyranny
> he spread wrongs all over and dictated them
> He is Aḥmad, who should never be praised[42]

In Damascus a manhunt on his aides ensued; Jazzâr's prisoners, including criminals, were liberated by what a chronicler called the mob and the *yerliyya*. Once again the city suffered from fighting between the various armed groups, including units in the service of the late pasha.[43]

The demise of the interior factions

The death of the ruler of Acre did not put an end to provincial factionalism and the division between the interior and the coast continued to play an important role. But the degree of violence and repression that

[41] SMH 46, 361–2, 1 Jumâdâ I 1214

[42] Al-ᶜAbd, *Târîkh*, pp. 110–12

[43] *Ibid.*, pp. 88–116; Dimashqî, *Ḥawâdith*, pp. 28–29; Shaṭṭî, *Rawḍ*, pp. 41–43; Shihâb, *Lubnân*, pp. 408–09

had accompanied provincial politics during Jazzâr Pasha's last years decreased. This was partly due to the more compassionate ways of Jazzâr's heir, Sulaymân Pasha, one of his former *mamlûk*s, who was also less ambitious.[44] Nonetheless, much of the energy of the governors of Damascus during the first seven years after the death of Jazzâr Pasha was spent in trying to curb the power of their counterpart in Acre. The status of the province of Tripoli continued to play a significant role during these years. It had become a dependency of Acre under Jazzâr Pasha, who had patronized the *dizdar*, the commander of the citadel of Tripoli, Muṣṭafâ Aghâ Barbar. To the dissatisfaction of the Porte this *aghâ* continued to receive support from Acre after Jazzâr Pasha had died. Several campaigns were launched against Muṣṭafâ Aghâ Barbar by Ibrâhîm Pasha al-Ḥalabî, ᶜAbdallâh Pasha al-ᶜAẓm and his successor in Damascus, Kunj Yûsuf Pasha. Even though the *aghâ* was ousted several times, he was always able to regain control over Tripoli and this pattern would continue into the 1830s.[45]

The ᶜAẓms ceased to play a prominent role in provincial politics in the first decade of the eighteenth century. ᶜAbdallâh Pasha served another turn in Damascus, but this last tenure was troubled by fighting among the Damascene military and, more importantly, by the Wahhâbî hold on the Hijaz. In the previous years the pilgrimage had become more problematic due to the Wahhâbî control over the holy shrines, but the Syrian convoy had been allowed entrance to Mecca, albeit only after handsome payments were made. In 1807 the pasha refused to give in to the demands of the Wahhâbî leaders, who would only allow the pilgrimage convoy from Damascus entrance to the holy shrines unarmed and without the ceremonial *maḥmal*, decorated camel-borne litter. The *maḥmal* of the Egyptian convoys was even set to fire that year.[46] For the first time since 1757 the 'Syrian' pilgrimage could not be performed. After his return, ᶜAbdallâh Pasha was transferred to Adana and later to Urfa.

His successor in Damascus was recruited from his own ranks, his former *delibaşı* and *mutasallim* of Damascus, Kunj Yûsuf Pasha, a Kurd who had served earlier in the Hama area. The new pasha inherited a

[44] Sulaymân Pasha even gained the epithet of al-ᶜÂdil, the Just, see ᶜAwra's history entitled *Târîkh wilâyat Sulaymân Pasha al-ᶜÂdil*, ed. A. Qayqûnî, Beirut 1979

[45] See, for the long career of Muṣṭafâ Aghâ Barbar, Khûrî, *Barbar*.

[46] Al-ᶜAbd, *Târîkh*, pp.131–32; Jabartî, *ᶜAjâ'ib*, VI, p. 363; Dahlân, *Khulâṣat*, p. 294

problematic situation and failed to solve the old problems. The pilgrimage came to a virtual standstill – except for small groups of pilgrims who adjusted to Wahhâbî ritual – and the area to the immediate south of Damascus became the target of Wahhâbî raiders. Kunj Yûsuf Pasha would be remembered for his religious policies, as well as those concerning public order; inspired, perhaps, by a Naqshbandî mystic and possibly in reaction to Wahhâbî successes, he instructed men to grow their beards and to refrain from smoking. He banned the performance of music and shadow theatre; the playing of games and eating sweets; and took action against alcohol consumption and prostitution. Dervishes which behaved indecently – naked dervishes – were ousted from town. Christians and Jews endured stricter enforcement of some old discriminatory Islamic rulings. These policies did not make the pasha popular and the dignitaries of Damascus pleaded the withdrawal of the instructions. In times of severe crisis, the authorities sometimes took similar measures. Kunj Yûsuf Pasha's moral offence was soon to fade out.[47]

The first and, in a way, only successful pilgrimage under the responsibility, but not under the command, of Kunj Yûsuf Pasha entered Mecca, albeit with only few pilgrims and without a *maḥmal* and an Ottoman banner. In 1809 the Wahhâbîs prevented pilgrims from visiting the tomb of the Prophet Muḥammad in Medina. After receiving payments the convoy waited in vain for admission to Mecca. Until 1813, the Syrian (and Egyptian) pilgrimage was suspended. After a large Wahhâbî raiding party looted several villages in the Hawran the career of Kunj Yûsuf Pasha in Syria came to a humiliating end; in 1810 he fled to Hama and then Latakia and finally sought refuge with Muḥammad ᶜAlî Pasha in Egypt.[48]

Sulaymân Pasha, heir to Jazzâr Pasha, was appointed to Damascus. His troops, reinforced by Druze forces, took control of the city. The policies of Sulaymân Pasha compared favourably to those of Jazzâr Pasha. Although he was engaged in an, at times violent, competition with Kunj Yûsuf Pasha, he was much less inclined to coercive action and much more to reconciliation. The news of his appointment had been received with some anxiety in Damascus. When Sulaymân Pasha's

[47] Al-ᶜAbd, *Târîkh*, p. 138–43; ᶜAwra, *Târîkh*, p. 94–95; Dimashqî, *Ḥawâdith*, pp. 37–41; Shihâb, *Lubnân*, pp. 524–26. See on the Naqshbandî sheikh, Hourani, *Shaikh Khâlid*

[48] Al-ᶜAbd, *Târîkh*, pp. 143–53; Shihâb, *Lubnân*, pp. 534–83; Dimashqî, *Ḥawâdith*, pp. 26–48; Mashâqa, *Mashhad*, pp. 103–9

choice for the office of deputy governor of the city – an *aghâ* who had served Jazzâr Pasha in his violent last year in Damascus – was announced, a revolt appeared to be imminent. Sulaymân Pasha gave in to the objections against his nominee and replaced him by a leading local *aghâ*, Darwîsh Aghâ ibn Jaᶜfar Aghâ, who had previously served under ᶜAbdallâh Pasha al-ᶜAẓm. This concession did not indicate that a strong and viable interior faction still existed. On the contrary, with the flight of Kunj Yûsuf Pasha to Egypt and the disintegration of his once quite formidable army, no provincial rival of any potency was left and there was no direct danger in recruiting able and experienced officers who had been attached to the interior factions in the preceding decade. The janissary commander of the citadel later replaced Darwîsh Aghâ.[49]

Sulaymân Pasha only served for about a year and half. Until his death in the late summer of 1819, he served as governor of the provinces of Sidon and Tripoli and does not appear to have had the ambition to recover the governorship of Damascus after 1812. Rising to power in the wider region, the governor of Egypt Muḥammad ᶜAlî Pasha, had sent his forces to the Hijaz to deal with the Wahhâbîs. After initial setbacks and at high costs, Muḥammad ᶜAlî Pasha's troops regained the holy cities for the sultan in 1812 and 1813.[50] Now that the pacification of the Hijaz and adjacent areas had become the responsibility of the governor of Egypt, the pressure on the governor of Damascus to campaign against the Wahhâbî tribesmen was relieved. Together with the final disintegration of the interior provincial factions, this allowed for a change of policy towards the province of Damascus. From early 1812, only non-locals were appointed to Damascus in order to bring the province under a stricter central control. The sultan of the time, Mahmud II, initiated this policy in Anatolia and the province of Aleppo. In September 1811, a former protégé of Sultan Selim III and officer in his new standing army had been appointed as governor of Aleppo. This governor, Muḥammad Râghib Pasha, was unable to bring the province of Aleppo

[49] Shihâb, *Lubnân*, p. 560; Al-ᶜAbd, *Târîkh*, p. 153

[50] Muḥammad ᶜAlî Pasha had first refused to fight the Wahhâbî movement. In 1811, however, he conceded to the pressure from the Porte. Al-Sayyid Marsot (*Egypt*, p. 198–202) refers to this campaign, which lasted until June 1815, as the pasha's first war of expansion. In this period Muḥammad ᶜAlî Pasha contemplated the idea of annexing the province of Damascus to his realm. The Wahhâbîs were forced to retreat into their heartland, the Najd. The pasha's attempts to establish control over the Najd had no lasting effect. In 1824 new campaigns were initiated to suppress the movement.

under his control and faced several uprisings. After the pasha had their leading sheikh killed while entertaining him as his guest, the Mawâlî revolted and the ᶜ*arab* avenged the death of Amîr Kunj, the son of Muḥammad Khurfân.[51] In the province of Damascus the change in policy was more successful and it produced at least one positive effect: factionalism acquired a local and usually petty nature. The period of intense and violent competition for the resources of the Syrian provinces, in particular those of the province of Damascus, a period which had started with the emergence of Jazzâr Pasha's military household in the 1780s, had come to an end. The factions of the interior, of which Kunj Yûsuf Pasha may be considered the last representative, had exhausted their means first. Notwithstanding their relative strength, the Acre faction also suffered from exhaustion. Sulaymân Pasha had inherited a domain which had been exploited well beyond the limit by Jazzâr Pasha during the last years of his life. Combined with war efforts related to the French invasion and the depression of trade with Europe, the extremely oppressive rule of Jazzâr Pasha had resulted in a decrease of economic activity in Acre and its hinterland and in the departure of a considerable part of its inhabitants.[52]

[51] See Bodman, *Factions*, p. 128–30 and Shihâb, *Lubnân*, pp. 584–85
[52] Philipp, *Social*, pp. 101–03

5. Local politics and violence

By the late eighteenth century the management of violence in the Syrian provinces had acquired a highly fragmented, but fluid nature. Local governors employed a wide variety of soldiers, varying from foreign mercenaries to locally recruited nomads. The troops were equipped for the collection of taxes and the maintenance of order, especially along the major lines of communication. In the province of Damascus, the latter task constituted a major concern in view of the all-important yearly pilgrimage. Troops employed in the area proved to be ill-equipped for resisting enemy forces; Napoleon's army experienced a near walkover in Palestine until the walls of Acre halted it and Wahhâbî warriors met with hardly any resistance. Local troops were better prepared for coercive action against the subject population, but the trade of a soldier was insecure following strong competition for local resources and heavy demands put forward by the Porte and their local representatives.

Soldier Pashas

The rotation of provincial rivals as governors of Damascus during the period 1785–1812 created an atmosphere of instability in which commanders of regular and auxiliary forces came to play an important role; for a number of decades a small group of proficient commanders constituted the continuum in local politics in inland Syria. These military had, of course, always been an important factor in provincial administration and politics. Many governors who served in the Syrian provinces had started their careers as professional soldiers, including the first generation of the ʿAẓm governors. All but one of the governors of Damascus who served between 1785 and 1812 were of humble soldierly background. The exception was ʿAbdallâh Pasha al-ʿAẓm, himself the son of a pasha. This is in marked contrast with the period 1744–1784, in which the sons of pashas had dominated the office.[1] A more typical

[1] The only important exception in this period was ʿUthmân Pasha al-Kurjî, who served in the 1760s. He was a former *mamlûk* of Asʿad Pasha al-ʿAẓm. He

career pattern was that of Kunj Yûsuf, a mounted *deli*, who started his career in the Hama area in the service of the most reputed *delibaşı* of the time, Mullâ Ismâ'îl (see p. 115). In the 1790s Kunj Yûsuf Aghâ served ᶜAbdallâh Pasha al-ᶜAẓm as *delibaşı* and may have accompanied him in that capacity when the pasha was taken captive by French troops.[2] Jazzâr Pasha, who endured the siege of Acre by French troops, engaged Kunj Yûsuf during his last term as governor of Damascus. After the death of Jazzâr Pasha, Kunj Yûsuf remained in Damascus, first in the service of Ibrâhîm Pasha al-Ḥalabî and, subsequently, again in the service of ᶜAbdallâh Pasha. By now a bey, he was appointed deputy governor when the pasha left for the Hijaz in his function as commander of the pilgrimage. After ᶜAbdallâh Pasha was humiliated by the Wahhâbî leadership – which refused the passage of the pilgrimage caravan to Mecca, even after the pasha had handed over the customary payments to the rich and poor of Mecca – Kunj Yûsuf replaced his former master in 1807. Other candidates for the office, in particular Jazzâr Pasha, his heir Sulaymân Pasha, Ibrâhîm Pasha al-Dalâtî and Ibrâhîm Pasha al-Ḥalabî were career soldiers; the first two were *mamlûk* soldiers, the third a *deli*, and the fourth a militiaman of a prominent sharîf of Aleppo.

The janissaries of Damascus

The prominence of the ex-soldiers after 1786 reflects the more violent character provincial rule had assumed. Apart from soldiers who made it to provincial governor, a broader stratum of influential *aghawât* existed. They included the commanders of both the *yerli* (local) and imperial janissaries of Damascus. Principle among the *yerli* chiefs were Darwîsh Aghâ ibn Jaᶜfar Aghâ, Muḥammad Aghâ ibn ᶜAqîl, Ḥasan Aghâ ibn Tîmûr, Ismâᶜîl Shurbajî[3] ibn Mahâyinî, and ᶜAbd al-Ghanî Aghâ al-Shâmlî.[4] Their position was vested in the capacity of the family

started his career as an *aghâ* in the Hama area. See Burayk, *Târîkh*, p. 81. Two of his sons served as governor of Damascus in 1783 and 1784.

2 Al-ᶜAẓm, *Al-usra*, p. 42; Dimashqî, *Ḥawâdith*, pp. 35–36

3 Shurbajî is the Syrian Arabic equivalent for the janissary rank of 'soup-maker'; commander.

4 See, on the Maydân, Marino, *Faubourg*. The author mainly offers statistical information derived from court records and gives some data on specific individuals. Some *yerli* families would retain their prominent position all through the nineteenth century, in particular the Mahâyinî and Shâmlî families of the Maydân. Schatkowski-Schilcher (*Families*, pp. 146, 149–50) gives some

households in rallying support on the provincial and central levels; official recognition of their local prominence was vital to their functioning.

The chiefs of the local janissaries occupied a variety of offices, and often acted as deputy governors. Darwîsh Aghâ ibn Jaᶜfar Aghâ had the longest career of all, serving the various governors appointed to Damascus from the early 1790s into the 1820s. Others had less successful careers; not long after Jazzâr Pasha had appointed Muḥammad Aghâ ibn ᶜAqîl as his deputy in Damascus, the *aghâ* died in the pasha's prison in Acre. In the wake of serious disturbances in Damascus (see below) Kunj Yûsuf Pasha had Ismâᶜîl Shurbajî ibn Mahâyinî and some of his sons arrested and strangled. In both cases the arrests and executions were followed by the confiscation of the wealth of the victims.[5] Notwithstanding the violent deaths of these *aghawât*, their families, especially the Mahâyinî, continued to play a prominent role in Damascene politics.

The career of a Damascene *aghâ* – though some were only second or third generation townsmen[6] – was normally more secure than that of an 'imperial' janissary colleague who resided in the citadel or in the castle of Muzayrîb to the south of Damascus. The citadel was the most solid expression of Ottoman power over the ancient city and served as its principal military bulwark. Muzayrîb was located strategically in the hinterland of Damascus: the Hawran, famous for its wheat. The castle also served as one of the main stations for the pilgrimage; large quantities of dry cakes, on which the pilgrims survived, were stored there. In cases of emergency, these supplies could serve other purposes, such as marketing the dry cakes in Damascus during food shortages. Consequently, Damascene authorities made sure that they maintained control over Muzayrîb.[7]

The distinction between imperial and local janissaries had become somewhat blurred by the late eighteenth century. For instance, some who came as imperial janissaries later joined the *yerilyya*. Moreover,

information on a number of families. More details on these and other *aghawât* are contained in the three main chronicles: Al-ᶜAbd, *Târîkh*; Shihâb, *Lubnân*; Dimashqî, *Ḥawâdith*.

[5] Al-ᶜAbd, *Târîkh*, pp. 95–96, 99–100, 137–38; Dimashqî, *Ḥawâdith*, pp. 25–27, 37–38

[6] The Al-Mahâyinî originated from the Hama area and the Shâmlî from the Shammar beduin.

[7] Burckhardt, *Travels*, pp. 240–46

locals were sometimes assigned to the command of the citadel and the fortress. The place of recruitment seems to have defined the latter's status as *yerliyya*, not necessarily the regional background of the recruit. In need of a more dependable military representation the Porte continued to dispatch *qûl,* fresh janissaries, to Damascus not only from Anatolia but also from Iraq. These troops were known as Mawâṣila (from Mosul) and Baghâdda (Baghdad). Apart from manning the citadel and fortresses, they were also enrolled in the urban musketeer units, the *tüfankci*s.

The careers of the *qûl* commanders appear to have been shorter than those of most of their local colleagues. When imperial janissaries turned against their masters, the sultan or his local representative, the governor, or were accused of doing so, they were subjected to rigid reprimands. The citadel provided them a sanctuary, but only as long as the provisions and internal cohesion of the *qûl* lasted. Aḥmad Aghâ al-Zaᶜfaranjî, Muḥammad Aghâ Urfa Amînî[8] and ᶜAlî Aghâ al-Baghdâdî, to mention three of the more influential imperial janissary commanders of the province of Damascus, were, like a handful of other imperial *aghawât*, strangled, hanged or put to death otherwise. While the officers often faced death penalties in the wake of revolts or other displays of disloyalty, their troops sometimes escaped to the villages or were collectively dismissed and banned. Thus they added to the ranks of roving soldiers in the countryside.

The last Janissary revolts in Damascus

Damascene *yerli* janissaries, long since, had ceased to contribute to the war efforts of the Ottoman empire. While until the early nineteenth century *yerli* commanders from Aleppo headed their units to the (Russian) front, their Damascene counterparts were most reluctant to comply with demand for military or police action outside of the city itself. Even the defence of the city was left to the imperial troops of the citadel; in 1771 when the troops of ᶜAlî Bey of Egypt attacked Damascus, the local janissaries did not resist, but the bey's soldiers failed to take the citadel.[9] Typically, hardly any *yerli* involvement occurred in the years of large scale regional campaigning following the French invasion of Egypt and Palestine and the Wahhâbî takeover of the Hijaz. It may be that the increased employment of various other military

[8] Arabic for *urpa amînî*, the controller of the barley provisions.

[9] Rafeq, *Province*, p. 260–71

units in and around Damascus, such as the *maghâriba* and the *deli*s, by the governors of the period curbed the remaining military capacities of the local janissaries. But they continued to use their arms in local disputes, especially during the decade in between 1798–1807. On several occasions they attacked the imperial janissaries or other military. ᶜAbdallâh Pasha al-ᶜAẓm faced several *yerli* revolts, in particular during his absence when touring the province or when heading the pilgrimage. Ibrâhîm Pasha, too, had difficulty controlling the situation in Damascus during his two terms in office. Jazzâr Pasha's troops were better equipped, but after his death the local janissaries took the lead in the manhunt on the late pasha's men and freed all prisoners. After 1807, Kunj Yûsuf Pasha restored order in Damascus by arresting a large number of leading *aghawât*, in particular among those circles which had cooperated closely with ᶜAbdallâh Pasha al-ᶜAẓm, among them Darwîsh Aghâ ibn Jaᶜfar Aghâ and a number of his relatives. Shortly thereafter, Ismâᶜîl Shurbajî ibn Mahâyinî and his sons were also taken captive. Most were bailed out of prison, but Ismâᶜîl Shurbajî was executed.[10] The precise motives of Kunj Yûsuf Pasha are unknown; he may have felt the need to demonstrate his power over the unruly city and he was certainly in need of cash; he had to prepare for a campaign against the Wahhâbîs. The pasha's moves, however, were not directed against the institution of the *yerliyya*; he selected his principal aide, his *kethüda*, from among them: Ḥasan Aghâ ibn Tîmûr.

In the following 25 years, Damascus witnessed only few janissary rebellions. The first occurred in 1812 when the commander of the citadel, ᶜAlî Aghâ al-Baghdâdî, refused to surrender the citadel to the new governor Sulaymân Pasha Silahdar; he surrendered after several days of siege and cannon firing. The rebel *aghâ* was strangled and his troops were given the option to leave the city.[11] A number of executions of leading *aghawât* in the following years suggests that other incidents happened, but the grounds for these punitive actions are unclear, except that most were executed during the insecure months of the transmission of power from one governor to another. In one case a chronicler remarked that Ṭâlib Aghâ the son of Muḥammad Aghâ ibn ᶜAqîl of the Maydân, was executed by a recently arrived governor because the victim '. . . was rich and famous'.[12] The pasha might well have retaliated

[10] Al-ᶜAbd, *Târîkh*, pp.135–37; Dimashqî, *Ḥawâdith*, pp. 37–38.
[11] Al-ᶜAbd, *Târîkh*, pp. 154–55
[12] Dimashqî, *Ḥawâdith*, p. 60

against this leading *yerli aghâ* for the way the Damascenes had treated his predecessor; when news of his dismissal arrived he was kicked out of town.[13]

In the 1820s conflicts and rebellions in coastal Syria – and even more so in Greece – attracted the attention of the authorities.[14] The rebellions caused some anxiety due to the movement of troops through inland Syria and the Greek insurrection in particular generated negative reactions against local Christians of the Greek rite. But by and large, the inhabitants of inland Syria experienced quiet times and both the population at large and the *aghawât* and their men remained unmolested in these years.[15] Another indication that political factionalism and the accompanying violence had indeed subsided to a considerable extent was the fact that the office of the *muftî*, the most prominent of local ulema, became much more secure. Until 1813 the office had often changed hands, but it did so only twice between 1813 and 1830. The first time in 1815 when the *muftî* ᶜAlî Efendi al-Murâdî died and was succeeded by his son Ḥusayn Efendi, whose prolonged tenure was interrupted for one year by Saᶜîd Efendi al-ᶜAjlânî, who was a son of Ḥamza Efendi al-ᶜAjlânî, the *muftî* who had served prior to ᶜAlî Efendi al-Murâdî.[16] It is of interest that the Murâdî family was able to dominate the office (well into the 1840s), while their former patrons, the Damascene ᶜAẓms, lost much of their past influence.

Even the news of the abolition of the janissary corps and the ensuing violent repression of the janissary mutiny in Istanbul in 1826 brought about some anxiety among the ranks of the janissaries in the Syrian provinces. In his efforts to build the *nizam-e cedid*, the new army, Sultan Mahmud II ran out of cash and time. As a consequence, the financial demands made upon the provinces increased sharply, leading to popular revolts in Homs and elsewhere.[17] Although some janissaries were involved in the disturbances, they were not janissary revolts. Some

[13] Shihâb, *Lubnân*, p. 631. Shihâb, too, stresses the innocence of the victim.

[14] The rebellion of ᶜAbdallâh Pasha of Acre in the early 1820s constituted the most formidable threat to central authority.

[15] The chronicler Dimashqî (*Ḥawâdith*, pp. 50–62) described the *wâlî*s of the time as *ᶜâdil* (just) or *ṣâhib ḥarakât* (energetic). In particular Ṣâliḥ Pasha who ruled for several years is characterized as just, gentle and intelligent, al-ᶜAbd (*Târîkh*, pp. 153–65) also judges them favourably.

[16] Shaṭṭî, *Rawḍ*, pp. 89–90, 129–30, and 199–203. See also Schatkowski-Schilcher, *Families*, p. 119

[17] See, for the revolt in Homs in 1826, Asᶜad, *Târîkh*, II, p. 370

attempts were made to transfer the janissaries of Damascus into the new army, but these attempts produced little effect. By and large the traditional military remained intact in Syria until the early 1830s. With the abolition of the corps, the division between local and imperial janissaries might have lost its relevance, but janissaries continued to function well into the 1840s on the local level.[18]

A series of less successful pilgrimages[19] and a change in fiscal policies caused Damascus to revolt in 1831. When the former grand vizier, Muḥammad Salîm Pasha, was ordered to suppress the revolt, the local janissaries might well have felt nervous; the new governor had been associated with the formation of the new army and was escorted by 5000 troops when he entered the city. After negotiations had failed Damascene janissaries attacked the governor's troops, forcing them to retreat to the citadel. Casualties were high and in the course of the fighting several governmental buildings and markets were put to fire. During the rebellion, which lasted for several weeks, some *aghawât* of the Maydân followed a more radical line than the inner-city notables, headed by the Ḥanafî *muftî*. When the governor surrendered to rebel forces, he was brought to the house of the late Muḥammad Pasha al-ᶜAẓm, where he stayed for some days. He was then moved to a house belonging to a Kaylânî on the pretext that he and his men would have more space to themselves, but it may well be that the ᶜAẓm were reluctant to entertain the governor given the hostile mood which prevailed in the city. At night the house was attacked and set on fire. The governor and his retinue were killed and their heads paraded through the city. Janissaries had now seized control of the city. In consultation with a number of leading ulema they restored public order and prepared for Ottoman retaliation. A new governor arrived, but he was unable to take charge. The population suffered from scarcity of food and exorbitant prices until relief supplies of wheat and other provisions were brought in from Hama and Muzayrîb. The pilgrimage was cancelled.

The invasion of Syria by the troops of Muḥammad ᶜAlî Pasha altered

[18] The same appears to have been true for Aleppo, see Bodman, *Political*, pp. 138–39. Koury (*Province*, pp. 183–84) argues that the division between local and imperial janissaries had now ceased to exist, but this will have depended on the prolongation or abolition of certain privileges on the local level. Moreover, the janissaries of the citadel – imperial janissaries – seem to have receive payments until the early 1830s (Dimashqî, *Ḥawâdith*, p. 51).

[19] Koury, *Province*, p. 187

the situation in Damascus drastically; in June 1832 his son Ibrâhîm Pasha and his impressive forces arrived in the vicinity of the city and met with little armed resistance. Uncertain about the pasha's actions, most *aghawât* and a number of ulema retreated to the countryside or to areas under loyalist control. One of the few *aghawât* who did not flee was the commander of the citadel; he handed the keys to Ibrâhîm Pasha and was pardoned. In the following days many refugee *aghawât* returned; eventually 75 of them, supplying about 1000 combatants, joined the Egyptian troops in their move to the north.[20]

The fragmented management of violence

In the Syrian provinces, janissary forces were tied to specific localities, towns or fortresses. They were not very mobile and some were even fully stationary, as in the case of the local janissaries in Damascus. *Deli* cavalry and the Maghâriba (Maghrebins) constituted the most formidable fighting units; the first serving mostly in the countryside and the second anywhere they were needed. D*eli*s were closely associated with Kurds. *Deli* commanders figured prominently in the households of the 'Aẓm governors, but in general the mounted *deli*s constituted the most important auxiliary force and a number of *delibaşıs* occupied vital positions.[21] The Maghrebin infantry and cavalry originated from the Maghreb. The employment of mercenaries from Northern Africa predates Ottoman times, but the numbers recruited in the late eighteenth century were unprecedented. The recruits were often sons of soldiers of the Dey of Algiers who were not enrolled in the Dey's army.[22] The Maghrebin forces substituted the so-called *sakbân* (dog-keepers) forces which had dominated in the late seventeenth and early eighteenth centuries and who were of Anatolian extraction. In line with regional tradition, the *sakbân* were not fully replaced and, until the early years of the nineteenth century, some units operated in the service of Jazzâr Pasha of Acre who was also the largest employer of Maghrebin forces.

The high demand for military and police services in the provinces offered yet other groups of soldiers employment, among them *arnâ'ûṭ*,

[20] See for a detailed account of the events, *Mudhakkirât*, pp. 22–56; see also, Dimashqî, *Ḥawâdith*, pp. 75–80; Koury, *Province*, pp. 189–98; Schatkowski-Schilcher, *Families*, 40–43

[21] This seems to have been the case in the province of Aleppo as well, see Bodman, *Political*, pp. 24–25.

[22] Rafeq, *Local*, p. 286

lewend and a variety of clan-based militia. *Arnâ'ûṭ* were recruited from the Balkans and operated in the Syrian provinces from the late eighteenth century onwards. Their more permanent presence in the region appears to have been closely connected with the career of Jazzâr Pasha, himself a Bosnian.[23] After his death their number decreased, but occasionally new parties of *arnâ'ûṭ* arrived. In 1808, for example, 500 *arnâ'ûṭ* who had been stationed in Egypt landed in Tripoli on the Lebanese coast. They had been hired to relieve the local strongman Barbar Aghâ, who was confronted by Kunj Yûsuf Pasha and had laid siege to the town. Upon their arrival the inhabitants of Tripoli escaped to the besieging troops of the pasha.[24] The *arnâ'ûṭ* were regarded as the most proficient military units and had a reputation of brusque conduct. They shared this reputation with the *levend*, cavalry auxiliaries from Anatolia. After their official disbandment in 1776, *levend* forces arrived in Syria and they '. . . did fear neither death nor ruin.' These qualities were greatly valued and they were engaged by several governors, among them Muhammad Pasha al-ᶜAẓm who hired about 300 *levend* cavaliers.[25] With the blessing of the Porte, Jazzâr Pasha contracted other *levend* units.[26]

It might well be that *deli*, *levend* and *arnâ'ûṭ* groups were partly organized by clan or common place of birth. This was certainly the case with beduin cavalry units from Egypt which were introduced in the Syrian provinces in the late eighteenth century. The ill-fated invasion of the troops of 'Alî Bey al-Kabîr of Egypt in 1771 brought about 300 horsemen of the Hawwâra tribe to the area in the retinue of Aḥmad Bey, the later Jazzâr Pasha. In the 1790s their number had increased to, perhaps as much as 1000 horsemen, who were instrumental in extending Jazzâr Pasha's control over Mount Lebanon and the coastal areas.[27] Fresh Egyptian beduin units entered Syria in 1831 and 1832 in the armies of Muḥammad Alî Pasha, who also employed Hinâdî beduin from Egypt. Hinâdî tribesmen had come to southern Syria earlier (in 1809) seeking employment. The cessation of the pilgrimage had deprived them of their livelihood, and they offered their services to

[23] The Syrian provinces had witnessed *arnâ'ûṭ* forces earlier. See Budayrî, *Yawmiyyât*, p. 50

[24] Shihâb, *Lubnân*, p. 536

[25] *Ibid.*, pp. 117–18; The French traveller Volney (*Voyage*, vol. 2, 375) reported that all villagers trembled when *levend* passed by.

[26] Cohen, *Palestine*, pp. 283–84

[27] Shihâb, *Lubnân*, pp. 146–48, 164–183, 205–208

Muḥammad Aghâ Abû Nabbût – which means Muḥammad Aghâ with the Club – one of the more influential commanders in the southern realms and then the governor of Gaza. Instead of hiring the beduin, he ordered them to leave his area; in the ensuing skirmishes, the tribesmen defeated his troops, thus demonstrating their proficiency.[28] Of the local beduin only the Mawâlî were employed as a police force on a regular basis; their chief headed a force of about 400 horsemen in the early nineteenth century.[29]

Locals in the Syrian provinces manifested themselves above all in irregular rural militia, in particular clan-based bands of the inhabitants of the mountainous and hilly regions. Communities in the coastal mountains and in hilly areas like Nablus in Palestine and Hawran to the south of Damascus had a marked military tradition and often showed great proficiency. Foremost among them were the Druzes of Lebanon and the Hawran. They constituted close-knit communities and demonstrated a striking capacity for feuding and fighting. Contrary to most other more militant communities, they ascended the parochial setting in which most other armed clans operated. Druze clan leaders and their men regularly played a significant role in provincial politics. On occasion they were contracted by the authorities for services of extra-local importance. In the early seventeenth century the Druze Emir Fakhr al-Dîn (II) and his troops even escorted the pilgrimage caravan to Mecca. Later Druze emirs of Lebanon did not compare to him in power, but several of them belonged to the more dominant actors in the region. Druze forces were involved in several larger military operations, including the suppression of the 1788 janissary revolt in Damascus and the occupation of the city by the troops of Ibrâhîm Pasha of Egypt in 1832 when the mixed Druze-Christian force of Emir Bashîr (II), who had sided with the pasha, entered the city first.

Other militia of consequence for the politics of both inland and coastal Syria included the men in arms of clans in the Nablus area[30] and the area in between Tripoli and Homs; ᶜAkkâr and Tell Kalakh. Some of the *aghawât* leading the villagers in arms were of janissary or sipahi background. ᶜUthmân Aghâ of the Jundî family, affiliates of the ᶜAẓms, and ᶜAbdallâh Aghâ al-Maḥmûd, head of the influential Danâdisha clan of Tell Kalakh, were both major actors in the Hama and Homs area

[28] *Ibid.*, p. 544

[29] See p. 25–7

[30] See Doumani, *Rediscovering*.

around 1800 and operated from what seems to have been a relatively secure rural base. The same was true of ʿAlî Bey al-Asʿad, the leading *aghâ* of the ʿAkkâr and for most of the time the associate of governors of Damascus in their strife with the Acre governors for the control of the province of Tripoli.

Most rural *aghawât* were tied to a specific locality, but many others had no strong local ties, among them military who had been recruited as *mamlûk* or as mercenary from outside the Syrian provinces or from nomadic groups. This does not imply that all *mamlûk*s and mercenaries lacked local ties. In Acre with its strong *mamlûk* household founded by Jazzâr Pasha, part of the *mamlûk*s established close relations with the locality, which they turned into their stronghold. In the case of quite a number of the *aghawât* and their troops, ethnicity rather than locality predominated in their relations and orientation. The population often identified them as ethnic groups: as Kurds, Turks, Maghrebins or *arna'uṭ*. The Kurds constituted the dominant ethnic group within various military formations.[31] The governors made extensive use of the services of both local *aghawât* and the more mobile 'ethnic' *aghawât*. The diversity of military forces operating in the provinces mirrored the fragmentation of the management of violence as well as an increase in the use of violence towards the close of the eighteenth century. Local and imperial janissary, musketeers, *sakbân*, Mawâlî and other forces were supplemented – and sometimes supplanted – by *deli*s, Maghrebins, *lewend, arnâ'ût*, Hawwâra and others. None of the governors of Damascus or Acre pursued military reforms. It is true that Jazzâr Pasha invested great sums in his armies, but he did so by engaging all available military specialists, ranging from Egyptian beduin cavalry to Afghan infantry. Unlike Muḥammad 'Alî Pasha, who arrived in Egypt at the time of Jazzâr Pasha's death, he did not implement any structural military reforms. Where Muḥammad 'Alî Pasha replaced a highly fragmented system by a unified system open to a broad local participation through conscription, Jazzâr Pasha deliberately maintained the distinctive character of the various troops at his disposal. Only in case of emergency did he combine them. In 1791, for example, his *deli*s, Hawwâra, *arna'uṭ, sakbân* and Maghrebin forces campaigned jointly in the

[31] In all local Arabic chronicles there are clear signs of a strong ethnic consciousness, especially in the case of the *aghawât* and their troops. Jazzâr Pasha made extensive use of Kurdish auxiliary forces. During his last year as governor of Damascus the city was ruled by his *akrâd*. See Shaṭṭî, *Rawḍ*, pp. 40–43

Shûf area in Lebanon. Together with some Druze and other bands, the campaign involved perhaps as many as 12,000 men.[32] The campaign was successful; the local Druzes who followed Emir Bashîr were subdued and their emir and his men had to seek refuge in the Hawran. Joint expeditions were not always a success; in 1794 Jazzâr Pasha dispatched his *deli*s and Maghrebins to the Matn area in Lebanon. Upon arrival they clashed with each other.[33]

Mullâ Ismâ^cîl, a warlord

One particular *delibaşı*, Mullâ Ismâᶜîl, was deeply involved in Syrian politics of the late eighteenth and early nineteenth centuries. He ranked among the most influential officers in the Syrian provinces.[34] He was a Kurd, but otherwise his origins are obscure. His followers were referred to as Mulliyya and those of his associate in Hama Barâziyya. Both the Mulliyya and Barâziyya are Kurdish tribes.[35] Mullâ Ismâᶜîl offered his services to all governors of Damascus and Acre during this period. During the suppression of the janissary revolt of 1788 he mediated between Ibrâhîm Deli Pasha and the commander of the citadel.[36] While serving ᶜAbdallâh Pasha al-ᶜAẓm he developed a special relation with the Hama area. By 1805, when ᶜAbdallâh Pasha was still governor of Damascus, Mullâ Ismâᶜîl had made a fortune and had taken up residence in Hama. Many sought his support or mediation. In his days the Hama area served as a place of refuge for many, including high-ranking non-local officials and Druze emirs involved in the numerous factional conflicts in Lebanon.[37] Others were sent to him in order to be kept in custody.

Naturally, Mullâ Ismâᶜîl was involved with several strongmen from areas adjacent to Hama, like Muṣṭafâ Aghâ Barbar of Tripoli and the Nuṣayrî headman of Ṣâfitâ, Ṣaqar al-Maḥfuḍ. Few of them could afford to be faithful allies in these times and Mullâ Ismâᶜîl, too, regularly

[32] Shihâb, *Lubnân*, pp.166–67

[33] Ibid., p.177

[34] Shihâb (*Lubnân*, p. 415) refers to him as 'kabîr aghawât al-dalâtiyya', the senior *aghâ* of the *deli*s.

[35] SMH and the chroniclers use Mullâ, Munlâ and Mullû interchangeably, which was not uncommon., and families of these tribes settled in the towns of the Syrian interior, including Hama, see Zakariyâ, *ᶜAshâ'ir*, p. 664.

[36] See p. 89–90

[37] See for example the case of Muḥammad Pasha Abû Maraq, Shihâb, *Lubnân*, pp. 435–36

changed sides, sometimes abruptly. In 1806, for example, Muṣṭafâ Aghâ Barbar ransacked the Ṣâfîtâ area after Mullâ Ismâᶜîl had withdrawn his support from Ṣaqar al-Maḥfûḍ.

The relation between Mullâ Ismâᶜîl and Kunj Yûsuf Pasha is of interest. The latter had started his career in the service of Mullâ Ismâᶜîl, but disengaged himself from his patron. Like his former master Kunj Yûsuf entered the service of ᶜAbdallâh Pasha al-ᶜAẓm and had a quick career. Mullâ Ismâᶜîl became, at least nominally, Kunj Yûsuf's inferior when the latter was promoted to governor of Damascus, but the veteran *delibaşı* followed his own interests.

On several occasions Mullâ Ismâᶜîl offered his services to Kunj Yûsuf Pasha. He campaigned with the pasha against Muṣṭafâ Aghâ Barbar in 1808, as well as against the local rulers of the Biqa valley, the Shiite Ḥarfûsh clan. Mullâ Ismâᶜîl also acted as a mediator in a number of disputes involving Kunj Yûsuf Pasha and various parties in Mount Lebanon and the Biqa valley. On behalf of the governor he restored the small town of Miṣyâf in the Hama area to its Ismaili inhabitants, after they had been expelled by the Nuṣayrî Rasâlina clan.[38] In 1810 Kunj Yûsuf Pasha's position in Damascus had become most awkward in the face of Wahhâbî incursions into southern Syria, local opposition to his rule and a military defeat at the hands of Sulaymân Pasha of Acre – who claimed the province of Damascus – and his Druze allies. The pasha called upon Mullâ Ismâᶜîl for military assistance. When it became apparent that Mullâ Ismâᶜîl had decided to throw in his lot with Sulaymân Pasha and remained in Hama, Kunj Yûsuf Pasha speeded up his preparations to escape to Egypt. His old patron allowed him to pass through his area in order to evade the area in control of Sulaymân Pasha. Mullâ Ismâᶜîl was duly rewarded by Sulaymân Pasha who replaced Kunj Yûsuf in Damascus; he was appointed his deputy governor (*mutasallim*) in both Hama and Homs.[39]

About a year after his appointment to Hama, Mullâ Ismâᶜîl fell from grace. He left Hama and sought refuge with the Mawâlî tribesmen. His departure was accompanied by apparently extreme violence, because news of disturbances in the Hama area shocked the public in

[38] Shihâb, *Lubnân*, pp. 501–02, 529, 534, 538, 541, 554–55

[39] Dimashqî, *Ḥawâdith*, pp. 45–46; Shihâb, *Lubnân*, pp. 556–59. Prior to his appointment as mutasallim, Mullâ Ismâᶜîl was referred to as *ḥâkim* (ruler) of Hama which might indicate that he had acted in an unofficial capacity.

Damascus.[40] He then established himself as a rebel chief in the fortress village of Qalᶜat al-Madîq, overseeing the entrance of the marshy Ghâb valley. Qalᶜat al-Madîq was located just outside of the Hama district and belonged to the province of Aleppo. Mullâ Ismâᶜîl maintained close relations with several local *ᶜarab* tribes who tended his huge flocks of sheep. He aligned himself with the self-appointed rulers of Jisr al-Shughûr, a small town in the northern Ghâb, and of Arîḥâ, an even smaller town in the northern Jabal Zâwiya. The thinly inhabited triangle in between these three places constituted a favoured retreat for insurgent *aghawât* and *ᶜarab*, given its remoteness from the city of Aleppo, the seat of the governor. The bravest among the European travellers, Richard Burckhardt, was so impressed by the stories told about Mullâ Ismâᶜîl – who was an old man when the young Swiss passed through the Ghâb valley – that he did not dare to enter Qalᶜat al-Madîq.[41] In 1811 the governor of Aleppo campaigned against a number of local *aghawât*, but his troops were defeated. His successor was more successful and in 1813 some of the leading rebel *aghawât* of the area escaped for the Lebanon. They then sought refuge with an *ᶜarab* tribe and later chose exile in Egypt.[42] In contrast to his former associates, Mullâ Ismâᶜîl made another comeback; he was even hired by Sulaymân Pasha Silahdar in 1813 to head the yearly tour to collect taxes in the province.

With the retreat to the fortress village of Qalᶜat al-Madîq his career had not come to an end, but during the second decade of the nineteenth century the provincial factionalism on which the warlord had fed subsided. The exclusion of the provincial factional leaders from the governorship of Damascus brought a higher degree of political stability to the Syrian interior, but circumstances in the countryside were far from ideal; the effects of the tribal shifts were strongly felt. The Hama area witnessed two major incidents involving *ᶜarab* tribes, and Mullâ Ismâᶜîl, who reputedly was respected and feared by the *ᶜarab*,[43] was a participant in both. In the spring of 1815 a number of ᶜAnaza tribes arrived from the Najd in the area to the east of Hama, among them the large Fadᶜân and their clients, the Sibâᶜa. Their arrival caused great alarm, not the least among the Ḥasana tribe which had recently

[40] Dimashqî, *Ḥawâdith*, p. 50. A Damascene Kurdish rebel *aghâ* who had escaped to the Hama area, was later executed (*ibid.*, p. 58).

[41] Burckhardt, *Travels*, p. 138. Apparently, the fortress had recently been evacuated by the janissary *muḥâfiẓ* troops.

[42] Shihâb, *Lubnân*, pp. 572, 581–98, 621–22

[43] (Stanhope), *Travels*, II, p. 89

established itself as the dominant tribe in the area. The Ḥasana, too, belonged to the ᶜAnaza, but to a competing faction. They mobilized the support of the large Wuld ᶜAlî, the dominant ᶜAnaza tribe in the area to the south of Damascus.[44] The tribesmen entered an exceptional coalition with Maghrebin and *arnâ'ûṭ* units from Damascus, local troops from Hama, the Biqa and ᶜAkkâr. Mullâ Ismâᶜîl and his cavalry were also engaged. The allies built up their forces in the Salamiyya area, to the southeast of Hama. A fierce battle followed which is said to have lasted for over two weeks. After suffering heavy casualties the Damascene troops retreated to Hama, later followed by Mullâ Ismâᶜîl and ᶜAlî Bey al-Asᶜad, the commander of the troops from ᶜAkkâr. Only the Ḥasana and Wuld ᶜAlî continued fighting until the Fadᶜân and Sibâᶜa withdrew to the north. The troops from Damascus and elsewhere returned home. Shortly afterwards when most troops had left the area, the Ḥasana and Wuld ᶜAlî, who now had their camps in the area to the west of Hama, became the target of retaliation raids of the Fadᶜân.[45]

In the spring of 1818 a second major incident occurred in the Hama area involving a completely different alliance. A tribal coalition had been forged which included the tribes that had clashed with each other three years earlier; for the occasion the ᶜAnaza had joined their forces. The local *ᶜarab* tribes, or more accurately their flocks, formed their main target. It was believed that Mullâ Ismâᶜîl had helped to bring about the coalition through his close relations with the Turkî tribe, a small but militant group. Salîm Bey al-ᶜAẓm, the *mutasallim* of Hama, went to Damascus to bring the matter to the notice of Ṣâliḥ Pasha, then governor. While on his return to Hama, the ᶜAnaza launched their long-awaited attack and carried off a huge number of sheep. The governor directed his troops to Hama and issued orders to have Mullâ Ismâᶜîl executed. The ᶜAnaza had retreated by the time the troops arrived. Mullâ Ismâᶜîl tried to open negotiations with the authorities, but was shot dead during a meeting with the Salîm Bey in the *sarâyâ* of Hama. Except for his personal belongings, his properties were confiscated. Ṣâliḥ Pasha distributed the thousands of sheep which had belonged to the dead *delibaşı* over the province. Mullâ Ismâᶜîl's family and followers were ordered to leave Hama for good, together with the following of his associate, the local *delibaşı* Bâkîr Aghâ al-Barâzî.[46]

[44] See on the tribes, p. 31–4

[45] *Ibid.*, pp. 607–08

[46] *Ibid.*, pp. 636–38; Dimashqî, *Ḥawâdith*, p. 62; SMH 43, pp. 197–98, 27

Mullâ Ismâᶜîl left no heir to his political and military legacy, even though some of his relatives or kinsmen may have returned to Hama. Bâkîr Aghâ al-Barâzî and his following were pardoned and allowed to take up residence in the Hama again in 1826 after a group of prominent inhabitants had petitioned the governor claiming that the *aghâ* had been falsely accused.[47]

The ᶜAẓms of Hama

After the retreat of Mullâ Ismâᶜîl to Qalᶜat al-Madîq the ᶜAẓm family re-established itself as the leading family of *aghawât* in the Hama area. For the next decade the *mutasallim* of the district was again to be recruited from the family. A resurgence of the power of the ᶜAẓms on the provincial level did not occur, although family was to produce one more pasha. In the early 1810s two of the senior pashas of the family retired to Hama, namely the army commander Nuṣûḥ Pasha and ᶜAbdallâh Pasha who had served his last term as governor in Urfa. He belonged to the Damascene branch of the family, but was ordered to settle in Hama.[48] At the same time the head of the Hama branch of the family, ᶜAbd al-Raḥmân Bey, died; he was succeeded by his son Salîm Bey. Little is known about the vicissitudes of the Damascene ᶜAẓms during these years, a clear sign that they had indeed ceased to play a role of significance in provincial politics.

Salîm Bey al-ᶜAẓm had secured the local pre-eminence of the family with the support of the governor of Damascus. The elimination of Mullâ Ismâᶜîl had relieved the area from a warlord who had figured prominently during the decades of violent provincial controversies. But the events had left their mark on the bey; the anxiety had made him ill. He went to Sidon on the Lebanese coast to recover, but died shortly

Rajab 1233, lists the personal belongings which Mullâ Ismâᶜîl left to his wife Zaynab; SMH 43, p. 213, early Shaᶜbân 1233, contains a copy of a *firmân ordering* the banishment of the Mulliyya and Barâziyya, as the two households were known, and p. 214 an order to that effect from the dîwân of Damascus, dated 24 Shaᶜbân 1233

[47] The family name Mullî occurs in a number of court records dating from the 1840s. The people involved include *aghawât*. See, for the edict concerning Bâkîr Aghâ, SMH 49, p. 234, dated 1242

[48] Shihâb, *Lubnân*, p. 603. Nuṣûḥ Pasha is referred to by Shihâb, as well as by Burckhardt, as Nâṣîf Pasha. He died in 1813 or 1815 and not in 1808/09 as Schatkowski-Schilcher believes (*Families*, 136–37).

after he arrived.[49] The *mutasallim* of Homs, Muḥammad Aghâ al-Jundî, the son of ᶜUthmân Aghâ, acted temporarily as governor of Hama, but after him three members of the ᶜAẓm family were appointed *mutasallim* consecutively.[50] The ᶜAẓms of Hama had not lost their ambition to pursue provincial careers. The refusal of ᶜAbdallâh Pasha – a former *mamlûk* of Jazzâr Pasha, who had succeeded Sulaymân Pasha in Acre in 1819 – to accept his dismissal in 1821 offered them the opportunity to further their interests. Armies were sent from the north to assist the then governor of Damascus in capturing and executing the rebel pasha of Acre. Over a hundred horsemen from Hama joined the military effort. In 1823, after Muḥammad ᶜAlî Pasha of Egypt had mediated between the Porte and ᶜAbdallâh Pasha, the crisis subsided and ᶜAbdallâh Pasha's hold on the province of Sidon was confirmed.[51]

Before ᶜAbdallâh Pasha revolted, he had been governor of both the Sidon and Tripoli provinces. However, once more, the central authorities undertook to detach the province of Tripoli from Acre of which it had become an often unruly dependency ever since the days of Jazzâr Pasha. The assignment to re-establish Tripoli as a province independent from Acre was given to Muṣṭafâ Pasha, the former governor of Aleppo, who had been transferred to Damascus and had headed the military efforts against ᶜAbdallâh Pasha in 1821 and 1822. During the rebellion of his patron, the veteran local strongman of Tripoli, Muṣṭafâ Aghâ Barbar, had escaped to Egypt, where he had been kindly received by Muḥammad ᶜAlî Pasha. His main local adversary was appointed in his place; ᶜAlî Aghâ al-Asᶜad of the ᶜAkkâr, who had been the candidate of

[49] Shihâb, *Lubnân*, p. 638

[50] SMH 43, p. 242, 3 Rabîᶜ II 1234 (Muḥammad Aghâ al-Jundî); p. 254, 11 Jumâdâ I 1237 (re-appointing ᶜAbd al-Qâdir Bey al-ᶜAẓm); p. 68, 1 Rabîᶜ II 1239 (appointing Sulaymân Bey al-ᶜAẓm); SMH 49, 12 Rabîᶜ II 1240 (appointing Muḥammad Bey al-ᶜAẓm)

[51] In a *firmân* ᶜAbdallâh Pasha was accused of having made common cause with the Druzes, the Shî'îs, Nuṣayrîs and with "ᶜarab culprits', SMH 43, 314–5, 30 Ramaḍân 1237. In fact the governor of Acre had fallen out with the governor of Damascus over the control of Nablus district and the financing of the ḥajj. During the revolt the *wâlî* of Damascus, Muḥammad Darwîsh Pasha, formally replaced ᶜAbdallâh Pasha until he himself was dismissed and succeeded by Muṣṭafâ Pasha, who acted as *wâlî* of Damascus, Sidon and Tripoli. After a settlement had been negotiated ᶜAbdallâh Pasha was reinstalled as *wâlî* of Sidon, but the districts of Yafa and Gaza were attached to Damascus. See, for the rebellion of ᶜAbdallâh Pasha, Shihâb, *Lubnân*, pp. 710–39; Al-ᶜAbd, *Târîkh*, pp. 167–80; Koury, *Province*, pp. 164–70; Mashâqa, *Mashhad*, p. 125

the central authorities for the office in Tripoli for some time and had replaced Muṣṭafâ Aghâ Barbar on several occasions before. ᶜAlî Aghâ depended to a considerable extent on the support of the governors of Damascus. In return for this support he offered military services to the governors of Damascus; for instance, he contributed with his large cavalry to the campaign against the Fadᶜân and Sibâᶜa. Now he was quickly replaced by the customs officer of Beirut, who acted at the same time as deputy governor (*qâyimmaqâm*) of Damascus. On his turn he was soon dismissed; Sulaymân Bey al-ᶜAẓm, the son of the late Salîm Bey, and then *mutasallim* of Hama, was appointed governor of Tripoli and, thus, became a pasha.[52] He also acted as *başbuğ al-jarda*, commander of the troops carrying provisions from Damascus to the returning convoy of pilgrims. This traditional combination of the two offices indicated that the governor of Damascus and commander of the pilgrimage, Muṣṭafâ Pasha, was, if not de jure, de facto his superior.

Sulaymân Pasha was quick to engage his relatives. He first appointed Aḥmad Bey, the son of ᶜAbdallâh Pasha al-ᶜAẓm, as his *qâyimmaqâm*, but soon replaced him with his own brother, Ḥusayn Bey. In Hama his cousin Muḥammad Bey al-ᶜAẓm succeeded Sulaymân as *mutasallim*.[53] On the surface the situation resembled that of a century earlier. The ᶜAẓms were holding office in Tripoli and Hama. However, it soon became evident that the family was far from regaining a leading position in the Syrian provinces. While Sulaymân Pasha headed the *jarda* in 1824, his brother Ḥusayn Bey faced a rebellion in Tripoli. The brothers had taken drastic measures to gain control over the town, causing many inhabitants to flee to the nearby mountains. When Ḥusayn Bey's men destroyed the house of a local family who was close to Muṣṭafâ Aghâ Barbar, a crowd attacked the bey. He escaped to the famous shrine of Sheikh al-Badawî to the north of the town. In order to recapture the town Ḥusayn Bey relied on the old network. He contacted ᶜAlî Aghâ al-Asᶜad of ᶜAkkâr and jointly they addressed ᶜAbdallâh Pasha of Acre, asking him to take action against Muṣṭafâ Aghâ Barbar, who was believed to have a hand in the revolt. ᶜAbdallâh Pasha ordered Muṣṭafâ Aghâ Barbar, who had returned from Egypt and stayed in Beirut at the time, to refrain from inciting the inhabitants of Tripoli against the ᶜAẓm

[52] He was appointed in the rank of *mirmiran*. In a later *firmân* the, then late, Sulaymân Pasha is referred to as former *wâlî* of Tripoli; SMH 49, p 70, 15 Rabîᶜ II 1240

[53] Shihâb, *Lubnân*, pp. 712, 756–57. For the excerpts of the letters of appointment, see Khûrî, *Barbar*, pp. 192–93; SMH 49, 12 Rabîᶜ II 1240

brothers and to keep away from Tripoli. In the meantime the sultan had ordered the head of Muṣṭafâ Aghâ Barbar to be brought to Istanbul. Muṣṭafâ Aghâ, then, had good reason to keep quiet. Sulaymân Pasha al-ᶜAẓm returned from the *jarda* in the summer of 1824. He fell ill and died shortly afterwards in Tripoli, where he was buried.[54] Sulaymân had been the last member of the ᶜAẓm family to become pasha. Ḥusayn Bey, the *qâyimmaqâm* of Tripoli, did not succeed his brother; instead ᶜAlî Aghâ al-Asᶜad was appointed governor of Tripoli. Ḥusayn Bey retired to Hama where he died some time later.

The containment policy of the central authorities – that is, the containment of provincial factions – had proved successful in inland Syria, but the developments in coastal Syria showed that the policy had its limitations. The Porte had been forced to confirm ᶜAbdallâh Pasha's position of strength in Acre. The appointment of ᶜAlî Aghâ al-Asᶜad, the headman of a local faction to Tripoli, marked the failure to disentangle the province from Acre. It is true that he was not a protégé of ᶜAbdallâh Pasha, but he and his ᶜAkkâr faction acted in the context of coastal factionalism in which ᶜAbdallâh Pasha occupied the central position. Eventually, the Porte did not persist in denying the predominance of the pasha of Acre. In 1827 ᶜAbdallâh Pasha again became governor of both Sidon and Tripoli; subsequently Muṣṭafâ Aghâ Barbar was restored as *mutasallim* of Tripoli.

Post-ᶜAẓm Hama

Muḥammad Bey al-ᶜAẓm, the *mutasallim* of Hama, died late 1824; he would prove to be the last *mutasallim* of the district recruited from the ᶜAẓm family. The most noted post-ᶜAẓm *mutasallim* of Hama was Faraj Aghâ. The origin and early career of Faraj Aghâ are unknown. He did not belong to one of the leading families of the area and may well have been a non-local. He was first appointed to Hama in May of 1826.[55] His career came into jeopardy two years later when he encountered strong local opposition to his rule. The merchants of Hama appealed to the governor of Damascus, accusing Faraj Aghâ of obstruction of trade, the imposition of illegal charges on silk, and the failure to repay forced

[54] Yannî, *Târîkh*, pp. 418–19; Khûrî, *Barbar*, 193–4; Shihâb, *Lubnân*, pp. 756–57. Muḥammad ᶜAlî Pasha of Egypt contacted ᶜAbdallâh Pasha of Acre, expressing his conviction that Muṣṭafâ Aghâ Barbar had no hand in the events, see *Maḥfûẓât*, vol. 1, p. 63

[55] SMH 49, p. 155, 14 Shawwâl 1241

loans. They also filed complaints against the commander of the musketeers and some other *aghawât*, who were likewise blamed for having imposed illegal charges. The merchants received the backing of the leading ulema, the local head of the descendants of the prophet (*naqîb al-ashrâf*), ᶜAbdallâh Efendi al-Kaylânî.[56] The opposition in Hama appears to have been connected with attempts on the part of the authorities to refuse the Kaylânî family their traditional hold on the office of judge. The first success of the local opposition had been the reappointment in 1828, at their request, of ᶜAbd al-Wahhâb Efendi al-Kaylânî as *qâḍî* at the expense of a non-local who had just been transferred to Hama. He had been the second non-local occupying the office since 1824. Shortly thereafter ᶜAbd al-Wahhâb al-Kaylânî was again dismissed and replaced by a non-local. Within two months, however, ᶜAbd al-Wahhâb Efendi was reinstated and when he died later that year, he was succeeded by a close relative, Sharaf al-Dîn Efendi al-Kaylânî.[57]

Relations in Hama remained tense and in the summer of 1829 the provincial authorities gave in to the dignitaries and merchants who refused to accept the affirmation of Faraj Aghâ in office. A senior provincial functionary of the province, Sulaymân Aghâ, the supervisor of the foundation of the Ḥaramayn, the Two Holy Sanctuaries (Mecca and Medina), was dispatched to Hama to conduct an inquiry into the finances of Faraj Aghâ and some of his officials. He showed that their exactions and malversations had amounted to nearly 800,000 qirsh (q.), a sum that exceeded the annual payment of fixed taxes to the treasury.[58] Notwithstanding the results of the inquiry, Faraj Aghâ was quick to return to office in Hama, succeeding ᶜAbd al-Ghanî Aghâ al-Shâmlî, a leading *aghâ* from the Maydân who served only very briefly in Hama.[59]

Seemingly, Faraj Aghâ had already established a name as a capable official whose ability to deal with the ᶜ*arab* tribes was one of his qualifications. The opposition to the rule of Faraj Aghâ should not only be regarded as an expression of strong local discontent against his

56 SMH 49, pp. 275–76, 17 Muḥarram 1244 (four orders from the *wâlî* Ṣâliḥ Pasha to Faraj Aghâ); p. 278, 27 Muḥarram 1244

57 SMH 49, p. 278, 27 Muḥarram 1244; SMH 49, p. 109, 3 Jumâdâ I 1241; and p. 271, 17 Muḥarram 1244; SMH 49, p. 238, [Muḥarram] 1245; SMH 49, p. 324, [Rabîᶜ I] 1245 and p. 356, [Rajab] 1245

58 SMH 49, p. 239 and 242, 30 Muḥarram 1245; p. 265, 11 Rabîᶜ I 1245. For the tabulation of the amounts levied on top of the legal taxes, see SMH 49, p. 250–3, dated early Ṣafar 1245. See for details pp. 178-182

59 SMH 49, p. 265, 11 Rabîᶜ I 1245; SMH 49, p. 357, 15 Rajab 1245

financial demands and the attempts to exclude the Kaylânîs from the office of *qâḍî*, but also as an expression of the more general sense of insecurity. After 1825, a year of drought, there were signs of growing unrest in several parts of Syria. Tribal pressure had again increased in the wake of the great plague of 1826 and the food shortages, which lasted well into the next year. The plague had ravaged much of Syria and the death toll had been very high, especially in the northern and central parts. To make matters even worse, locusts devoured much of the standing crop. In the summer of 1827 *ʿarab* tribes, which had suffered greatly from the epidemic, besieged the town of Hama in search of food. Troops from Damascus were sent to expel them.[60] Evidently, Faraj Aghâ, like many other *aghawât*, had to operate under difficult conditions.

[60] Shihâb (*Lubnân*, pp. 787–90) claims that half of the population of Aleppo, Hama and Homs perished, most likely an inflated estimate

6. The Fiscal Regime

The fundamental issue underlying competition for office-holding in the provinces of the Ottoman empire was access to revenue. The sole individual in the empire having an inalienable right to the revenue was the sultan, but he had to delegate considerable power to his servants in the provinces in order to enable them to function properly. The exercise of control over these office-holders was problematic and a constant concern of the central authority. Moreover, the fiscal system was elaborate; a multitude of taxes, levies and fees existed, which were assessed in various ways. Local variation in the composition and collection of the revenue was marked, but also in specific localities custom and privilege had given rise to differences in the fiscal treatment. The basic principles of the fiscal order, however, showed less complexity; the main taxes comprised levies on produce and transport, and the mode of production – agricultural, horticultural, animal husbandry, artisanal or otherwise – determined to a large extent the methods of assessment and collection. In addition to levies on produce, three other major types of revenues existed: firstly, fees collected in order to finance specific official duties and obligations; secondly, impositions related to military efforts and natural calamities; and thirdly, the capitation tax resting on non-Muslims. This chapter contains a detailed description of the revenue system in the Hama area. The next chapter deals with the collection of the taxes and their allocation in the context of the financial policies of the state.

The court and taxation in the Hama district

The district (*sanjaq*) of Hama constituted a rich source of revenue; it yielded more than any other district attached to the governorship of Damascus. In the years 1839 and 1842 the Hama district yielded about 200 per cent more than the neighbouring district of Homs and 30 per cent more than the district of Nablus, which was the second in importance among the districts of the province of Damascus.[1] The

[1] F.O. 195/196, n. 73, Damascus, 5 October 1842. In this consular report the

records of the religious court (*maḥkama sharᶜiyya*) of Hama contain a wealth of data concerning the local fiscal regime of the late eighteenth and early nineteenth centuries, but there are no data for each and every year. The involvement of the court with the fiscal regime was largely limited to times of political or economic problems, when the central or provincial authorities involved the local judge in the implementation of measures taken to overcome these problems. The enactment of fiscal reforms, too, was entered into the books of the court. The most detailed documents concern tax tabulations and regulations issued in the wake of the crisis of 1818, when ᶜAnaza tribes confronted local tribes of Hama. Another series of highly informative documents were entered into the books in 1829 when an influential segment of the population of Hama refused to accept the reappointment of Faraj Aghâ as *mutasallim* on the grounds of the imposition of illegal charges. For several other years valuable documents have survived, for example for 1788, when some taxes were reduced in order to halt village desertion caused by the Mawâlî uprising and the ensuing military campaigns, and for 1806, when the provincial authorities undertook to adjust some deviations from the fiscal regulations in the district. Provincial financial authorities conducted a remarkable investigation after the evacuation of Syria by the troops of Muḥammad ᶜAlî Pasha, comparing the yields of the traditional fiscal regime (1831–32) to the much higher revenue generated by the Egyptian authorities (1839–40). The fiscal regime described here is the regime which had come about by 1818 and which remained by and large unchanged – only the rates of some major impositions changed – until the occupation of Syria by the troops of Muḥammad ᶜAlî Pasha of Egypt in 1832.[2]

revenue of all the districts of the provinces of Damascus, Tripoli and Sidon are given. For the earlier decades no such figures are available, but the figures given by Cohen (*Palestine*, table 5 and 7) for the province of Sidon for the late eighteenth century suggest that Hama was a comparably rich source of revenue.

[2] This chapter is primarily based upon the following tax tabulations and regulations: SMH 46, pp. 74–76, 15 Rabîᶜ I 1203 (1788); SMH 43, p. 153, dated 1220 [Jumâdâ I] (1805); SMH 43, 174–187, 7, 15 and 19 Rabîᶜ I 1233 (1818); SMH 49, pp. 326–29, 23 Rabîᶜ I 1245 (1829); SMH 51, pp. 316–27, undated [Ramaḍân 1257], which includes the figures for 1248 (1831–32) and 1256 (1839–40) and SMH 51, pp. 425–28, dated Jumâdâ I 1257 (1841). Numerous references to taxes are to be found in other documents. The identification of certain levies was at times troublesome due to missing or illegible (mainly due to mildew) lines.

The variety of impositions

Well over fifty different taxes, fees, dues and other impositions are recorded in the records of the Hama court for the late eighteenth and early nineteenth centuries. They include designations for taxes in general or for a number of related impositions, though some of these also had a specific meaning, referring to one single tax.[3] To complicate matters, some impositions were known by different names. Many other levies consisted in the more minor charges like the various tolls. This wide variety of taxes and the relative lack of consistency in the use of fiscal terms correlate to the relatively low degree of rationalization within the traditional Ottoman administration. Numerous taxes were imposed to cover specific expenditures of the administration. Moreover, like other rulers the Ottoman authorities had always shown a remarkable inventiveness in the pursuit of their material claims on the population.[4]

In the literature on the Syrian provinces most attention has been paid to taxation in earlier periods, in particular the sixteenth century, mainly concerning Palestine (Singer, *Palestinian*, Mantran et Sauvaget, *Règlements*, Heyd, *Documents*, Lewis, *Land tenure*; Cohen and Lewis, *Population*, Abdulfattah and Hütteroth, *Historical*, Venzke, *Tithe*, Murphy, *Regional*. Studies on the central financial bodies and politics, too, concentrate on earlier periods, but especially Darling, *Revenue-raising*, is of use for later periods, too. For the late eighteenth century, Cohen, *Palestine*, deals extensively with the finances of Jazzâr Pasha. Also of value is Rafeq, *Land tenure*, although it deals with the 1840s when changes in the fiscal system had occurred. Given regional variation in taxation studies on other parts of the empire (for example on Egypt, ʿAbd al-Raḥîm, *Rîf*) are only helpful to some extent. Although nearly all taxes could be identified, the nature and magnitude of some remains obscure. Due to the local variation in the fiscal regime and the diversity of the fiscal vocabulary, there is some danger in ascribing the function of a certain tax in another locality to an imposition of the same name which was collected in the Hama district

[3] Especially in the case of the extraordinary taxes (see below) several general terms were used: *bad-i hava*, *kharj* or *khawârij*, *ṭarḥ* and *jawâyiḥ*

[4] Some taxes were abolished after the Ottomans had taken possession of the Arab lands, but others were adopted from their Mamlûk predecessors. The fiscal regime which prevailed in Syrian provinces during the sixteenth century appears to have been less complicated than that in later periods, but our knowledge of the local fiscal regime in the sixteenth century is to a large extent derived from the central archives. The central authorities were obviously less concerned with local differentiation

The authorities distinguished between four basic types of revenue in the Hama district:

1) *amwâl mîriyya* and *takâlîf ᶜurfiyya*: regular taxes and customary levies
2) *khawârij*: extraordinary impositions
   ᶜawâyid: fees to which a number of local office-holders were entitled[5]
3) *dhakhâyir*: levies in cash and kind related to military efforts and natural calamities
4) *jizya*: the capitation tax payable by non-Muslims

In the Hama district a clear distinction was made between the taxes which had to be remitted to the state's treasury, the *khazîna ᶜâmira*, and levies collected for the support of office-holders. They were administered separately. The extraordinary levies in times of war and revolt were also administered separately. The *khawârij* compensated for a variety of expenses that were not, or only partly, covered by the treasury. The first category of extraordinary taxes had acquired a regular aspect in the sense that they were levied each year, at more or less regular rates. The magnitude of the second category of extraordinary charges depended on the occurrence of war, revolt and natural disasters and varied sharply.

The taxes, which were remitted to the treasury in the province of Damascus, were largely earmarked for the financing of the pilgrimage. The paradox in the flow of revenue was that the income of the treasury was spent in the province and never reached Istanbul, whereas a large share of the levies which were collected to support office-holders was transmitted to the sultan and the grandees of the state in Istanbul on whose backing appointments in the provinces depended.

The *amwâl mîriyya*

Once part of the province of Tripoli, the district of Hama was attached to the governorship of Damascus in the 1720s when Ismâᶜîl Pasha al-ᶜAẓm, former governor of Hama and Tripoli, was promoted to Damascus. He was granted the district of Hama as a leasehold for life

[5] A number of officials engaged in the pilgrimage were paid from the treasury. These officials were not part of the local administration, but were functionaries of the central institutions of the state. See below.

(*mâlikâna*) in his capacity as commander of the pilgrimage (*amîr al-ḥajj*). The income of the treasury from the district was allocated in its entirety to this vital operation and to some related religious occasions. The taxes which were remitted to the treasury consisted in two main components: the *murattabât Ḥijâziyya* and the *amwâl mîriyya*. The term *murattabât Ḥijâziyya*, the Hijaz impositions, refers to the pilgrimage to Mecca and Medina, which are in the Hijaz. The *amwâl mîriyya*, or simply *mîrî*, comprised primarily taxes resting upon the usufruct of state-owned properties, in particular agricultural land. The *mîrî* charges constituted the largest component of the total revenue and primarily consisted in levies on produce.

The *murattabât Ḥijâziyya* comprised the *takâlîf ᶜurfiyya*, customary levies which covered the expenses of officials who were involved with the *ḥajj*. The most prominent of these were the dignitaries who had come from Istanbul in procession, headed by the *sürre emini*, who was in charge of the presenting gifts to the rich and poor of Mecca and Medina. With the arrival of the procession in Hama, the governor of Damascus assumed the responsibility of the *ḥajj*.[6] As his delegate, the *mutasallim* of Hama had to see to the well-being and safety of the procession until it had reached the district of Homs. The retinue of the *sürre emini* included the *mücdeci başı*, his chief emissary, and the *saka başı*, who supervised the supply of water to the pilgrims. Their expenses are listed among the *takâlîf*. The *takâlîf* also accounted for the letters of exchange of the *mashâyikh al-ḥajj*, religious dignitaries who accompanied the lay people on their way to the holy shrines, as well as the *taqâdim*, camels offered as presents to dignitaries. Listed as *takâlîf* were also the *ᶜîdiyya*, *bashâyir* and *salâmiyya*, all relating to gifts to the sultan and high officials on the occasion of specific events in the course of the pilgrimage: the *ᶜîdiyya* refers to the *ᶜîd al-aḍḥâ*, the feast of Immolation; the *bashâyir*, to the good tidings of the safe arrival of the pilgrimage convoy to the Holy Shrines; and *salâmiyya*, the safe return of the convoy to Damascus.

The *takâlîf* comprised impositions which corresponded with specific religious exercises, but these charges were not prescribed by religious law. The term *takâlîf* was normally used in combination with *ᶜurfiyya*, denoting that these charges were rooted in sultanic law.

Sultanic law likewise defined the *mîrî*. Occasionally the *murattabât* and *mîrî* were referred to jointly as *qisṭ sulṭânî*, the sultan's share.[7] *Mîrî*

[6] See, for the organization and financing of the *ḥajj*, Barbir, *Ottoman*.
[7] See, for example, SMH 43, p. 357, Rabîᶜ I 1238

designated all that belonged to the sultan as the head of the ruling house. The ideology of the state did not allow for formal limitations on the powers of the sultan, but in fiscal practice *mîrî* referred first and foremost to state-owned arable land, *arâḍî mîriyya*. When collected or assessed in kind, the *mîrî* was referred to as *qism*, a proportion of the harvest. Most agricultural land was considered the personal property of the sultan and the villagers or others who were entitled to its usufruct (*taṣarruf*) were liable to the *mîrî*. These peasants produced the bulk of the revenue.[8]

The *mîrî* did not necessarily correspond to the right of usufruct of state-owned properties. In the Hama district the *mîrî* also rested on the agricultural land which was held in mortmain; *waqf* holdings. Nor was the *mîrî* an exclusively rural tax. In practice, a variety of impositions was included in the *mîrî*. Most of these concerned fixed charges resting upon commercial and economic activities, such as market dues (*iḥtisâb*) and slaughterhouse rights (*mâl qaṣṣâbkhâna*). Also the tax resting on urban real estate, the *iʿâna*, was listed among the *mîrî* charges. In the Hama area the *iʿâna* financed the *manzil*, the postal service and resting house.[9] Apart from these more substantial charges, a number of small taxes were usually listed under the heading of *mîrî*, varying from the church tax (*mâl kanâyis*) to the animal fat tax (*samniyya*).

The *murattabât Ḥijâziyya* and the *mîrî* constituted the mass of the income of the treasury from the Hama district. Other taxes, which were remitted to the treasury, included the wedding tax, the pasture fees, the goat tax, and tolls levied on bridges.[10] The duties on imports of livestock, wool, tobacco and silk also contributed to the income of the treasury. The rates of these *rusûmât*, as they were called collectively, were fixed per head or volume.[11] Finally the payment to the leading sheikh, the *amîr*, of the Mawâlî, the so-called *muwassaṭa*, had to be compensated; the expenditure was distributed over the villages of the

[8] See on categories of landholding, Rafeq, *Land tenure*; Reilly, *Properties*.

[9] The real estate was referred to as *musaqqafât* and probably included commercial and artisanal properties only. Note that the term *iʿâna* was also used for war levies.

[10] The *ʿursân*, the *kiṣlak* (winter pasture fee) and *qayẓiyya* (summer pasture fee), the *aʿdâd mâʿiz*, and the *ghafr* respectively.

[11] The separate duties are referred to as *bac*. Unfortunately, the records contain no figures on the total amounts of the *rusûmât* collected. The relative importance of these charges is likely to have been small, given the low rates, for instance 1 q. for each camel or cow.

districts of Hama, Homs and Maʿarra, and was part of the income of the treasury of Hama.[12]

Levies to support office-holders

The total amount of levies to support office-holders and to make up for some expenses of the local government roughly equalled the sum collected as *takâlîf* and *mîrî*. A number of the office-holders had the right to collect fees, referred to as *ʿawâyid*.[13] The amounts varied according to rank and the number of troops. At least some of the fees were payable on a monthly basis. The *aghawât* who were entitled to levy *ʿawâyid* included the commanders of the janissary cavalry (*garib yiğit ağasi*), of the musketeers (*tüfenkçi başı*), and the *qassâm aghâ*, chief of the military who collected the important proportional tax on agricultural produce (see below). The latter was, at least in the late eighteenth century, entitled to take a fixed amount for both the primary crops, wheat and barley, and the secondary crops, like lentils and chick peas.[14] The superintendent of the expenditures (*wakîl al-kharj*) also had the right to collect fees.[15]

The district governor (*mutasallim*) was not entitled to collect *ʿawâyid*. He will have had various sources of income and direct access to various components of the revenue. He acted in the capacity of the tax collector (*muḥaṣṣil*) on behalf of the governor of Damascus, which might well have entitled him to collect the so-called *fâyiḍ* or a comparable fee.[16] In

---

[12] See p. 36

[13] According to Redhouse, it simply means 'items of income and revenue; fees.' These fees are known to have pressed hard upon the population, but few details are known for other parts of Syria. Cohen (*Palestine*, pp. 224–26) found some references to a tax called *ʿawâyidât* but fails to identify it.

[14] SMH 46, pp. 75–77, 21 Rabîʿ I 1203. The secondary crops are called *shakâyir*. Later no such distinction appears to have been made.

[15] See for these officials, pp. 76–77

[16] The *muḥaṣṣil* was entrusted with the collection of the taxes payable to the treasury by local tax farmers (see below). In the letters of appointment the *wâlî* directed the *mutasallim* of Hama to the *taḥṣîl al-amwâl*, the collection of the taxes. The term *muḥaṣṣil* as such is not used in the Hama records. The only reference to the *fâyiḍ* in the Hama records for the period within the context of the finances of the local administration is in SMH 49, p. 468, 20 Shaʿbân 1247, dealing with an amount of wheat and barley charged on top of the amounts of seeds which had been distributed over the villages earlier and had been repaid by the villagers. See for numerous, but confusing, references to the *fâyiḍ* Cohen,

many cases the district governor was a principal tax farmer in the area. When recruited from the ʿAẓm family, his income was derived from a variety of sources, in particular commercial activities anchored in extensive *waqf* holdings. Mullâ Ismâʿîl, too, was not solely dependent on privileges connected to office-holding. However, these privileges were central to their functioning. The *ʿubûdiyya*, 'servitude' tax, constituted one of the main extraordinary levies. The *ʿubûdiyya* aimed at compensating the district's governor for one of the largest expenditures he had to make yearly: the payment to the governor of Damascus to express his servitude and to procure his (re)appointment. In his turn the governor made similar payments to the sultan and the grandees of the state.[17] The exact magnitude of the *ʿubûdiyya* in the Hama area is unknown, because it was tabulated jointly with some other levies, but there is little doubt that it constituted the main imposition collected for the support of office-holders, not only in the Hama area. For instance, emir Sulṭân Ḥarfûsh paid 200,000 q. as *ʿubûdiyya* to Sulaymân Pasha of Acre to secure his appointment to Baʿalbak.[18]

The *ʿubûdiyya* and *ʿawâyid* were tabulated jointly with two other charges: the *khidma* and the *ʿawna*. The *khidma* was a minor duty levied by the local treasury department, amounting to 2.5 per cent of the aggregate of taxes resting upon a fiscal unit.[19] The nature and magnitude of the *ʿawna* is obscure.[20]

Palestine; Shaw, *Old and New*; ʿAbd al-Raḥîm, *Rîf*. The term *fâyiḍ* was sometimes used interchangeably with *ḍamm*, another very broad term, see p. 134

[17] Shihâb *Lubnân*, p. 581. See on the *ʿubûdiyya* collected by Faraj Aghâ, SMH 49, p 242, [Muḥarram 1245].) See also Cohen, *Palestine*, p. 226; Koury, *Province*, p. 176

[18] The high amount of 200,000 paid by Amîr Sulṭân (see the previous note) to obtain the much smaller Baʿalbak district gives an indication of the magnitude of the *ʿubûdiyya*. The amount of taxes resting upon the slaughterhouse of Hama in 1795 amounted to 12,000 q. of which 8250 q. *mîrî* and 3750 q. *ʿubûdiyya*, see SMH 46, pp. 237–38, dated Ramaḍân 1210. A similar ratio occurs in some excerpts from tax farm contracts from the ʿAkkâr region in *Uṣûl*, p. 26; see also ʿAwra, *Târîkh*, 224, 243

[19] One *miṣriyya* out of every *qirsh*, there are 40 *miṣriyya* in a *qirsh*.

[20] The *ʿawna* may have been a tax payable in lieu of forced labour services. In Egypt the tax was a component of the *barrânî* charges, levied to cover the expenses of local government; ʿAbd al-Raḥîm, *Rîf*, p. 132

Composite tax assessments

The tradition of linking impositions with specific expenditures was one of the reasons of wide variety of taxes. The traditional inclination of the authorities to tap on additional sources of revenue in order to satisfy their financial needs added to the number of impositions. Moreover, the authorities showed a marked reluctance to formally abolish old taxes or to replace them with more general impositions. Instead they undertook to cluster a number of taxes in order to facilitate their assessment and collection. These composite impositions concerned mostly, but not solely, *mîrî* taxes that were remitted to the treasury. There were two major composite impositions: the *mâl muqâṭaᶜa* and the *mâl faddân*. The first defined the fiscal category of the *muqâṭaᶜa*s, rural and urban tax farms. The second was of importance for the tax assessment of the villages of the plain which were distributed over four fiscal categories: the *ḥâṣil*, the *maqṭûᶜ*, the Turcoman and the *quṭuniyyât* villages.

Tax farming was a common feature of the Ottoman fiscal regime. The general word for the farming of taxes was *iltizâm*, whereas a *muqâṭaᶜa* concerned a specific fiscal unit which was put to auction, farmed out and administered separately. A *muqâṭaᶜa*, then, did not refer to each and every village, tribe, quarter or craft organization of which the taxes were farmed, but to specific entities.[21] The fiscal treatment of these *muqâṭaᶜa*s differed from that of other categories in the Hama area.

The more substantial rural *muqâṭaᶜa*s comprised several clusters of villages and farms in the western periphery of the district, in the foothills of the Nuṣayrî Mountains. The largest was Ḥiṣn al-Akrâd, the famous Crac des Chevaliers, the others being Jabal Kalbiyya, Miṣyâf and Ḥazûr. They were usually, but not always, farmed by local *aghawât* or headmen, but occasionally well-to-do inhabitants of Hama or Homs bid for these farms. Only two single villages, situated in the western part of the district as well, constituted separate *muqâṭaᶜa*s: Kafrûn and Baᶜrîn. The urban *muqâṭaᶜa*s included a number of offices which regulated and taxed activities in the field of commerce and industry. The *iḥtisâb*, the market inspection and duty office, and the *qaṣṣâbkhâna*, the slaughterhouse, constituted the two major urban *muqâṭaᶜa*s. Other less valued *muqâṭaᶜa*s encompassed the leaseholds of the roasting house, the weighing house, the small Jewish quarter, a number of shops, a bath

[21] When the taxes resting upon a village, etc., were farmed out, the word *muqâṭaᶜa* was never used. The collection of the taxes of a village was given in *iltizâm* to an individual. See, for example, SMH 48, p. 276, [Rajab 1236]

and some waterwheels, all of these state property.[22] The last category of urban *muqâṭaᶜas* concerned the farming of the taxes resting on urban gardens and orchards, churches, the administration of the *jizya* (see below), the dye-pits and on some of the smaller craft organizations: the fishermen, string makers and drummers.

Mîrî levies constituted the main component of the *mâl muqâṭaᶜa*. On top of the *mîrî*, a sum referred to as *ḍamm* rested on most *muqâṭaᶜas*. The *ḍamm* was a blanket term denoting any amount which was levied in addition to the original or an earlier tax assessment. An increase of the tax rate following, for example, the debasement of the currency, would be entered as *ḍamm*. Payments to make up for the difference between calculations based on the Islamic lunar year and the solar financial year counted as *ḍamm* as well. The *ḍamm* often included an additional amount of *mîrî*, but apart from an increase, it could refer to any other tax imposed on top of the *mîrî*, including the *ᶜubûdiyya*, *ᶜawâyid* and other charges which were not remitted to the treasury.

The proportion of the *ḍamm* varied substantially from one *muqâṭaᶜa* to another, depending largely on the magnitude of the original tax assessment. Regularly, the *ḍamm* was used to adjust differences in tax treatment. The *mâl muqâṭaᶜa* of the village of Baᶜrîn, for example, comprised 103 q. of *mîrî* and 1500 q. of *ḍamm* in both 1818 and 1829. Clearly the large amount of *ḍamm* compensated for the very low original *mîrî* assessment. Another indication of the use of *ḍamm* as an adjustment to the more general practice of revenue raising lies in the fact that the charge rested almost exclusively on the rural and urban *muqâṭaᶜas* which, unlike other fiscal categories, were not liable to the *takâlîf*. Often introduced as being a temporal imposition, the *ḍamm* tended to become permanent. In some cases it was even included in the general mîrî assessment; in the case of the *muqâṭaᶜa* of the slaughterhouse on which 13,406 q. of *mîrî* rested, no *ḍamm* was entered for years, but an earlier amount of *ḍamm* imposed on the tax farm had become part of the 'old' *mîrî*.[23] Given the broad application of the term, it is doubtful that the

[22] In the tabulation of 1829, the Jewish quarter was simply referred to as [the rents of] the *maḥallat al-mîrî*. Why this quarter was state-owned is open to speculation; perhaps the state had taken possession of the houses after its Jewish occupants had migrated.

[23] The tabulation of 1818 distinguished between *mîrî qadîm* and *ḍamm al-mîrî*. The tabulation of 1829 distinguished between *aṣl al-maṭlûb* and *mîrî murattab*. In 1795 the *mâl muqâṭaᶜat qaṣṣâbkhânâ* included *ḍamm* for an amount of 250 q. See SMH 46, pp. 237–38, Ramaḍân 1210

increase of amounts labelled *ḍamm* correlated to an increase in productivity of certain *muqâṭaᶜas*. It has been argued that the increase of *ḍamm* payments by Jazzâr Pasha of Acre to the central state reveal an upward economic trend, but it is more likely to have been effected by the financial demands of sultan of the time, Selim III, who initiated some fiscal reforms.[24]

The *mâl faddân* constituted the other major composite imposition in the Hama area and was payable by the large majority of villages of the Hama plain. It concerned a tax assessment in proportion to the acreage. The *faddân*, or span (Turkish *çift*), was not a fixed square measure but represented the area which could be ploughed by one or two yokes of cows or oxen during the season, which lasted for about 28 days in the Hama area. In other areas of Syria, the *faddân* often represented the amount of land which could be ploughed in one day. The Hama area appears to have been unique in that a double *faddân* was used.[25] But not only 'four cows' or two span *faddân* figure in the Hama records; also 'six cows' and 'eight cows' *faddân* are mentioned. Moreover, people distinguished between the species of draught animals used; for instance a *faddân* ploughed by the strong Syrian cow will have been larger than one worked with the smaller, but hardier, Anatolian cow.[26]

The *mâl faddân* represented the amount of fixed regular taxes resting upon the acreage, and by multiplying the number of *faddân* of a village by the *mâl*, the total amount of regular taxes payable by a village was assessed. The villages and farms of the Hama plain had been categorized into four groups: the revenue villages (*ḥâṣil*)[27] numbering about 73, the 'fixed sum' villages (*maqṭûᶜ*) (ca. 20), Turcoman (ca. 19) and cotton villages (*quṭuniyyât*) (3). The *mâl faddân* always included the *takâlîf*, and in the case of the villages of the *maqṭûᶜ*, Turcoman and *quṭuniyyât* categories the *mîrî* was also included. Technically all three categories

[24] Cohen (*Palestine*, pp. 211–26) argues that, contrary to the *mîrî*, the *ḍamm* (*ẓamm*) figures are indicative of economic trends. However, the distinction between the two is blurred. See on the fiscal reforms of Selim III, Shaw, *Old and New*.

[25] Anderlind, *Ackerbau*, p.54

[26] See, for instance, SMH 48, p.46; 55, pp. 330–33; 59, pp. 27–28; 60, p. 297; 63, p. 435. In the early twentieth century the *baqar shâmî*, or Syrian cow, was not the most common cow in the Hama district, but the *baqar qalîṭî* or *anâdûlî* was more common. See also Kurd ᶜAlî, *Khiṭaṭ*, vol. 4, pp. 185–86

[27] Hâṣil has various but interrelated meanings: produce, harvest, (total) revenue, and granary.

were *maqṭûᶜ*, which merely denotes that they were liable to a fixed amount of impositions. The rate of the *mâl faddân* varied from one category to the other, but some variation with a single category existed as well.

The *mâl faddân* of the largest category, the revenue villages, consisted of the *takâlîf* only. On top of the *mâl faddân*, they paid the *mîrî* in proportion to the crop, the *qism* or *ḥabbat al-ḥâṣil*. The division between villages which were liable to a fixed amount only and villages which paid a proportion of the crop on top of a fixed amount not only predates Ottoman but also Islamic times. In some areas of Syria the latter category was still known by its (Arabized) Greek name, *dîmûs* (from *dèmosion*), in the sixteenth century and possibly later.[28] The proportions levied varied in the Hama district. In 1788 the rates for most of the *ḥâṣil* villages were set at 2/6 or 2/7 of the crop, but some paid less. Later the rates were reduced to 1/6, 1/7 or 1/8.[29] The reduction of the rates was designed to stimulate peasants to continue farming. The *qism* rested on the primary crops of wheat and barley, as well as on the secondary crops of dura or sorghum, chickpeas, lentils and its near relative, *kirsinna*. The collected cereals and pulses were stored in the local *anbâr*, the state's granaries. The contents of Hama granaries formed a highly strategic resource of provincial power; the wheat fed urban populations and the barley the animals, passing pilgrimage convoys and armies.

Remaining tax assessments

The methods of tax assessment of rural and urban *muqâṭaᶜas* and the villages of the plain show a clear degree of fiscal rationalization; a multitude of impositions had been condensed to one single amount in cash, combined, in the case of the revenue village, with a proportional levy in kind. The remaining three fiscal categories of the district – the villages of the Jabal Gharbî, the *ᶜarab* tribes and the craft organizations (*aṣnâf*) – were treated differently. In the Jabal Gharbî, a small area located to the west of the town, in the foothills of the Nuṣayrî Mountains, the *takâlîf* were assessed separately for each of the fifteen villages, but the *mîrî* was fixed upon the Jabal Gharbî as a whole. The

[28] Mantran et Sauvaget, *Règlements* p. 5; Lewis, *Studies*, p. 484; Venzke, *Tithe*, pp. 260–61

[29] Prior to 1788 the rates had been higher. The expression used was: two (or one) out of every six (or seven or eight) *ḥabba*, grain, see SMH 46, pp. 74–75, 15 Rabîᶜ I 1203; SMH 43, p. 384, 13 Shawwâl 1214

reverse was true for the fiscal treatment of the local ᶜ*arab* tribes. In their case the *takâlîf* were assessed collectively and subsequently divided among the individual tribes. The tribes were also liable to the *a*ᶜ*dâd ghanam*, the sheep tax. This tax resembled the *qism* in that a proportion of the livestock was taken. The Hama records contain hardly any details on the sheep tax, which suggests that the collection of this tax might not have fallen within the authority of the *mutasallim* of Hama. On top of the *takâlîf* and the *a*ᶜ*dâd ghanam* the tribes were liable to two small charges; the pasture fees and the animal fat tax (*samniyya*). For five out of the 24 tribes, these charges were assessed at a fixed sum, the others paid per tent or volume respectively.[30]

In the case of the craft organizations – collectively known as *ṭawâyif* (sing. *ṭâyifa*) – of Hama, the financial authorities distinguished between *aṣnâf* (sing. *ṣanf*) and *ḥirfa* (plur. *ḥiraf*). The distinction in fiscal treatment might indicate that the *ḥiraf* were organized differently from the *aṣnâf*, but the differentiation might have been rooted in older privileges or practices.[31] Over 40 craft organizations existed in Hama and most were entered under the heading of *aṣnâf*. The *aṣnâf* were assessed collectively and were liable to the appointment fee of the sheikhs.[32] This imposition amounted to nearly half of the total amount of taxes resting upon these craft organizations of weavers, coppersmiths, weaponsmiths, charcoal burners, druggists and saddlemakers, to mention only some of the more important. The *ḥiraf* were not subjected to an appointment fee; they paid *takâlîf* only. They comprised some major occupational groups, like the millers and dyers.[33] For unclear reasons Christian merchants (*khwâjkiyya*) and even Christians in general (*naṣârâ*) were also entered in the list of *ḥiraf*. Whether this inclusion is an indication

[30] In 1818 the winter camping (*qishlâq*) was set at 5 q. per tent. The summer camping fee (*qayẓiyya*) is listed in tax tabulations, but no rates are given.

[31] In the literature no reference was found to a possible distinction within the craft organizations of the Arab provinces of the empire. On the craft organizations see Raymond, *Artisans*, vol. 2, pp. 505–82; Marcus, *Middle East*, pp. 162–77; Rafeq, *Maẓâhir*; Khoury, *State*, pp. 137–39, 225–27

[32] Called the *paha-i libsât mashâyikh al-aṣnâf*.

[33] The *ḥiraf* included the *ṭaḥḥâna* (millers), the *kayyâla* (corn measures), the *saqqâya* (water carriers), the *naḥḥâla* (beekeepers), the *makâriyya* (muleteers), *sabbâghîn* (dyers) and the unidentified *raddâda*. The *basâtina* (market gardeners) were referred to as *jamâ*ᶜ*a* or *ṭâyifa*, but were treated as the *ḥiraf*.

of the existence of a clear division of labour along confessional lines remains to be investigated.[34]

When compared to their European counterparts, the artisanal organizations in the Ottoman empire generally observed more lenient regulations and often allowed freer competition. Moreover, they were more exposed to interference by the authorities. Indicative of official concern about the functioning of the artisanal system was the appointment of heads (*baş*) to the most important occupational groups; the butchers and bakers, who provided the urban population, including the officials and the troops, with food. The head supervised the distribution of meat and bread. As a consequence, these two groups were treated in a different manner by the financial authorities. The butchers belonged to the *qaṣṣâbkhâna*, the slaughterhouse, which was not a single building, but an institution comprising nine butcher shops.[35] The slaughterhouse figured among the more important urban *muqâṭaᶜa*s and their head, the *qaṣṣâb başı*, acted its leaseholder. Apart from the *mâl muqâṭaᶜa*, the slaughterhouse was liable to a monthly payment of 900 q. The bakers, headed by the *ekmekçi başı*, were not organized as *muqâṭaᶜa*. They paid a monthly charge of 200 q.[36]

The distribution of the burden of taxation

The distribution of the taxes over the different fiscal categories in the Hama district was uneven. Some segments of society were treated with comparative leniency, whereas others were assessed at amounts that appear to have been disproportional to their number or economic value. Differences in tax treatment originated from various considerations. Economic value and viability mattered as much as the needs of the administration, but tradition, privilege and religious principles had also helped shape the fiscal system.

The synopsis of the revenue of the district for the year financial year 1248 (1831–32) in table 2 shows that the amount of taxes which was remitted to the treasury and the amount of levies collected for the support of office-holders were balanced. The synopsis also shows that about

[34] In the early Ottoman period, Christians in Hama worked, among others, as goldsmiths, blacksmiths, silk weavers, doctors and dyers. See Rafeq, *Maẓâhir*, p. 37

[35] SMH, 46, pp. 237–38, dated Ramaḍân 1210

[36] Three smaller occupational groups – the fishermen, stringmakers and drummers – were also dealt with separately and subjected to *mîrî* only.

Table 1. Distribution of impositions for the year 1248

A: number of villages or tribes (year 1245)
B: taxes payable to the treasury
C: levies to support office-holders
D: total of B and C
E: percentage of the grand total

fiscal category	A	B	C	D	E
I. Rural					
ḥâṣil villages*	73	169,916	202,367	372,283	24
Jabal Gharbî	15	62,212	78,211	140,423	9.1
Turcoman villages	19	53,434	49,961	103,395	6.7
maqṭûᶜ villages	20	23,175	28,730	51,905	3.4
quṭuniyyât villages	3	14,715	12,452	27,167	1.8
*muqâṭaᶜa*s		138,254	372,411	510,665	33
ᶜarab tribes**	24	49,836	62,012	111,848	7.2
					(85.2)
II. Urban					
*muqâṭaᶜa*s		140,124	17,379	157,503	10.2
crafts		59,213	12,470	71,683	4.6
		710,879	835,993	1,546,872	
		46 %	54 %	100 %	
including the *qism**		820,879	835,993	1,656,872	
		49 %	51 %	100 %	

*Also liable to the *qism* which amounted to a cash value according to official prices of ca. 110,000 q. in the year 1246

**Also liable to the *aᶜdâd ghanam*, no aggregate figures available

Sources: A: SMH 49, pp. 326–29, 23 Rabîᶜ I 1245; B and C: SMH 51, pp. 316–17, n.d. [Ramaḍân 1257] (which includes the figures for 1248)

85 per cent of taxes entered in the books in cash, was paid by the rural population.[37] When the *qism*, the proportional tax on the agricultural yields, is included, the relative share of the rural population rises to at least 90 per cent. Of course the amounts of cereals and pulses collected

[37] The year 1248 (1831/32) has been selected because it is the only year for which total amounts of levies for support of office-holders are known. Note that years given in tax tabulations relate to *mâlî* or *shamshî* year, a solar year beginning in March.

Table 2. The *qism* collected in 1246 in *makkûk*

320	wheat	= 76,800 q.
163	barley	= 20,864 q.
47.5	dura	= 6,840 q. (sorghum)
24	kirsinna	= 4,224 q. (related to lentils, fodder)
30.5	chickpeas	= ?
8.5	lentils	= ?

Source: SMH 49, pp. 449–50, 15 Rajab and 15 Jumâdâ I 1247

as *qism* varied with the yields. In 1830 the crops collected as *qism* represented a value of about 110,000 q., that is, according to official prices and not to the market value. The official price of wheat, the main crop, had hardly changed since the turn of the century, notwithstanding a high rate of inflation. In 1800 the price of a *makkûk* of wheat had been fixed at 224 q. and three decades later it had been augmented with a mere 26 q. to 240 q., or 30 per cent or less of its value on the market.[38] Subsequently, the actual contribution to the treasury by the revenue villages was considerably higher than the synopsis suggests. The disparity between official price and market value was a rich source of hidden revenue.

Given the absence of a reliable indication of the number and the distribution of the population of the Hama district, any remark made on the relative fiscal burden remains speculative. It seems highly unlikely that only about 10 per cent of the district's population lived in the town of Hama. According to the first somewhat more precise estimate of the district's population which dates from 1851, 35 to 40 per cent of the population lived in the town of Hama.[39] The proportion of the rural population may well be deflated in this estimate, but nonetheless there is reason to believe that by contributing about 90 per cent of the total

[38] SMH 46, p. 376, 15 Ramaḍân 1214. In 1244 the official prices of wheat and barley were identical to those of 1247, see SMH 49, p. 322, 29 Jumâdâ I 1244 and p. 450, 15 Jumâdâ I 1247. The market value of a *makkûk* of wheat fluctuated between 190 q. and 640 q. in the early 1820s and between 700 q. and 1120 q. in the 1830s.

[39] The *makkûk* of Hama constituted 16 *shunbul* and 1 *shunbul* equaled 3.5 *kayl Islâmbûlî*.

revenue, the rural population carried a considerably higher tax burden than the townspeople.

Table 3. Comparison of tax distribution over five rural categories

A. average number of *faddân* per village

B. *mâl faddân*

C. average amount of taxes per *faddân*

D. average amount of taxes per village

	A	B	C	D
Jabal Gharbî	–	–	–	9361.5
quṭuniyyât	21.7	225	417.3	9055.7
ḥâṣil	25.2	110	261.5	6589.2
including *qism*	170	379.7	9568	
Turcoman	16.4	150 or 225	331.8	5441.8
maqṭûᶜ	14.8	100	175.4	2595.3

Sources: A: SMH 49, pp. 326–29, 23 Rabîᶜ I 1245; B and C: SMH 51, pp. 316–17, n.d. [Ramaḍân 1257] (which includes the figures for 1248)

The tax treatment of the villages varied considerably (see Table 2). The *maqṭûᶜ* villages clearly received a preferential treatment. The rationale behind the comparatively lenient rate of 110 q. per *faddân* is obscure.[40] The *maqṭûᶜ* villages and farms were scattered over the plains and inhabitants depended for their livelihood on the production of cereals and pulses, just like the other peasants on the plains. In the recent past a number of revenue villages had been illegally entered into the books as *maqṭûᶜ*. In 1806 the *dîwân* of Damascus ordered the *mutasallim* to restore these villages to their original state (*ḥâṣil*) and subsequently the number of *maqṭûᶜ* villages had dropped from 44 to 14 by 1818.[41]

The revenue villages carried a far heavier tax burden. The rate of the *mâl faddân* resting upon these villages was relatively low, but on top of the fixed amount they were liable to *qism*. The average of 9568 q. per village includes the value of the *qism* according to highly conservative

[40] In 1851 the French consular agent in Hama estimated that the rural population in the Hama district numbered 60,000. He put the urban population at 35,000 to 40,000. See ADN/CE, Beyrouth, c. 44, 8 March 1851, Tripoli.

[41] It may be that the mainly small *maqṭûᶜ* villages and farms were the remnants of the *timar*s, the old cavalry fiefs. There is no reference to *timar*s in the Hama records for the relevant period.

official prices for the year 1830; for this year this meant that they paid *qism* to the value of about 60 q. per *faddân*, but when the market value of the crop collected as *qism* is followed, this amount should be tripled or even quadrupled. Because the *qism* was levied in proportion to the harvest, the fiscal regime of these villages was, to a degree, adapted to the uncertainties of dryfarming. It is unknown whether the harvest of 1830 was below or above average.[42]

In the case of the Turcoman villages, economic conditions were taken into consideration. Most Turcoman villages paid a *mâl faddân* of 225 q., but the villages situated to the east of the Sultanic Road were liable to a lower rate, 150 q. This reduced rate reflected the poorer conditions of agriculture in areas bordering the steppe and desert. The three cotton villages (*quṭuniyyât)* belonged to the more prosperous farming communities of the area. They were situated on the fertile banks of the ᶜÂṣî river in the near vicinity of the town of Hama. A number of waterwheels carried water to their gardens and fields. Apart from cotton, they supplied a variety of fruits and vegetables to the town's population. The relative prosperity of these villages might explain the comparatively heavy tax burden.

Religion and taxation

The villages of the Jabal Gharbî were not treated with leniency by the fiscal authorities and carried a heavy tax burden. The villages in question were all small vineyard and orchard villages which produced syrup (*dibs*) and raw silk for the local market. The inhabitants adhered predominantly to the Nuṣayrî faith and, perhaps, their persistence in following this schismatic rite helps to explain the heavy fiscal demands. In the early Ottoman period the Nuṣayrîs were subjected to a discriminatory capital tax, the *dirham al-rijâl*.[43] No such separate charge was payable by them in the period under discussion, but the tradition that these apostates had to pay for their corrupt tenets might have influenced the tax assessment. The Nuṣayrî faith was not confined to

[42] SMH 43, p. 161, 4 Ramaḍân 1221

[43] Two years earlier the quantity of cereals stocked in the granary was less than half of the amount collected in 1830, but it is uncertain whether the stock represented the *qism* of the year 1828. In 1825 the granary contained considerably more. In that year an amount of cereals for the value of 95,040 q. was taken from the granary of Hama by the governor of Damascus. See SMH 49, p. 222, 29 Jumâdâ I 1244; p. 107, 25 Rabîᶜ II 1241; p. 114, 11 Jumâdâ I 1241

this small area. A number of *ḥâṣil* and *maqṭûᶜ* villages were inhabited by Nuṣayrîs as well, but more importantly, Nuṣayrîs made up the large majority of the population in the rural *muqâṭaᶜa*s. These *muqâṭaᶜa*s made up the single largest source of revenue due to a disproportionate amount of levies collected in the support of office-holders. These levies constituted roughly half of the total tax burden resting upon most rural categories, but in the case of the rural *muqâṭaᶜa*s their presence constituted no less than 73 per cent.[44] However, it remains unclear as to whether the Nuṣayrîs were discriminated against by the fiscal authorities on religious grounds. In principle, apostates had no legal rights and any discriminatory imposition which would have been levied from the Nuṣayrîs lacked the backing of religious law. According to Islamic law they should not be tolerated at all. Yet, society had become accustomed to their continuing presence, including the legal authorities who allowed them access to Islamic court.[45]

In the case of the Christians and the Jews[46] who, as People of the Book, enjoyed a protected but subordinate status (*dhimma)*, the levying of a discriminatory poll-tax, the *jizya*, followed old religious prescriptions. The Ottoman authorities paid special attention to the *jizya*, because of its religious relevance.[47] On top of this tax, Christians and Jews in the Hama area were subjected to two other discriminatory charges, the church fee (*mâl kanâyis*) and a toll payable to guards who manned checkpoints at the entrance of town and at bridges (*ghafr dhimmiyyîn*). The latter charges were rooted in tradition rather than Islamic law and were unsubstantial. The *jizya* payable by two large Christian villages had been fixed (*maqṭûᶜ*) for the village as a whole, a practice which ran contrary to the prescription of religious law, but

[44] Mantran et Sauvaget, *Règlements*, p. 76

[45] Compared to 42 per cent for the *ḥâṣil*, 46 per cent for the *quṭuniyyât*, 48 per cent for the Turcoman, and 55 per cent for the *maqṭûᶜ*, Jabal Gharbî and the *ᶜarab* (see table 1).

[46] See, on the Nuṣayrî communities and their position in the area, Douwes, *Knowledge*.

[47] In the early Ottoman period a small number of Jews lived in Hama and in some of the predominantly Christian villages, see Yûsuf, *Rîf*, pp. 41–12. Later the large majority of Jews migrated elsewhere, in particular to Aleppo. In the mid-1830s some Jewish Aleppines had commercial interests in Kafr Buhum, a village which had earlier comprised a small Jewish community, see SMH 50, p. 14, [Jumâdâ I 1251]. Other Jews converted to Islam; the last Jewish convert was recorded in the Hama record in 1831. See SMH 49, p. 455, 20 Jumâdâ II 1247

which was not uncommon.[48] The sums made up about 2 per cent of the total amount of taxes resting upon these villages, demonstrating that these rural Christians were treated with relative clemency. The Christians of the town of Hama were assessed properly, that is per capita, according to the number of adult males. The number of Christians liable to pay the *jizya* in 1825 amounted to 333, divided over the wealthy (33), those having an average income (268) and the working poor (32). The *jizya* of the town of Hama was tabulated jointly with that of Homs, which had a slightly larger Christian community. The total for the two towns amounted to 14,415 q.[49] Due to the devaluation of the Ottoman currency and the increasing financial needs of the state, the rates of the *jizya* were regularly reassessed and by the early 1830s the rate showed an increase of 100 per cent compared to 1825.[50]

Preferential fiscal treatment could be motivated by religious ideals as well. *Waqf* holdings, which were vital for the upkeep of mosques and other religious and public facilities, profited considerably from lower tax rates and frequent exemptions and the same was true for a number of religious dignitaries who owned land in some villages. The old Islamic tithe (*ᶜushr*) hardly occurs in the Hama records, but if it is mentioned, the small charge rested upon some of these pious holdings. Other *waqf* holdings, in particular on the plains, were liable to the more common impositions like the *mâl faddân*.

However, the person who secured the largest tax exemption on the land tax was the *mutasallim*.[51] The Ottoman fiscal system was not a product of religious calculations. As elsewhere, fiscal policies were ruled

[48] E.I.2, vol. II, p. 562. As a rule the *jizya* was remitted to the treasury in Istanbul and administrated by the *qâḍî* on the local level. Whether this was the practice in early nineteenth-century Hama is doubtful. The scarcity of references to the tax in the court records suggests that the *qâḍî* was hardly involved in its collection. The edict of 1825 was addressed to the *mutasallim* and the inclusion of the *khidmat jizya*, an administration fee, in the district's tax tabulations may indicate that the provincial authorities were in charge of its administration. The 1825 edict was signed by the *qâyimmaqâm* of Tripoli, the province of which Hama once had been part.

[49] E.I.2, vol. II, pp. 563–64

[50] SMH 49, p. 83, 5 Muḥarram 1241

[51] The last reassessment had taken place in 1824 when the rate was augmented by no less then 50 per cent; *tartîb qadîm* 9610 + *ḍamm* of the year 1240, 4805 = 14,415. This increase corresponds with the rates given in E.I. 2 vol. II, p. 364. In 1828 the *jizya* payable by the two large Christian villages of Mḥarda and Kafr Buhum, amounted to 450 q. and 350 q.

by considerations of necessity, tradition, privilege and coercive power. *Jizya* payments constituted an important share of the revenue in areas with large Christian populations, but in inland Syria Muslims constituted the large majority of the population. Nevertheless, vested in religious tradition, the *jizya* had acquired a distinct symbolic meaning; attempts to impose a capitation tax on Muslims met with strong opposition and even the rumour of such a reform could contribute to a violent response against the authorities, as happened in Damascus in 1831.[52]

The costs of military efforts

The frequency and magnitude of military efforts and natural calamities was relatively high in the late eighteenth and early nineteenth centuries. In times of natural calamities such as drought, locusts, earthquakes and plagues, the administration imposed additional levies or raised the rate of some of the regular taxes.[53] The more frequent misfortunes were, however, war and revolt. The recurrence of revolts and wars pressed hard upon the population. Smaller and larger armed disturbances and revolts, entailing frequent movement of troops, accompanied provincial factionalism. Attempts to protect the cultivated areas in some years against *ᶜarab* incursions involved further military efforts.

Several events entailed massive movements of troops, such as the invasion of ᶜAlî Bey of Egypt and, even more so, the French invasion of Egypt and Palestine. In the early 1820s the refusal of ᶜAbdallâh Pasha of Acre to accept his dismissal led to a massive mobilization when troops from Aleppo, Adana and elsewhere were ordered to lay siege to the pasha's stronghold. Apart from the contributions to the military efforts, the district of Hama was affected by wars and revolts because it was situated on the Sultanic Road, along which many troops passed. The Hama area was occasionally the scene of frays which provoked the higher authorities to intervene militarily. Military campaigns in the Hama area included the expeditions against the Mawâlî in the 1770s,

[52] In 1818 three rural *waqf* estates in the near vicinity of Hama were exempted for one third of the *mâl faddân*. The village Ṭayyibat al-Gharbiyya, belonging to the *waqf* of the Sayyidnâ Khâlid (ibn al-Walîd) mosque in Homs, was the only village in the relatively prosperous area to the southwest of Hama which secured tax exemptions. The dignitaries referred to are the *muftî*, the *naqîb*, and two religious sheikhs. Salîm Bey al-ᶜAẓm acted as *mutasallim* in this year; SMH 43, p. 187, 15 Rabîᶜ I 1233

[53] See p. 146

fighting between troops of ʿAbdallâh Pasha al-ʿAẓm and Jazzâr Pasha in 1804, and the campaigns against ʿAnaza beduin in 1815, 1818 and 1827.

Local troops were regularly called upon by the governor of Damascus, or others, to contribute in provincial military efforts, in particular in the days of Mullâ Ismâʿîl, but the supply of food, fodder and transport to the passing troops or to the troops on the battlefield constituted the main contribution of the Hama district to the military efforts in general. In more peaceful years as well, supplies were demanded, for instance by ʿAbdallâh Pasha al-ʿAẓm when he prepared to leave for Damascus to succeed Jazzâr Pasha as governor in 1795. The provisions were referred to as *dhakhîra* or, more often, its plural *dhakhâyir*.[54] In many years, the *mutasallim* of Hama received orders from the governor of Damascus or Aleppo, or directly from Istanbul, to prepare provisions for troops which were about to pass through the district. A list of the demanded items and quantities was attached to the order, but sometimes the *mutasallim* was simply ordered to prepare plentiful provisions. A whole range of items could be requested, including coffee, tobacco and wax, but flour, dry cakes, barley, sheep, and mules and camels for transport constituted the main components of the provisions.[55]

The engagement and movement of troops involved high expenses, which were only partly covered by the treasury. The deficit had to be made up by the districts. For that purpose an extraordinary levy was imposed, simply called *dhakhîra* or *dhakhâyir* after the provisions, or after the purchase of the provisions, *mubâyaʿa*. The provisions were usually bought locally. The officer in charge of the purchase, the *mubâyaʿajî*, carried some cash with him, but most of the expenses which he incurred were recovered from the villages, the town and the tribes. The distribution of this burden followed, at least partly, the method of assessment of the regular taxes. The villages of the plains, for example, contributed in relation to the number of *faddân*.[56]

The magnitude of the *dhakhâyir* levies, of course, varied from one year to the other, but it appears that the Hama district had been

[54] The impositions *jawâyiḥ* and *ṣawâyib* are referred to occasionally. Both terms translate to 'calamities', see for example SMH 43, 254, 11 Jumâdâ I 1237, and p. 357, late Rabîʿ I 1238. However, *jawâyiḥ* was also used in the broad meaning of 'extraordinary tax'.

[55] Sometimes the equivalent *dhukhra* was used.

[56] See for a list of twenty different items ordered by the newly appointed *wâlî* ʿAbdallâh Pasha al-ʿAẓm, SMH 43, p. 231, 9 Jumâdâ I 1210

earmarked for a fixed yearly contribution to the upkeep of the armies, which had to be augmented in the case of actual warfare. In 1818 provisions of barley and wheat of a value of 51,250 q. were transported to Tripoli to be shipped, an amount which matched that of 1802.[57] In 1831 the amount of what appear to have been mostly regular *dhakhâyir* levies, added up to 86,266 q. The rates had been established by the newly appointed governor when he passed through Hama on his way to Damascus.[58] This imposition might have been identical with the *safariyya*, the well-known charge levied to support war efforts.

During wars and insurrections the demands for provisions could skyrocket. The largest contributions to war efforts were made at the time of the French occupation of Egypt and coastal Palestine.[59] Imperial and provincial troops heading south to expel the French invasion army camped for two days near Hama. They were provided with food and fodder during their short stay, as well as with supplies which would last the troops until they had arrived in Damascus.

The main order of the *mubâyaᶜajî* of the imperial troops included cakes, flour and sackcloth for packaging. The quantities of wheat for the production of flour and cakes were specified and the *mutasallim* was warned not to have the flour mixed with straw and earth. With the acquisition of thousands of sheep, the troops did not only enjoy nutritious biscuits but fresh meat as well.

The effort was tremendous by all standards and not to be surpassed in the coming years.[60] Some months later a second order for the imperial troops was sent to Hama, demanding the delivery and transport of identical amounts of cakes and fodder to Damascus. No sheep were ordered this time. The delivery was delayed because the *mutasallim* complained to his superiors that the district was unable to carry the burden. The governor acknowledged that the demands pressed hard upon the district and reduced the demands of wheat and barley. The district was also relieved from the cost of transport; camels would be

[57] SMH 43, p. 82, 11 Ṣafar 1215

[58] SMH 43, p. 235, dated 1233 and p. 131, 29 [?] 1217.

[59] SMH 49, pp. 442–3, 29 Rabîᶜ I 1247

[60] The following is based upon: SMH 46, p. 277, 13 Dhû al-Qaᶜda 1213; p. 312, 11 Rabîᶜ II 1214; p. 353, 11 Dhû al-Qaᶜda 1213; p. 354, 10 Dhû al-Ḥijja 1213; pp. 357–59, 1 Rabîᶜ II 1214; p. 360, 28 Rabîᶜ II 1214; p. 365, 24 Jumâdâ I 1214; p. 369, dated 1214; p. 376, 15 Ramaḍân 1214; SMH 43, pp. 73–74, 19 Muḥarram 1215; p. 82, 11 Ṣafar 1215; p. 84, 15 and 19 Ṣafar 1215; pp. 85–86, 27 Ṣafar 1215; pp. 93–94, 12 Rabîᶜ II 1215

Table 4. Provisions for the imperial troops in 1799–1800

	Quantities	Value (q.)
Wheat	ca. 705 *makkûk*	90,241
Barley	946 *makkûk*	77,054
Sheep	5533 head	35,632
Cloth		7,500
Milling/baking/packing/ administration		52,967
TOTAL EXPENSES		253,394
From the *mubâyaᶜajî*		61,062
dhakhîra		41,551
treasury		1,987
TOTAL AMOUNT COVERED		104,601
DEFICIT (to be made up by the district)		148,793

Source: SMH 46, pp. 358–59, 1 Rabîᶜ II 1214

sent from Damascus. The *mutasallim* was told that no further favours were to be bestowed upon the district.[61]

In times of war, the authorities required a large contribution from the *aᶜyân* and other well-to-do members of the local community, especially from the merchants. In 1799 several people were lumped together as *arbâb nuqûd*, the moneyed, and duly charged. They were not only forced to contribute financially, but they, or rather a number of them, also had to take heavy losses on their merchandise. The *mubâyaᶜajî* purchased the army provisions at prices well below the official fiscal price and far below the market prices.[62] In 1799 a price of 128 q. and 80 q. per *makkûk* of, respectively, wheat and barley was offered, less than 60 per cent of the official price. The reduction of the amounts of wheat and barley almost a year later was accompanied with a reduction of the prices. Now, the *mubâyaᶜajî* offered in compensation only 84 q. and 56 q. respectively.

An odd twenty years later the refusal of ᶜAbdallâh Pasha of Acre to

[61] This amount comprised a sum of 13,125 q. labelled *dhukhra*, 12,756 q. labelled *darâhim dhakhîra* and 15,670 q., the value of sheep collected 'in addition to the *dhakhîra*'.

[62] Apparently part of the deficit was financed from other sources, because eventually 118,628 q was imposed on the district.

resign brought havoc on the population of the Hama area. In 1821 troops which had been ordered to bring his head to Istanbul passed through Hama on their quest. They had to be supplied with provisions. Cavalry from Hama joined the military campaign. Half a year later the *mubâyaᶜajî* placed a second order for the troops which were now besieging Acre. Complaints about the magnitude of the demands had been dismissed by the governor, although he admitted that the population of Hama was, impoverished due to the earlier movement of troops; these were days of hardship for all, he argued.[63] The demands of wheat were moderate compared to those during the French assault on Acre, and even though the amounts of barley and sheep stayed behind as well, they were again enormous.

Table 5. Dhakhâyir demands during campaigns against ᶜAbdallâh Pasha

Wheat/flour	ca. 160 *makkûk*	camels 100
Barley	ca. 590 *makkûk*	mules 150
		sheep 3667

Source: SMH 43, p. 323, 27 Shawwâl 1237, p. 335, end of Dhû al-Ḥijja 1237, and p. 20, 7 Ṣafar 1238

The expenditure for the military increased sharply in the second half of the 1820s as a result of the reorganization of the armies and the Balkan wars. The elimination of the janissary corps had left many officials and officers in the empire with a strong sense of insecurity about their future position. The building of the new standing armies, notably the *mansure*, required high investments and time. Both fell short. The desperate attempts of Sultan Mahmud II to acquire additional income to finance his ambitious military reforms included the imposition of new charges or the reimposition of old ones. The most substantial imposition was the substitute tax for military service and expenditures (*badal maṣârif al-ᶜaskar*), announced in all towns and villages in 1827.[64] In 1829 the town of Hama alone was earmarked for no less than 252,631 q. Earlier, the tobacco duties had been increased to

[63] The deficit nearly equalled the income of the treasury in the district in 1805, SMH 43, p. 153, dated 1220

[64] The rent of 667 camels for the transport of the provisions had been imposed upon the district. The rent of one camel was assessed at 50 q. The total amount of rent imposed upon Hama was 33,350 q. Nearby Homs had to supply another 333 camels and Damascus 1,000. See SMH 43, pp. 73–74, 19 Muḥarram 1215 and p. 82, 11 Ṣafar 1215

help cover the military expenses.[65] These were temporary impositions meant to satisfy the urgent needs. Another new imposition was the *badal anfâr ᶜaskar*, the substitute conscription tax, apparently only payable by the villages in the Hama district at its introduction in 1829. The introduction of the conscription constituted one of the most important military reforms.[66] The actual conscription was delayed and in lieu an amount of 4000 q. was payable for each technical conscript. The Hama villages had been earmarked for 50 conscripts and hence 20,000 q. of *badal* was demanded.[67] Eventually the *badal anfâr ᶜaskar* was to survive as a tax payable by non-Muslim subjects only, because they were exempted from serving in the sultan's army.

The limits of taxation

In the pursuit of their financial and provisionary goals, the authorities encountered a number of obstacles. The yields of agriculture were relatively low and unstable. The crops on the rain-fed land, predominantly wheat and barley, were vulnerable to changes in weather conditions and to hazards like locusts and mice; subsequently the yields varied considerably from year to year and crop failures occurred with some regularity. Later in the nineteenth century, the peasants in the Hama area even reckoned with one crop failure in every five years.[68] In the second half of the eighteenth century, agricultural production had decreased and notwithstanding the recovery during the first decades of the nineteenth century, the rural economy remained fragile. Scarcity meant that the administration was almost permanently confronted with inadequate resources and found difficulty in organizing the taxation because of the high costs involved for collection, storage and transport. Evidently the authorities realized that the demands made upon the districts in times of war, revolt and military reform harmed the local economy, but the integrity of the state could not be compromised. In

[65] A document dealing with arrears payments states that the *mubâyaᶜajî* paid the 'following *aᶜyân*', among them two members of the Kaylânî family and the merchant family al-Ḥâjj Zayn. See SMH 43, p. 119, 11 Rabîᶜ 1217. See also Inalcik, *Centralization*, p. 49 and Khoury, *State*, pp. 54–55

[66] SMH 43, p. 345, 7 Ṣafar 1238

[67] Shihâb, *Lubnân*, p. 788

[68] SMH 49, p. 364, 12 Ramaḍân 1245. No figures are given for the villages, the rural *muqâṭaᶜa*s and the tribes. SMH 49, p. 230, 19 and 27 Rajab 1242, on the extra charge on the *gumruk dukhkhân*.

the late eighteenth and early nineteenth centuries the empire was under severe threat, both from without and within. At the centre the initial response to the problem of inadequate resources was to lay the blame on local and provincial officials. These officials could easily become the targets of the higher authorities of the state. The rights of the officials in the provinces to a share of the revenue were only acknowledged to a certain degree, but many were usually able to appropriate a considerable share. However, it was not mere greed that motivated the servants of the sultan in the province to apply the methods which were often considered as unjust; they had to enlarge their income in order to strengthen their capability to serve.

7. The logic of injustice; Fiscal and financial policies

Revenue extraction lay at the heart of Ottoman administration and ideology, in particular after the empire had ceased to expand and the ruling house was confronted with internal challenges and serious budgetary difficulties. The doctrine of Circle of Justice contained the vision of permanently productive sources of revenue to be tapped and protected by the ruling class. The idea gained popularity among the Ottoman elite at a time of deep crisis: the critical economic conditions and Celali uprisings of the late sixteenth and early seventeenth centuries. The Circle of Justice served as a tool to analyse the crisis and to develop policies aimed at the recovery of the state.[1] But also prior to these critical evaluations, fiscalism dominated Ottoman political thinking.[2]

Taxation constituted the major method of surplus extraction, but it was not the only method. Nor was taxation merely a method of surplus extraction; it was an instrument to regulate the relations between the resources and the population, and also the relations of power.[3] In these functions taxation was supplemented by various other instruments. In the case of the peasant population, obliged to remit a substantial share of their produce to the state, their relations with the authorities were determined by the mechanisms of tax assessment and collection; one could even argue that taxation formed the basis of rural social order.[4] But the relationship was reciprocal – certainly in the ideology of justice – and the authorities had a clear interest in the protection of the well-being of the peasantry, because '. . . an empty treasury reflected poverty

[1] See, for a discussion of the (changes in the) ideology, Abou-El-Haj, *Formation*, and Darling, *Revenue-raising*, pp. 281–306

[2] *Economic*, vol. 1, pp. 44–45

[3] See for a general discussion of taxation Eisenstadt, *Political*, pp. 123–26; Tilly, *Coercion*, 87–89

[4] *Economic*, vol. 1, pp. 69–70; Singer, *Palestinian*, p. 87

in the countryside, and filling it again necessitated meeting the needs of the peasant producers.'[5]

The concepts of justice and oppression

It did not escape the central authorities that much of the wealth of the Ottoman domains was appropriated by those who served them in the provinces. The administration of justice implied that the population had to be protected against excessive demands of the local administrators and military. According to Ottoman ideology this required the maintenance of the absolute power of the sultan, because without sultanic rule the application of the divine law, the *shar*ᶜ, was not guaranteed.

Orders emanating from higher authority normally contained a general reference to the application of the *shar*ᶜ, also when the ruling involved appears to be entirely 'sultanic'. The frequent borrowings from the Islamic legal tradition in sultanic regulations demonstrate the perceived oneness of the two legal systems. Illegal and oppressive actions were often coined *bidᶜa*, and the perpetrator *khârijî*, both terms with a strong religious bearing, the first denoting an unlawful innovation according to the *shar*ᶜ, the second a renegade and rebel against the legitimate ruler. The latter category was a broad one and included those who committed grave sins, such as apostation, highway robbery, abuse of power, causing of disorder, deserters, and of course, rebels against sultanic rule.[6] Not unsurprisingly, the Wahhâbîs were considered the '*khawârij* of our time'.[7] Jazzâr Pasha, after having disobeyed orders from Istanbul, was called '. . . the object of the anger of God, his exalted prophet and his beneficent successor (*khalîfa*).'[8] In a verdict issued against ᶜAbdallâh Pasha of Acre when he refused his dismissal, the pasha was not only customarily branded a *khârijî*, but was also was accused of having made common cause with an unfaithful coalition of Druzes, Shiites (*rawâfiḍ*), Nuṣayrîs, and ᶜ*arab* 'culprits', and subsequently sentenced to death.[9] Apart from being part of official and legal terminology, the religio-political idiom had long since become part and parcel of the common

[5] Darling, *Revenue-raising*, pp. 289–90

[6] In (contemporary) *sharᶜi* terms: *al-khârij* ᶜ*alâ imâm al-ḥaqq*, see Ibn ᶜÂbidîn, *Radd*, vol. 3, pp. 308–13

[7] *Ibid.*, p. 309

[8] Shihâb, *Lubnân*, pp. 362–63

[9] SMH 43, pp. 314–15, 30 Ramaḍân 1237

vocabulary. The death of the principle aide of Jazzâr, the *deli* Shaykh Ṭaha, was celebrated in a poem in which he was called a Yazîdî, a non-Muslim sectarian.[10] Decades earlier, the death of another *aghâ* gave rise to an outburst of joy in Damascus; one of the leading ulema declared him to have been more tyrannical than Nimrod and gave permission to the population to throw stones at his grave, "just like people do in the Hijaz with the grave of Umayyad caliph Yazîd ibn Muᶜâwiya", whose troops defeated and killed Ḥusayn the sacred son of ᶜAlî.[11] Other words derived from the religious tradition which were used frequently in the context of corruption and violent rule include *kufr*, or disbelief, *ḍalâl*, or error, *fitna*, or fighting among Muslims.

Reference to words and images having a religious bearing was the accepted way to define a wide variety of offences in these, seemingly, strong terms, including what must have been more minor offences, such as accepting small bribes. Just like in Byzantine times, the verdicts, laws and chronicles have to be treated with care concerning alleged acts of injustice and tyranny.[12]

The income and expenses of the provincial officials

Many accusations of abuse of power occurred in the process of revenue extraction. In their efforts to secure an income which would enable them to administer their areas adequately and to further their careers, provincial officials applied both legal procedures and methods which were not sanctioned or were even strictly forbidden. The higher authorities often took a lenient position with regard to the legitimacy of certain actions of their servants, because it was through them that they retained their material and moral claims on the subject classes. But the dispensation of justice required the timely imposition of sanctions against those who had overtly transgressed the boundaries of proper conduct, however fluid these boundaries were. This principle served the central state as an important instrument to contain provincial power groups and to press its own material claims on them.

Officials in the province had good reason to be inventive when it came to ways of augmenting their income. The tax income of a province often fell short of the actual expenses of the governor and other senior

[10] Shihâb, *Lubnân*, p. 426. He was a Kurd and, in fact, might have been of Yazîdî background.

[11] Ibn al-Siddîq, *Gharâ'ib*, p. 58

[12] Cameron, *Mediterranean*, p. 82

officials. Russell estimated in the mid-eighteenth century that the regular revenue of the governor of the province of Aleppo was barely sufficient to cover two thirds of his annual expenses.[13] The governor of the province of Damascus, with its particular fiscal regime focussed on the yearly pilgrimage, was also confronted with budget deficits. Given the great importance attached to the pilgrimage extra-provincial sources were drawn upon, but the governor had to utilize other means of income derivation as well. Although the central authorities showed a degree of flexibility with respect to the financing of the pilgrimage, they played down the magnitude of the expenses. The formal allocation of funds to the pilgrimage remained unchanged over long periods, notwithstanding rampant inflation.[14] By denying the provincial officials adequate regular funding to perform their duties, the central state relieved itself from the difficult task of making ends meet. Income derived from personal investments in the local economy, or from loans, or income derived by more coercive means constituted badly needed supplements. This very common phenomenon is sometimes approached from a different angle; Barbir, for instance, puts much weight on '. . . the central government's flexibility in handling revenue problems.'[15] In practice this flexibility often came down to leaving the handling of these problems to others. One of the consequences of this policy was that the central accountancy had limited control over the provincial finances. This deficiency in the central administration allowed senior provincial officials room for manoeuvring and manipulation, but their policies lacked a secure financial as well as sound legal base. Given its limited hold of the provincial finances, the central administration had every reason to keep the position of the senior provincial officials insecure.

The governors and other high-ranking officials had no alternative other than to increase their income from the province in order to make up the budget deficits and to protect their interests. A variety of means were at their disposal. The function of the state in the economy was such that office-holders had the opportunity to turn economic resources to their own use.[16] They also used the more manifest political resources

[13] Russell, *Natural*, vol. 1, pp. 315–16. Alexander Russell worked as a physician for the British factory in Aleppo until 1753.

[14] See for the financial base of the pilgrimage Barbir, *Ottoman*, pp. 110–25. The amount of revenue allocated to the pilgrimage in 1796 was identical to that of 1764.

[15] *Ibid*, pp. 118–19 and 125

[16] This central authorities were well aware of this use, see Thomas, *Naima*, p. 88

and these methods were often of a coercive nature. The most common sources of additional income were investments in the spheres of the urban and rural production and commerce by establishing partnerships or by acquiring landed or commercial properties, the monopolization of the marketing of certain commodities, the forcing of loans, imposition of additional levies, confiscations, and bailing out.[17] Not all of these methods were illegal, but some obviously were, whereas others were only permissible in certain circumstances. Combined with the near absolute claims of the sultan on his servants, the controversial nature of quite a number of current revenue policies gave the central authorities ample pretext to intervene into provincial finances.

The state and the economy

In the Ottoman tradition, economic policies were aimed at three major issues: to preserve the fiscal prerogatives of the state, to guarantee the supplies to the armies, and to protect the supplies of necessities to the large urban populations.[18] Agriculture received most state attention, but through monopolies, market regulations, the custody of urban craft organizations and charitable endowments, the state intervened extensively in the internal market. The state carried a great responsibility for the distribution of goods from agricultural and pastoralist producers, as well as for the preservation of the conditions required for the continuation of agricultural production. The doctrine of the Circle of Justice clearly defined this responsibility.[19] The state provided the incentives for the production of an agricultural surplus by granting peasants the permanent use of land on the condition that they cultivated

[17] For a concise discussion of the office- and provincial households' strategies, including a number of illustrations obtained from various parts of the empire, including the centre, see Göçek, Rise, pp. 50–56 and 60–65.

[18] See, for a short discussion of Ottoman economic thinking, *Economic*, vol. 1, pp. 44–54, vol. 2. pp. 710–23

[19] See p. 3–4. The economy of the empire can be defined as a peasant economy, which means that most production takes place in agriculture and that the peasant household constitutes the dominant unit of production. The household in peasant economies produces first and foremost to satisfy its subsistence needs and is reluctant to produce surplus. Structures of kinship, religion and/or political power provide the stimulus to surplus production and its distribution. See Sunar, *State*, pp. 65–68. See for the concept of the peasant economy, Thorner, *Peasant*.

it. As the guardian of God's domains[20] the state owned most land – in inland Syria particularly dry-farming land. The usufructuary rights to the *mîrî*, state-owned, land were generally well protected and, subsequently, the peasants' right to subsistence were as well.[21] The tax reductions and the provision of loans, ploughing animals and seeds figured among the instruments to stimulate peasants to continue producing. Peasants who left their land and village could be returned by force, a policy which was not undisputed; according to Islamic law peasants were free to leave their land and within the religious establishment, opposition to the forced return of peasants and fining of fugitive peasants existed.[22] Given that the taxes were imposed collectively on the village community, the community had an interest in the return of fugitives.[23] In the district of Hama the taxes resting upon the villages were assessed in relation to the land and not to the number of adults or households, thus binding the peasants to the land. When peasants had left their land and ceased paying taxes (*taᶜaṭṭul al-mîrî)*, others had the opportunity to occupy the land and claim its usufruct.[24]

The economic policies of the state were conservative, aimed largely at the conservation of the existing productive units, also in the case of urban industries. The craftsmen, for example, were protected from competition by the state's custody of their corporations that had the obligation to maintain the quality of the products. The ideal was that everyone, peasant and craftsman alike, held on to his occupation and remained within his particular productive units, the village community or the craft organization.[25] Only the attitude towards nomadic producers was different. They were often encouraged to take up a sedentary mode of production. This policy was not motivated by economic considerations as such, but reflected the state's ambition to control nomadic groups and to safeguard public security in the rural areas and along the lines of communication.

The exchange of goods, the market, was also regulated by the state to

[20] See, for the concept of the guardianship of the state, Johansen, *Islamic*.

[21] Islamoglu-Inan, *Peasants*, pp. 58–64

[22] Seikaly, *Land*, pp. 404–05; Abdel Nour, *Traits*, p. 75; Aladdin, *Fatwâ-s*, pp. 18–20

[23] See Rafeq, *Land*, p. 382. The remaining fief (*timar*) holders in the countryside of Damascus shared this interest. See Rafeq, *Economic*, p. 668. See also Hansen, *Economic*.

[24] See, for instance, SMH 48, p. 276, [Rajab 1236]

[25] This was embedded in the ideal of the Bounds (*hudud*), see p. 3

a considerable extent. Prone to protect the urban consumers, competition was restrained by the fixing of prices of a large number of necessities and by checking on their quality and quantity through the market inspection (*iḥtisâb*). Restrictions on the flow of goods were common in order to prevent shortages in necessities for the armies and the urban populations. Monopolies on the manufacture and sale of certain commodities followed from the same consideration. Other monopolies had been established out of fiscal considerations. Finally, the Ottomans paid much attention to charity institutions in the cities in view of the masses of urban poor. These institutions, which distributed alms and food, and offered (limited) health services, played a role of some significance in the urban economy.

The central role of the state in the economy forced the office-holders in the province to engage in economic activities; moreover, this offered them ample opportunity to secure additional income. The relative weight of the economic resources which were at the disposal of provincial office-holders varied. The establishment of viable partnerships or other commercial relations with peasants, pastoralists, craftsmen and traders could only be pursued with a measure of success when a governor or other senior official had knowledge of the local economic fabric. If he was a total stranger to the province, he might well have been reluctant to invest in its agriculture, animal husbandry or urban industry. But for much of the eighteenth and early nineteenth centuries hardly any governor was appointed to the province of Damascus who lacked a reasonable degree of familiarity with the area. The career expectation of a governor also will have influenced his commercial activities. When he would have reason to believe that he would serve for at least a few terms, investment in the local economy became more attractive. The ʿAẓm governors were a case in point. They made great fortunes out of various commercial enterprises ranging from cereal production and animal husbandry to overland trade.

Monopolies and market manipulation

Monopolies offered office-holders an instrument to prevent bread riots and other manifestations of the unbalanced distribution of goods, but also the monopoly of the marketing of cereals, meat, cotton and other commodities often served to strengthen their economic interests. Traditionally, the state granted the monopoly of the trade of certain commodities, like salt, tobacco, timber, candles, soap and wine, in given areas to individual merchants, including foreigners, but office-holders also competed for these monopolies.[26] Commodities like wheat, meat and cotton did not normally belong to the category of state monopolies, but especially these commodities attracted the attention of the governors of Damascus, Acre and Aleppo.

The commercial interests of the governor were further advanced by the fiscal system. The major share of the amounts of grain collected in the Hama area was at the disposal of the governor of Damascus and it is highly likely that the same was true for the grain collected in Homs, the Hawran and other districts. Part of the wheat was marketed by the governor in order to convert it into cash; the remainder being in stock or shipped to Istanbul or elsewhere. Through their hold on major cereal producing areas like Hama, the ᶜAẓms controlled a considerable part of the internal cereal market. In concert with some Damascene cereal traders, they were able to manipulate the market by withholding supplies in times of plenty and by selling off their stock and pile in times of dearth. Asᶜad Pasha al-ᶜAẓm, the governor of the mid eighteenth century, was very successful in manipulating the price of grain and bread to his own profit. However, he did not actually monopolize the trade. The heads of craft organizations, like the millers, bakers and butchers, and other interested parties, often cooperated with the governor and other high officials in manipulating the prices of the commodities.[27]

It might have been common to establish a monopoly, but this policy could easily provoke opposition from influential segments of local society. Many families of some standing had interests in tribes, villages, crafts, and their respective produce. But of special importance were the Damascene cereal traders, who were often *aghawât* and tax farmers of the hinterland of Damascus, the Marj and the Hawran. The cereal production in the Hawran was second in importance only to that of Hama. Any governor had to take the interests of the Damascene cereal traders into account. Also the entanglement of the craft organizations and the local military in Damascus put a restraint on the economic policies of a governor. In pursuit of his commercial goals, a governor had to be careful not to arouse popular discontent, in particular not in the Maydân where the *yerliyya* resided. Damascenes complained about the price manipulation of the market by Asᶜad Pasha al-ᶜAẓm, but he was

[26] See Inalcik, *Ottoman*, pp. 128, 132, 137 and Shaw, *History*, vol. 1, pp. 60, 120, and 159

[27] Rafeq, *Economic*, pp. 657–58

careful enough not to provoke bread riots. It was essential for a governor not to totally disregard the interests of the common people and to temper popular feelings against him by occasional acts of fairness and generosity. Asʿad Pasha used the surplus of grain in Hama area on several occasions to relieve the population of Damascus by selling his wheat at a modest price.[28] When he was transferred to Aleppo, he soon gained popularity, because he lowered the price of wheat and supplied the city from his own granaries. When after some months the news spread that he was to leave for Sivas, people demonstrated against his departure.[29]

The one governor who neglected the interests of the public at large was Jazzâr Pasha of Acre. He established a wide range of monopolies in the province of Sidon, and suppressed any opposition against his policy.[30] He pursued a similar monopolistic policy when he was in office in Damascus and met with a strong local opposition when he initiated this policy; his first term in office ended after leading Damascenes had petitioned the Porte complaining about the imposition of a monopoly on wheat trade.[31] Contrary to his hold on the province of Sidon, his grip on the province of Damascus was never secure and the monopoly policies were never fully implemented there. In his economic policies Jazzâr Pasha is likely to have followed the example of his former master, ʿAlî Bey of Egypt, and to a certain extent that of Ẓâhir al-ʿUmar, who operated in the Acre region under much more favourable economic conditions. Jazzâr Pasha's economic policies influenced later governors, like Kunj Yûsuf Pasha of Damascus, who, was however, unsuccessful.[32] The renowned governor of Egypt, Muḥammad ʿAlî Pasha, resorted to this system of exploitation as well and carried it to its limits.[33]

Loans and additional impositions

The enforcement of loans was an authorized method of raising capital. However, when a governor or other functionary failed to repay a loan,

[28] Rafeq, *Province*, p. 203; Budayrî, *Ḥawâdith*, pp. 74 and 157

[29] See Russell, *Natural*, vol. 1, pp. 341 and 404

[30] Cohen, *Palestine*, pp. 21–23; Gibb and Bowen, *Islamic*, vol.1, pp. 67–68; Philipp, *Social*, p. 98, p. 102

[31] See p. 91

[32] In Aleppo similar attempts were made, for example by the establishment of the monopoly of wheat by Khûrshîd Pasha in 1820. See Bodman, *Political*, p. 28

[33] Owen, *Middle East*, pp. 64–76; al-Sayyid Marsot, *Egypt*, pp. 145–60

he committed a breach of contract. It was not uncommon for him to refuse or to be unable to settle a contracted debt and it was often doubtful whether the claimant was able to recover the debt without the support of higher authority. The central state applied this method of fund raising as well, particularly in times of war, and issued orders to provinces to contract loans.[34] At the time of the campaigns against the French occupation army in Palestine and Egypt, the commander of the imperial troops imposed large sums on several members of the ᶜAẓm family of Damascus, some of their associates and others, amounting to 300,000 q. The then *mutasallim* of Hama, ᶜAbd al-Raḥmân Bey al-ᶜAẓm, had also been forced to make a loan (of 40,000 q.). These loans were later recovered by the governor of Baghdad.[35] The promissory notes issued by the treasury in return for a loan were often difficult to redeem for cash, and consequently, local opposition to the enforcement of loans was generally strong.[36]

Office-holders also resorted to ways to enlarge their income by the mere abuse of their power: outright extortion of money and kind, soliciting bribes on top of legal fees, the imposition of new taxes without the sanction of the central authorities, upgrading existing tax rates, as well as manipulating interest rates, prices and weights. The refusal of a proper compensation or any compensation at all for services of various types occurred frequently as well. While governor of Damascus, Jazzâr Pasha had quite a number of well-to-do Damascenes arrested and then bailed out.[37] These means of exploitation were collectively referred to as *ẓulm*, acts of injustice. Likewise, outright profiteering by market manipulations and the exclusion of the local trading community were considered unjust acts.

The use of force by provincial officials was only unlawful when it concerned the extortion of amounts on top of the legal rates. People who were reluctant or unable to pay their share of taxes could be subjected to various methods of persuasion. The governor of Damascus toured in most parts of his province with his private army in order to compel local

[34] In 1786, for example, the *wâlî* of Damascus, Ibrâhîm Deli Pasha, instructed the *mutasallim* of Hama to contract loans from its population following an order from the Porte, SMH 46, p. 123, [Rajab] 1201

[35] Al-ᶜAbd, *Târîkh*, pp. 68–70

[36] See, for example, Murâdî (*Silk*, vol. 1, p. 224) for the exile of three religious dignitaries from Damascus after they had opposed the forcing of loans by the *wâlî*.

[37] al-ᶜAbd, *Târîkh*, pp. 23–24

officials and tax farmers to meet their liabilities. This custom was referred to as *dawra*, the tour. The district of Hama, being attached as the leasehold for life (*malikane*) to the governorship of the province, was normally not visited during this tour. The taking of hostages from the relatives of officials and tax farmers constituted another widely practised method of compulsion. Beating constituted the main physical argument to compel people to pay.

The policies of the central authorities

The allocation of insufficient revenue resources to the officials and their households was only one of the ways in which the central authorities sought to control them; another way to deplete the resources of the officials and their households was the confiscation of their economic resources.[38]

These measures constituted a major instrument in containing these groups, but could not always be pursued with success. In pressing its political and material claims on the servants in the province, the central administration relied on the combined use of various other instruments.

The withholding of adequate regular financial resources served as a valuable instrument to restrain the power of senior provincial officials, although it may not have been intended as such at first. Their endeavours to augment their income in order to administer the province properly and to further their interests and careers, were accompanied with transgressions of written and unwritten laws. Legal action could be taken against them at any time and this constant threat served to intimidate the provincial administration into a loyal attitude. The intimidation also restrained many an official from the more excessive methods of exploitation, although some, like Jazzâr Pasha, proved difficult to intimidate. When the policies of provincial authorities produced social unrest, the central authorities regularly intervened. For instance, a governor could be called to account for the sums exacted on top of the amounts established by law. Moreover, the risk that an official had to account for even more than he had collected in reality by illegal means was far from hypothetical.[39] The tradition of petitioning the imperial council (*dîwân*) against acts of injustice perpetrated by senior officials

[38] For a concise discussion, including a number of illustrations from various parts of the empire, including the centre, see Göçek, *Rise*, pp. 56–60

[39] Russell, *Natural*, vol. 2, p. 316

was an important element of the tradition of exerting a constant pressure on provincial office-holders.

In actual practice the central authorities often took a lenient position towards the unauthorized actions of those who served them. These practices had become an organic part of the administration and no viable alternatives were at hand. They often turned a blind eye to market manipulation, exactions and other 'unjust' measures, and much remained unpunished. From the point of view of the central authorities the main disadvantage of the system was that the actual income of provincial officials, and thus the magnitude of the provincial revenue, remained somewhat obscure. The means to manipulate the provincial budget were manifold, in particular because the central state had little control over the expense side. Numerous officials were able to enlarge their income and divert a considerable part of it to their own private use. The central authorities were always suspicious of the financial dealings of their inferiors in the provinces. The distrust was mutual, because the sultan could act at will and many governors and others were obsessed by possible actions or intrigues against them.

Functionaries of the treasury department were regularly sent to provinces to audit the accounts, but it often proved difficult to conduct a proper investigation into the finances of the senior provincial officials as long as they remained in office. It had become routine to conduct an inquiry into the provincial finances after a governor had been dismissed, transferred to another post or had died, but even then it often took a long time before an inquiry was concluded. Local authorities were regularly involved in the inquiries. In 1799 Jazzâr Pasha's *mutasallim* in Hama, ᶜAbdallâh Aghâ al-Maḥmûd, was ordered by the Porte to instruct the judge of the Hama court to prepare a tabulation of taxes collected during the reign of Ibrâhîm Deli Pasha, who had been dismissed a decade earlier. In the same year the properties in the district of Hama of yet another former governor of Damascus, Muḥammad Darwîsh Pasha, who served in 1782–83, were subjected to an official investigation.[40] Of course, most officials would eventually be found guilty of manipulation of some sort. Many officials and their heirs were indebted to either the treasury or their proclaimed victims including individuals, often traders, but also to entire quarters, craft organizations, villages or tribes.

[40] SMH 46, pp. 330–31, 8 Shaᶜbân 1213 (Ibrâhîm Deli Pasha had acted as *wâlî* from 1787 to 1790); SMH 46, p. 352, 13 Ṣafar 1213 (on Muḥammad Darwîsh Pasha)

Confiscation of part of their properties or inheritance normally followed. Inquiries following accusations of abuse of power, too, often resulted in confiscation. The imperial household depended strongly on income generated by confiscating the wealth of provincial – and central – officials and notables; those who held no formal offices, but acted as tax-farmers or otherwise, attracted the attention of higher authority if they accumulated considerable wealth.[41]

Many officials left their office in a hurry when news about their dismissal arrived – and some even earlier – in order to evade prosecution and confiscation. In principle, a deposed governor was obliged to reside in the provincial capital until his accounts had been audited.[42] Usually, governors and others had converted part of their wealth into cash, gold and precious stones, which were easily hidden or transported. Another method to protect one's possessions against confiscation was to convert property in, in principle, inalienable *waqf* holdings or to invest in existing *waqf* holdings. The low tax demands resting upon *waqf* property constituted an additional advantage. In the legal establishment opposition was voiced against some of these transactions, but especially the ᶜAẓm governors had applied this method widely.[43]

Part of the inheritance of most, if not all, of the ᶜAẓm governors was subjected to confiscation by the state. The most famed governor of the family, Asᶜad Pasha, was even killed in preparation for the confiscation of a large part of his wealth, including 78 looms of striped and silk-cotton cloth, 2 inns, 236 shops, 42 vegetable gardens, 3 bathhouses, 7 farms, 20 houses, 2 mills, and 4 coffee houses.[44] The officials in charge of the confiscations had the houses of the ᶜAẓms, as well as those of their associates, thoroughly searched, breaking down walls and digging up gardens. They forced relatives and aides of the pasha to cooperate by imprisoning and flogging them.[45] The central authorities were more reluctant to infringe upon *waqf* holdings. The *waqf* holdings in the districts of Hama and Homs belonging to Asᶜad Pasha, appear to have

[41] See Göçek, *Rise*, pp. 57–59, 62–65. She mentioned the case of a certain Kürd Mehmed Agha of Damascus in 1799; perhaps it concerned Muḥammad Aghâ Urfa Amînî, who was executed around that time.

[42] Gibb and Bowen, *Islamic*, vol. 2, p. 47

[43] Rafeq, *Province*, pp. 180–1 and *Economic*, pp. 669–72

[44] Göçek, *Rise*, p. 53

[45] Budayrî, *Ḥawâdith*, pp. 57–59 (Sulaymân Pasha), p. 219 (Asᶜad Pasha), p. 235 (Saᶜd al-Dîn Pasha); Burayk, *Târîkh*, pp. 70–71 (Asᶜad Pasha)

been left largely untouched.[46] His slaves and *mamlûks* did not escape confiscation, however, and were carried off to Istanbul.[47]

Presents and patronage

In order to further his career, a senior provincial official depended strongly on networks which included people from the entourage of the sultan and high officials of the state.[48] In order to be reconfirmed in office or to be promoted to a more prestigious position, these officials needed intelligence on the political mood at the centre. Above all, the good offices of a grandee of the state were required. The ruling elite of Istanbul comprised – often unstable – factions, each with its own patronage networks. The removal or death of any member of the imperial elite could easily affect the careers of officials connected to him. Their chances depended on the degree of loyalty shown to their patron, and naturally to the sultan, his trustees and other prominent functionaries, who were all keen to protect their respective privileges. Loyalty, or in Ottoman terms servitude (*ᶜubûdiyya*), was best expressed in cash payments referred to as gifts.[49] Often a relation existed between the magnitude of the gifts forwarded to Istanbul and the potential revenue of a province.

Impressed by the apparent venality of the patronage regulations, some authors hesitate to acknowledge the legality of the presents and the impositions used to finance them, but it would be wrong to assume that all payments in the context of patronage were bribes and therefore illegal.[50] The payments to the sultan and the members of the imperial council had been legalized in the mid-seventeenth century. The presents were financed by what had become regular taxes by the second half of the eighteenth century and possibly earlier. In the Syrian

[46] SMH 46, p. 360, 28 Rabîᶜ II 1214. In this year, 1799, the *waqf* holdings of Asᶜad Pasha were exempted from further impositions levied in support of the war efforts.

[47] Burayk, *Târîkh*, p. 71

[48] The Ottoman word for networking, or patronage relations, is *intisab*. See Shaw, *History*, p. 166 and 170; Findley, *Bureaucratic*, pp. 34, 39 and 121; Barbir, *Ottoman*, p. 39

[49] In their correspondence with the sultan, governors normally opened with the confirmation of their servitude or devotion to him (ott. *ubudiyyet*, ar. *ᶜubûdiyya*). The payments were referred to a *hediye* (ar. *hadiya*); see also ᶜAwra, *Târîkh*, pp. 224, 243

[50] Gibb and Bowen, *Islamic*, vol. 2, pp. 6 and 48–49

provinces a tax simply referred to as *ᶜubûdiyya* was collected for that purpose.[51]

The presents, which were payable annually, were substantial. Unfortunately, there are no figures available for the province of Damascus for the late eighteenth and early nineteenth centuries. Muḥammad ᶜAlî Pasha of the large and prosperous province of Egypt transferred 740,000 q. as presents to the imperial household, the grand vizier and other high officials in 1827. The distribution of the presents is likely to have reflected the actual balance of power at the centre – and the relative strength of the sultan of the time, Mahmud II – rather than the ideological order of the state. Nearly 70 per cent of the amount was forwarded to the court. The swordkeeper of the sultan and the grand vizier received 50,000 q. each, but the chief *muftî* (*şeyhülislam*), in the ideological order their superior, was presented with only 25,000 q. A number of other high-ranking officials were paid 15,000 q. or less.[52] The total amount of Muḥammad ᶜAlî Pasha's 'presents' exceeded the annual income of the treasury from the district of Hama. Apart from the regular presents, which also included gifts on the occasions of religious festivals, other more informal payments were made.

It is of interest to note that a self-reliant governor-general like Muḥammad ᶜAlî Pasha continued to send such large sums as 'presents' to Istanbul, despite his disputes with the sultan over a compensation for his military services. It appears to have been highly unusual for provincial governors in the period under consideration not to honour the financial claims which were put forward by the central authorities. Jazzâr Pasha of Acre, who certainly did not pay heed to each and every order emanating from Istanbul, never refused to honour the financial demands made upon him.[53] Their willingness to pay demonstrates their dependence on support in the capital, but also their acquiescence in the system which allowed them to exploit their provinces in their own right.

But, however timely payments were made, the position of any senior official remained insecure. In his relation with the Porte, suspicion of the intentions of his imperial masters played a significant role. The sultan had the authority to depose anyone at will. An occasional display of his absolute power was required in order to remind his servants that their prerogatives were limited, if not futile when compared to his. The

[51] See p. 132. In Egypt the levies related to the presents were included in the *barrânî* taxes. See ᶜAbd al-Rahîm, *Rîf.*

[52] *Maḥfûẓât*, vol. 1, p. 95, n. 231 (15 Muḥarram 1243)

[53] Cohen, *Palestine*, pp. 237–38

decapitation in 1758 of the capable and loyal Asᶜad Pasha al-ᶜAẓm, whose principal offence seems to have been his prosperity, had left its mark on the Syrian provinces. The execution was generally regarded as an arbitrary act, but the fairness of sultanic will was beyond open dispute. Its arbitrariness bestowed upon it a supernatural dimension typical for traditional absolutist rule. The basic idea remained that no official had a right to professionally generated wealth. The paradox enclosed in the system is striking; a governor being the most senior provincial official, wielded very extensive powers within his province, but enjoyed hardly any rights.

The governor and local administration

The powers of the governor of the province (*wâlî*) were extensive, but not exclusive. The central authorities had been careful to separate some authority from the governorship, most notably the jurisdiction of the *sharᶜ*, religious law, and the administration of the treasury, the office of the *defterdar*. In principle, each and every subject in the province could address the imperial council and by doing so evade the governor's authority in non-*sharᶜ* affairs as well. In particular the religious *aᶜyân* petitioned the imperial council; they were considered to be the guardians of the religious and moral traditions, and by extension, of local traditions. They often voiced the protests of the local commercial class. The effects of their petitions depended very much on circumstance, but they were generally immune from arbitrary punishment.[54] The authorities certainly paid heed to the common values of society. Exceptions to this rule occurred. Jazzâr Pasha, once the victim of a petition by the *muftî* of Damascus, showed less respect for the religious establishment and had several *muftî*s put to death. These killings ranked high among the long list of his outrages against social and moral order.[55] The office of treasurer (*defterdar*) belonged to the more secure offices in the province, normally held for extensive periods. Little controversy existed between the governors and the treasurers during the late eighteenth and early nineteenth centuries, which suggests that the treasurer did not figure as a major check on the activities of the governor.[56]

The policy of the central authorities toward the province of

[54] Gibb and Bowen, *Islamic*, vol. 2, pp. 110–11

[55] See p. 92

[56] The *defterdar* served from 1736 until 1746, Fatḥî al-Falâqinsî, used the office in his struggle for power with the ᶜAẓms. He was executed and not

Damascus was focussed on the organization of the yearly pilgrimage to the holy shrines of Mecca and Medina. In silent recognition of the strenuous nature of this effort, the Porte had abandoned the principle of swift rotation of the governors during most of the eighteenth century. When a governor had given proof of his ability to organize the pilgrimage, he would normally be maintained as governor and commander of the pilgrimage (*amîr al-ḥajj*) for longer periods. This allowed him to extend his control over the officials and tax farmers in the province and to initiate commercial activities that would enlarge his income.

The governor spent most of his time organizing the finances, contracts, supplies and troops for the pilgrimage. In this he depended upon a body of officials and tax farmers. Many people, in different capacities, were involved in the levying of taxes, all of whom had a right to a certain share or fee. The distinction between officials and officers, on the one hand, and tax farmers, on the other, was blurred because many officials and officers acted as tax farmers. Basically, the province comprised a number of large tax farms (*muqâṭaʿas*), most of which were in the leasehold of the governor.[57] The governor farmed out the collection of taxes in most *muqâṭaʿas* to other individuals or, occasionally, communities. Among the more important tax farmers were the senior provincial officials, like *kethüda*, the governor's chief lieutenant and the second in command, his secretary, and the treasurer. Like the governorship, the positions of *kethüda* and treasurer constituted in fact tax farms.[58] The secretary often occupied an important position within the system of exploitation of the province. ʿAbbûd Baḥrî of Homs, for example, when serving as secretary to ʿAbdallâh Pasha al-ʿAẓm had been granted the tax farm of numerous villages.[59]

imitated by others in later years. See Rafeq, *Province*, pp. 149–54 and 164–69; Barbir, *Ottoman*, pp. 86–89

[57] Non-resident high officials occasionally enjoyed the leasehold of a cluster of villages or even small districts in return for, mainly military, services to the sultan. The leasehold of expensive, but lucrative tax farms, like the *gumruk* (customhouse), could also be granted to the grandees of the state.

[58] See Barbir, *Ottoman*, p. 118

[59] ʿAbbûd Baḥrî is an older brother of the most famous scion of this family, Ḥannâ Baḥrî the financial aide of Ibrâhîm Pasha, the son of Muḥammad ʿAlî Pasha of Egypt. Their father, Mikhâ'îl Baḥrî already had a career in the service of Ẓâhir al-ʿUmar of the Galilee, and Jazzâr Pasha. ʿAbbûd started his career in the province of Sidon. He moved to Damascus when Sulaymân Pasha was appointed to Sidon. He became one of the closest associates of ʿAbdallâh Pasha

In outlying districts like Hama, the tax farmers were often local officials, officers and members of prominent local families. The district of Hama was normally granted as a leasehold for life (*malikane*) to the combined governorship of Damascus and command over the pilgrimage.[60] The *mutasallim* was his representative and enjoyed extensive powers locally. The group of tax farmers (*multazims*) was limited. The urban based tax farmers included members of the two most prominent local families, ʿAẓm and Kaylânî, from which local functionaries were recruited. Also *aghawât* families, like Jijaklî, Turkumân and Barâzî, were involved in the farming of taxes. Members of these families served in the local military as well. Evidently, the combination of office-holding and tax farming was the dominant feature in the exploitation of the district. Rural *aghawât* also regularly acted as tax farmers of the villages in which they resided, in particular in the case of Turcoman villages.

Not all villages of the Hama area were farmed by the more powerful well-to-do locals. The village community or the village sheikh acted as *multazim* with some frequency.[61] In 1802 the taxes of over half of the Turcoman villages to the south of Hama were farmed by the villagers. This might have implied that no prominent official, ulema or merchant had committed himself to collect the amount of taxes imposed on the village and that this task now rested upon the communities themselves.[62] In the *muqâṭaʿa*s of the western periphery of the district

al-ʿAẓm. ʿAbbûd also served under Kunj Yûsuf Pasha, although their relation was strained due to the efforts of Kunj Yûsuf to convert ʿAbbûd to Islam. In 1810 they fled to Egypt together. ʿAbbûd continued his career as *kâtib*, now to the *dîwân* of Egypt, see Dimashqî, *Ḥawâdith*, p. 36; Asʿad, *Ḥims*, vol. 2, pp. 392–93; Philipp, *Syrians*, p. 25 and 65

[60] It is unclear whether this was still the custom after 1826. In an edict of that year on the military reform of the provinces following the abolition of the janissary corps, it is stated that '. . . not the entire [revenue of the] province of Damascus is allocated to the organization of the *ḥajj*, but only that of the districts of Jerusalem and Nablus'. See *Maḥfûẓât*, vol. 1, p. 75

[61] For example, the villages of Nîṣâf, Ḥaydariyya, Kafr Kamra and Khirbat al-ʿAwj in, and near, the Jabal Gharbî and ʿAqrab and Akrâd Ibrâhîm in the southern Waʿr, see SMH 48, p. 276 [Rajab 1236]; SMH 49, p. 345, 13 Jumâdâ II 1245 and p. 483, p. 483, 25 Dhû al-Qaʿda 1248

[62] SMH 43, p. 120, 26 [?] 1217. The Turcoman villages in question are referred to as those of which the taxes were not guaranteed. The *multazims* of the remaining Turcoman villages are referred to as *arbâb*, the owners (of the tax farm).

the local Nuṣayrî, Ismaili or Turcoman headmen usually acted as tax farmers. The position of these headmen was not always secure. Apart from local competition, *aghawât* of Hama occasionally competed for these tax farms.[63] The leaseholds of some villages in the Hama district were granted to senior provincial officials or close associates, of the governor.[64]

As the representative of the governor, the *mutasallim* bore the overall responsibility for the timely and full collection of the taxes which were remitted to the treasury, as well as of most extraordinary levies. The *ᶜawâyid* were collected separately by those who were entitled to these fees, but the *mutasallim* had to see to their proper collection. This was true for the collection of the proportional agricultural tax (*qism*), which was not collected by the tax farmer of the village, but by the *qassâm aghâ* and his men.[65]

The tax tabulations did not include the gains, or losses, of the tax farmers. In normal practice a tax farmer pledged a certain amount of taxes to the treasury when these were put at auction. The amount pledged was recorded in a contract (*şartname*) and usually an advance payment was demanded. The governor or his council (*dîwân*) granted the tax farm, but this power could be delegated to the *mutasallim*.[66] The tax farmer ran a considerable risk. It was not unusual that he was unable to raise the required sum. In the late eighteenth and early nineteenth centuries many tax farms proved to be unprofitable and the authorities had difficulty in interesting people to bid for the right to collect taxes,

[63] For instance, the Ismaili headman of the *muqâṭaᶜa* of Miṣyâf, Mîr Mulḥim, had lost his traditional rights, at least temporarily, to Khalîl Aghâ Jijaklî in the early 1820s, SMH 43, p. 33, 1 Shaᶜbân 1238. In the late 1820s the *muqâṭaᶜa* of Turcoman Ḥazûr was farmed by an *aghâ* of Maghribi origin, SMH 49, p. 333, 22 Rabîᶜ I 1245

[64] The villages of Ṭayyibat al-Aᶜlâ, Miṣîn, and Tall al-Râm had been in the lifetime leasehold of Muḥammad Efendi al-Murâdî, the secretary of the *dîwân* of Damascus from 1786 until 1799 (SMH 46, 355, 5 Ramaḍân 1213). In 1805 ᶜAbdallâh Pasha al-ᶜAẓm granted the *mâlikâna* of al-Jannân to his relative Nuṣûḥ Pasha (SMH 43, pp. 153–54, 9 Jumâdâ I 1220). These *mâlikâna*s had in common that they concerned villages which suffered from depopulation

[65] See, on these officials and taxes p. 131–2

[66] See, for example, SMH 43, p. 254, 11 Jumâdâ I 1237, the *dîwân* granting of the *iltizâm* of the village of Dayr al-Ṣalîb and its satellite farms (*mazraᶜa*s) to Muḥammad Ghârib Bey (al-ᶜAẓm). In 1805 the *wâlî* ᶜAbdallâh Pasha al-ᶜAẓm ordered the *mutasallim* to grant the *iltizâm* of villages suffering from depopulation to any interested party, see next note.

especially those resting upon the villages which suffered from depopulation.[67] It appears from the attempts to interest people in the farming of the taxes of villages which were in poor shape, or even depopulated, by offering favourable conditions, that a tax farmer was not merely expected to collect taxes, but also to invest in the village or at least to create the conditions for the return of peasants by taking such a village into his care. A tax farmer, then, seems to have shared the responsibility of keeping a village productive.

The claims of local officials

Local authorities received regular warnings from the governor or his council not to exceed the proper rates of taxes and fees and to refrain from levying new, illegal charges, usually referred to as *bidʿa*.[68] The high frequency of the edicts of this type seem to indicate that illegal demands were habitual and that the recurrent admonitions had little effect. It is of interest to note that the edicts were hardly ever directed against tax farmers as such.[69] This seems to be somewhat surprising, because any tax farmer would be after a return on the capital invested – under conditions which were often not very favourable. Opportunities existed to manipulate the outcome of the *ḥisâb*, the tax computation of a village, but the court records of Hama do not provide sufficient information on the methods tax farmers applied in order to compensate their financial efforts other than simply demanding more than their legal share. No indication was found that a tax farmer was permitted to levy fees on top of the amount of taxes fixed by the authorities, but it might well be that not all impositions were included in the tax farm contract.[70] When villagers had failed to meet their liabilities towards a tax farmer, the tax farmer had to bring the case either to the attention of the *mutasallim* or

[67] SMH 43, p. 154, 9 Jumâdâ II 1220

[68] Singular *bidʿa*, and, although hardly used in the documents, in full *bidʿa muḍarra*, the Islamic term for an innovation which runs contrary to the (spirit of the) law. See for example SMH 46, p. 215, 20 Ramaḍân 1209, one of the few documents in which *bidʿa muḍarra* is used. Also *iḥdâthât* and *ḥawâdith* were used in this sense in several documents.

[69] The only instance in which they (i.e., the *multazims*) were specifically referred to is in an edict on the tax rates of the *maqṭûʿ* villages. See SMH 43, p.179, 19 Rabîʿ II 1233

[70] Cohen, *Palestine*, p. 211

to the court.[71] In the court the judge applied the formal tax rates. Apart from farming the taxes he would often act as a banker to the villagers or as their partner in agriculture, by supplying ploughing animals and seed. Instead of actually farming the taxes, the well-to-do sometimes preferred to advanced the payment of the taxes resting on a village as a loan to the villagers and sometimes made the payment to the treasury.[72]

Given the scarcity of warnings against the possible abuses of tax farming, it seems safe to assume that tax farming did not figure among the main instruments of exaction. Nearly all warnings against abuse of power were directed against local officials and the same goes for petitions presented to the governor by the population. It is true that officials often acted as tax farmers, but the main offences comprised the imposition of excessive rates of fees, in particular *ᶜawâyid*, the levying of illegal charges and the refusal to give proper compensation for lodging, food and fodder. In other words, officials and officers were susceptible to taking advantage of their status and of the fact that they commanded or had access to armed units. Tax farmers who did not hold any formal office, and certainly the petty village sheikhs amongst them, could easily become victims of the rapacity of some of the *aghawât*. Not only the common people suffered from exactions. The more well-to-do were regularly forced to make payments referred to as *rashwa*, normally translated as bribe.[73]

The information contained in the Hama records conforms largely to the more general picture presented in the contemporary literary sources. Acts of oppression were nearly always ascribed to the military officeholders and their troops, who imposed all sorts of additional charges in both cash and kind at will and regularly physically harassed people.[74] Other functionaries, like the local judge,[75] the *muftî*s, or the non-military

[71] See, for example, SMH 43, p. 357, 29 Rabîᶜ I 1238

[72] See, for example, SMH 49, p. 27, 15 Rabîᶜ II 1240 and p. 250, end Ṣafar 1245

[73] See, for example, SMH 49, p. 403, 22 Ṣafar 1246, when the *mutasallim*, Faraj Aghâ, is forbidden to demand *rashwa* from a certain effendi, who farmed the taxes of one of the villages of Ḥiṣn al-Akrâd.

[74] The western travellers of the time repeated this common notion. In their accounts, the illegal demands are often referred to as *avanias*, an in origin Italian word, which is occasionally used in Arabic sources as well, but not in the Hama court records.

[75] The *qâḍî*s-in-chief in the provincial capitals regularly resorted to malversation. See, for example, Russell (*Natural*, vol. 1, pp.317–20), who expresses a negative view on the administration of justice by this official in Aleppo.

tax farmers belonged to the class of people whose malversation paled in comparison with those committed by the men of the sword.

Analogous to their superiors, the local *aghawât* did not act out of mere greed. The provincial authorities paid little heed to the actual expenses of local administration and in this they followed the example of their imperial overlords. The collection of taxes which had to be remitted to the treasury was given precedence over the collection of other impositions, notably those which were meant to cover the expenses of local officials. The magnitude of the expenses of their inferiors often was disregarded and high payments were demanded from them in order receive appointments. Consequently, it was left to them to make ends meet. The way the local office-holders sought compensation for their expenses and attempted to enlarge their personal income varied. Like their superiors, they combined legal with illegal methods. Most legal methods had in common that they carried an at times considerable risk, because they required capital investments. This was true for farming of taxes and for commercial activities such as the establishment of partnerships and the making of loans. Nonetheless, investments in local agriculture and animal husbandry, as partners of villagers and tribes or otherwise, occurred frequently.[76] Investing in real estate, mainly shops in or gardens around Hama, required high initial investments. Although the lease of shops and irrigated gardens was lucrative, only long-time resident officials and their families, like the ᶜAẓm, the Kaylânî, ᶜAlwânî and the merchant families Kûjân and al-Ḥajj Zayn, acquired extensive properties. The ᶜAẓm and Kaylânî families owned or controlled, either as freehold or *waqf*, numerous shops, houses, and agricultural land along the ᶜÂṣî river, as well as stretches of rain-fed agricultural land in the vicinity of the town and some mills and waterwheels.[77] Both families,

[76] To give two examples: 1) the former *mutasallim* of Hama, and last pasha of the ᶜAẓm family, Sulaymân Pasha ibn Salîm Bey, owned 78 oxen, 190 farming utensils (ploughs etc.) and 5 storage rooms in the village of Khân Shaykhûn and had another 20 oxen in partnership with a local *aghâ*. See SMH 49, 1, 5 Rabîᶜ I 1240. 2) Two *aghâ*s, one of them of the Jijaklî family, entertained a partnership (*sharika*) with the village sheikh of ᶜAwj, and the capital invested in the village amounted to 45,530 q., see SMH 49, p. 388, 16 Dhû al-Ḥijja 1245

[77] The landed *waqf* holdings were largely situated on, or near to, the banks of the ᶜÂṣî, especially to the north of the town (Balḫusayn area). However, the Kaylânî family also controlled *waqf* estates near Miṣyâf in the western fringe of the district, leasing it to locals. See SMH 43, 33, 1 Shaᶜbân 1238

but especially the ᶜAẓms, possessed real estate in other parts of Syria as well.[78]

The central authorities regarded the wealth of the *aᶜyân* in the provinces as a source of additional revenue. In times of urgent financial need, the locally prominent, in particular former high officials and their heirs and those who enjoyed privileges like the life leasehold of land, were forced to remit considerable sums to the treasury or to the purse of the officer in charge of the provisions (*mubâyaᶜajî*) of the imperial army. In 1799, for example, 12 per cent of the expenses incurred by this officer was covered by extraordinary levies resting upon the *amlâk* and *awqâf* of Hama, the habitual reference to the properties and estates of the wealthy.[79] ᶜAbdallâh Pasha al-ᶜAẓm, when governor of Damascus, ordered his *mutasallim* in Hama not to exclude the properties of his relatives in the district when he demanded supplies for his troops in 1806.[80] The forcing of loans constituted another method to draw upon the resources of the *aᶜyân*.

The ᶜAẓm and Kaylânî families had a long tradition of office-holding. At times, their wealth constituted a target of the central authorities, but they were in the position to mobilize support and to obtain preferential treatment. The heirs of Asᶜad Pasha al-ᶜAẓm, for example, procured an imperial decree in 1799 ordering the cessation of any further demands on their properties concerning the war efforts against the French.[81] In 1818, when several tax rates were reduced following the *ᶜarab* incursions in the area, the property holders (*arbâb al-amlâk*) were granted additional tax exemptions.[82] Others lacked the relative security of tradition and wealth. A number of families of *aghawât* were in the process of acquiring a foothold in the area during the first decades of the nineteenth century, like the Jijaklî, Barâzî, Ṭayfûr and Turkumânî. In the early decades, the Jijaklî family had the most extensive commercial interests of these *aghawât* families.[83] Later in the century, some of these

[78] In 1844 the heirs of Muḥammad Bey al-ᶜAẓm (d. 1825) divided – or redivided – his real estate, which included 21 shops in Maᶜarra, a bath, 3 shops and an olive orchard in Tripoli, 2 guesthouses in Homs and 2 shops in Damascus, SMH 50, pp. 225–26, Dhû al-Qaᶜda 1259

[79] SMH 46, p. 376, 15 Ramaḍân 1214

[80] SMH 43, p. 148, 28 Shaᶜbân 1221

[81] SMH 46, p. 360, 28 Rabîᶜ II 1214

[82] SMH 43, p. 178, 19 Rabîᶜ II 1233

[83] See, for some *sharika* (partnership) relations between the Jijaklîs and villagers, SMH 48, p. 142, 18 Jumâdâ II 1235; SMH 49, p. 388, 16 Dhû al-Ḥijja 1245

families, in particular the Barâzî and Ṭayfûr, were to be counted among the small group of the very wealthy local families.

For those who were not blessed with tradition and wealth, the more coercive methods of income derivation seemed more effectual, certainly as a start. This is not to say, of course, that members of the ᶜAẓm and Kaylânî families always obeyed the laws and that no non-local official established legal commercial relations. ᶜAbdallâh Aghâ al-Maḥmûd, who served as *mutasallim* under Jazzâr Pasha, was quick to enter into partnerships with several villages.[84] This *aghâ*, however, was not totally unfamiliar with the area, being a native of the adjacent district of Homs. Earlier, Jazzâr Pasha ordered him to refrain from burdening the local trading community with forced loans (without his consent) and exactions in kind.[85]

Exacting amounts of cash and kind from the population on top of the legal charges constituted the easiest method to secure supplementary income. The high frequency of official warnings against this practice served as a constant reminder to the local officials that they acted against the law and that legal action could be taken against them. The careful tabulation of the legal impositions resting upon the district defined the formal claims of the state and served as an instrument to discipline the local body of officials, officers and troops and to moderate their demands. That the relation between the tabulations and the actual amounts collected was at best hypothetical, appears to have been of secondary concern.

The fees

The right to payments for the military office-holders in the Hama area were not unrestricted. The *ᶜawâyid*, one of the main extraordinary impositions, was meant to furnish an income to a number of them and to compensate them for their expenses. Most, if not all of these *aghawât* commanded a military unit. Their troops had to be paid out of the *ᶜawâyid*. The rates of these fees were fixed by the council of Damascus at a conservative rate. The *ᶜawâyid* were occasionally reduced, some by no less than 50 per cent. These reductions often coincided with the reduction of other impositions like the proportional tax on cereals and pulses (*qism*) and the fixed sum of taxes resting upon agricultural land

[84] SMH 43, p.'97, [Jumâdâ II] 1215
[85] SMH 46, p. 259, 13 Ramaḍân 1213

(*mâl faddân*) and were meant to revitalize the ailing rural economy.[86] In 1822 the large category of revenue villages were even exempted from the fees payable to the collectors of the proportional agricultural tax (*qassâmiyya*); the villages were exempted from all impositions levied on top of the regular taxes which were remitted to the treasury.[87] Another method to tone down the claims of the local *aghawât* was to ignore the devaluation of the Ottoman currency. The amounts of *ᶜawâyid* payable to the *qassâmiyya* in 1818, for example, were identical to those in 1824. Their commander. however, had demanded higher amounts.[88] The rates of the *ᶜawâyid* remained unchanged until the early 1830s, when they were abolished. Whereas the rates of *ᶜawâyid* were frozen, the rates of some regular taxes were increased, although major charges like the *mâl faddân*, too, remained unchanged.[89]

Local officials fell back on a traditional method to gain a proper compensation, or more: the collection of the so-called *miṣriyyat al-fard*. When taken in kind it was referred to as *ḥabbat al-fard*, a measure (of grain) from each. It is possible that the *ᶜawâyid* had been recently introduced to replace the practice of collecting the *miṣriyyat al-fard*, which roughly translates as 'a penny from each' and constituted a type of poll-tax.[90] The high frequency of directives in which the local officials were instructed to refrain from taking the *miṣriyyat al-fard* from the population indicates that its collection remained customary, at least well into the 1820s in the Hama district. In Damascus the levying of the charge appears to have been suppressed earlier; its inhabitants were

[86] In 1788 the rates of the *qism* as well as the *ᶜawâyid* payable to the *qassâmiyya* were reduced. See SMH 46, pp. 74–75, 15 Rabîᶜ I 1203. In 1818 the rates of a number of impositions were reduced, including the *ᶜawâyid* of the *garib yiğit ağasi*, *tüfenkçi başı*, the *haznadar* and the *wakîl al-kharj*. See SMH 43, pp. 179–80 and 187, 19 Rabîᶜ II 1233

[87] SMH 43, p. 255 3 Jumâdâ I 1237

[88] SMH 49, p. 16, 3 Rabîᶜ I 1240

[89] One of the regular taxes which was increased by nearly 100 per cent was the *iᶜâna*. See SMH 49, pp. 177–78, 17 Shaᶜbân 1241. The rates of the *jizya*, the poll-tax payable by Christians and Jews, were usually adapted to the devaluation of the currency, as well as to the increasing financial need of the state. Compared to 1816 this charge had been increased by 50 per cent in 1824 and by 200 per cent by 1829. See vol. 2, p. 564

[90] The phrase '. . . do not charge anyone with the *miṣriyyat al-fard* other than (or on top of) the specified fixed amounts [of *ᶜawâyid*] mentioned previously . . .' seems to establish a relation between the *miṣriyyat al-fard* and the *ᶜawâyid*. See SMH 43, p. 177, 19 Rabîᶜ II 1233

disturbed by the introduction of a poll-tax by the Egyptians in 1832, because '. . . it had been long since that the *miṣriyyat al-fard* had been taken from them.'[91] In particular the *aghawât* who were entitled to *ᶜawâyid* had difficulty in conceding that they were not or no longer authorized to demand these contributions. The provincial authorities also called upon the population not to give in to the demands for the *miṣriyyat al-fard*.[92]

Hardly any figures are extant which would enable us to disclose the actual expenses of *aghawât* who were entitled to levy *ᶜawâyid*, like the *garib yiğit ağasi*, the *tüfenkçi başı* and the *qassâmiyya*. According to Burckhardt 300 to 400 cavalrymen were normally stationed in the town of Hama, but unfortunately he does not tell us whether these concern *garib yiğit* forces, *deli*s or other mounted troops.[93] Not only is the number of troops in the service of the various local commanders unknown, but little is known of their pay as well. In 1818 the *garib yiğit ağasi* was entitled to 1000 q. monthly, an amount which would have allowed him perhaps 40 to 60 mounted troops; the *tüfençi başı* was entitled to 750 q. monthly, perhaps sufficient for the pay of up to 75 musketeers.[94] Apart from regular military forces, commanded by

[91] *Mudhakkirât*, p. 67. The Egyptian tax was called *farda*. In this source *miṣriyyat al-fard* is used once in the meaning of an (illegal) increase of the prices on the markets in Damascus (p. 60).

[92] In the literature, hardly any reference to the *miṣriyyat al-fard* is made. The charge may have been similar to the *ḥaḍriyya* mentioned by Cohen (*Palestine*, pp. 264–65) and defined as 'a few *akces* from each' taken by the *wâlî*. The income of Ibrâhîm Deli Pasha comprised *miṣriyyat al-fard* collected in the Hama area (SMH 46, 330–1, 8 Shaᶜbân 1213). This *wâlî* had prohibited the local *qassâmiyya* to levy the same charge (SMH 46, pp. 74–75, 15 Rabîᶜ I 1203). ᶜAbd al-Raḥîm (Rîf, pp. 136–38) lists a tax called *fard(a)* among the illegal charges in late eighteenth-century Egypt. The charge is occasionally referred to as *qirsh al-fard*. See SMH 43, p. 179, 19 Rabîᶜ II 1233

[93] Burckhardt, *Travels*, p. 147.

[94] See SMH 43, p. 187, [Rabîᶜ I] 1233. In the mid-nineteenth century the *tüfenkçi*s in Hama received a monthly pay of 20 q., see SMH, 53, p. 292, 3 Dhû al-Ḥijja 1268. In the late eighteenth-century Aleppo the pay of a *deli* amounted to 10 q. monthly and that of a *tüfenkçi* 5 q. See Bodman, *Factions*, pp. 23–24. In 1826 a yearly income of 500 q. was considered the minimum for the upkeep of a cavalryman. Almost a decade later a soldier in the Egyptian army received a pay of 20 *para* (*miṣriyya*) a day (which would make 182.5 q. a year), which fell short of the minimum of 1 q. needed daily to support a family, see *Maḥfûẓât*, vol. 1, p. 80 and vol. 3, 96

officers who had the right to collect *ᶜawâyid*, at least one auxiliary force was normally stationed in the district, the *deli*s, who were neither paid out of the treasury, nor had the right to collect fees. The presence of these troops was a common source of anxiety among the rural population, because they often failed to receive their pay from their patrons, mainly governors.

Faraj Aghâ's exactions

Being the most senior local official, the *mutasallim* controlled more resources than any other in the district. The early career of Faraj Aghâ may serve as an example of the politics of financing local administration. The origins of Faraj Aghâ are obscure, but given the strong local resistance to his (early) rule, it seems unlikely that he was a local.[95] He was first appointed *mutasallim* in Hama in 1826. At the time of his appointment he was reminded by the council of Damascus that the *qassâmiyya* in his service should not exceed the fixed amounts of *ᶜawâyid* payable by the population.[96] A little later he received the warning not to charge interest on the delivery of seeds from the granary to the peasantry.[97] The complaints of the peasants were followed by a more influential segment of local society, the merchants. They petitioned the governor, accusing Faraj Aghâ of obstructing trade in general, levying illegal charges on silk, and failing to repay forced loans. They also accused the commander of the musketeers and some other *aghawât* of demanding illegal fees. The merchants were backed by the head of the descendants of the prophet (*naqîb al-ashrâf*), ᶜAbdallâh Efendi al-Kaylânî. After the governor had attempted to mediate between the parties, he conceded to the demands of the local community. In 1829 Faraj Aghâ was dismissed and a senior provincial functionary, Sulaymân Aghâ, the supervisor of the *waqf* endowments of the Ḥaramayn (the two holy cities) in the province, was dispatched to Hama in order to conduct an inquiry into the financial dealings of the Faraj Aghâ and some of his aides.[98]

The outcome of the inquiry of Sulaymân Aghâ was clear. It showed

[95] See p. 122–4

[96] SMH 49, p. 157, 15 Shawwâl 1241

[97] SMH 49, p. 222, 11 Rajab 1242

[98] See, for the petitions and the replies by the *wâlî* and *qâyimmaqâm* of the province of Damascus, SMH 49, pp. 275–76, and p. 278, 17, [?], and 27 Muḥarram 1244, and p. 239 and p. 242, late Muḥarram 1245

Table 6. The exactions and malversations of Far Aghâ and his men

A. The income of Faraj Aghâ and some of his officers derived by (allegedly) illegal means

B. The legal regular taxes payable to the treasury in the same year

	A.	B.
Urban units		
craft organizations	155,770	79,685
quarters	16,557	3,950
market inspection	11,701	33,917
	184,028	117,552
Rural units		
revenue villages	189,450	174,205
Turcoman villages	14,368	45,232
fixed amount villages	3,863	20,250
cotton villages	2,649	10,463
Jabal Gharbî villages	72,818	64,283
tax farms	58,185	150,240
ᶜ*arab* tribes	82,728	51,400
	424,061	516,073
Other		
inheritance of *aghawât*	75,797	
granary	55,570	
sundry taxes (incl. ᶜ*ubûdiyya*)	31,832	
miscellaneous	21,848	10,426
	185,047	
TOTAL	793,136	644,051

Source: SMH 49, pp. 250–52, dated [Ṣafar] 1245 and pp. 326–29, 23 Rabîᶜ I 1245

that '. . . by way of injustice, violation and tyranny . . .' Faraj Aghâ and some of the senior local officers,[99] including his principal aide ᶜUthmân Aghâ, had collected 793,136 q. in cash and kind. Of that amount nearly 700,000 q. had been pocketed by Faraj Aghâ himself. Sulaymân Aghâ had based himself largely on the accounts of victims, which included

[99] Namely the *odabaşı*, the *tüfenkçi başı*, and the *wakîl al-kharj*. See for these offices, pp. 76–77

almost any single quarter, craft, village and tribe. Apart from that, the investigator had used the books of the local treasury and granary. Whether the inquiry had been conducted properly remains difficult to answer, but the fairness of the exercise is of little interest here and Faraj Aghâ's alleged rapacity finds some support in other sources.[100] Later in the century, villagers occasionally refer to the greed of Faraj Aghâ in their lawsuits.[101]

The income derived by illegal means by Faraj Aghâ and his men exceeded the annual amount of the taxes which had to be remitted to the treasury by over 20 per cent. The lion's share of the total amount consisted of exactions taken from craftsmen, villagers and tribesmen. The high contribution of the craft organizations to the pockets of the officials helps explain the strong urban opposition to Faraj Aghâ. In the case of the rural categories it is of interest to note that the villages liable to a fixed amount (*maqṭûᶜ*) were treated with leniency, both by the treasury and by Faraj Aghâ. The opposite is true for the dozen of small villages of the Jabal Gharbî, which not only constituted a rich source of income for the treasury, but also for the *mutasallim* personally.

The magnitude of the exactions might be seen as indicative of the degree of control over the various segments of the population. The high contribution of the *ᶜarab* tribes, for example, reflected the strong influence Faraj Aghâ exercised over the tribes, a prerequisite for any successful *mutasallim*. A remarkable feature of the distribution of the exactions from the villages is that those in the near vicinity of Hama either had been forced to pay moderate sums relative to the legal charges, or even nothing at all. The partly Nuṣayrî village of al-Rabîᶜa, for example, had not been visited by the *mutasallim* or one of his officers. Several members of the Kaylânî family maintained close relations with this village, the fields of which bordered on the land belonging to the town.[102] Prominent families of Hama had considerable interests in these villages and it is likely that their relations with the villages near Hama protected

[100] Namely in the records of the Egyptian administration of Syria. See Sâlim, *Ḥukm*, pp. 67–68

[101] SMH 55, 282–3, 23 Rabîᶜ I 1274 (1857); SMH 60, p. 284, 7 Rajab 1283 (1866)

[102] Its taxes had been farmed by Muḥammad ᶜAlî al-Kaylânî in the early 1820s, and possibly later, SMH 43, p. 357, 30 Rabîᶜ I 1238 and SMH 49, p. 37, 5 Jumâdâ I 1240. The relationship between the family and the village continued well into the twentieth century.

the inhabitants from excessive demands, at least by Faraj Aghâ and his men.

Economic conditions undoubtedly played a role in the case of other villages. The highest demands had been made upon some villages in the fertile and well-watered plain to the west of the town, including two large and relatively prosperous Christian villages. The Muslim village of Talldû had been forced to make the largest contribution both in absolute and relative terms: 35,350 q. compared to 9130 q. of taxes remitted to the treasury. It is evident that religious bias did not influence the size of the amounts taken. Even the village of Ṭayyibat al-Gharbiyya, which was part of the *waqf* holdings of the principal mosque of Homs, had been forced to pay 6800 q. compared to the amount of 3190 q. remitted to the treasury.

Sulaymân Aghâ had not only traced numerous exactions, but also had found malversations at the expense of the treasury. The single largest amount concerned a part of the inheritance of Ḥusayn Bey al-ᶜAẓm, who acted as the deputy governor of Sulaymân Pasha al-ᶜAẓm, the late governor of Tripoli (1823–24). The finances of Sulaymân Pasha had been subject to an inquiry earlier and his debt to the treasury had apparently been settled, but Ḥusayn Bey, too, owed a debt to the treasury and so did his brother Muḥammad Bey, a former *mutasallim;* in 1826 Faraj Aghâ had been ordered to confiscate part of the inheritance. The inquiry showed that Faraj Aghâ had indeed confiscated coins, cereals, sheep, cows and horses from the inheritance, but had failed to remit 48,134 q. of their value to the treasury. He had also withheld from the treasury 23,163 q. out of the debt of the treasurer (*haznadar*) of Sulaymân Pasha al-ᶜAẓm.[103]

Faraj Aghâ had taken full advantage of the central position he occupied as *mutasallim*. He had left few opportunities unused. He had failed to remit part of the substantial impositions like the *ᶜubûdiyya*, the *dhakhîra*, the *safariyya*, and the recently introduced substitute conscription tax (*badal al-anfâr al-ᶜaskar*). The wheat and barley stored in the granary had not escaped him either. Even the commander of the musketeers and of the Janissary barracks, the finances of whom were also scrutinized by Sulaymân Aghâ, figured among his victims. Compared to their superior, these two officers and the superintendent

[103] SMH 49, p. 1 and 33, 15 Rabîᶜ II 1240 (on Sulaymân Pasha and Muḥammad Aghâ Qudûr); p. 121, 13 Jumâdâ II 1241 (on Muḥammad Bey (see also p. 33 undated) and Ḥusayn Bey); p. 251, dated 1245. The debt of Muḥammad Bey amounted to only 15,300 q.

of expenditures had satisfied themselves with moderate amounts, which were probably more in line with the old *miṣriyyat al-fard*, a few pennies from each villager, craftsman or tribesman. Faraj Aghâ's trustee and right hand, ʿUthmân Aghâ, was accused of having extorted nearly 57,000 q., a considerably higher amount than those taken by his colleagues.[104]

The apparent rapacity of Faraj Aghâ was unprecedented. Earlier incidents of this type of abuse of delegated power in the Hama district do not compare to the extortions of this *mutasallim*. ʿAbd al-Qâdir Bey al-ʿAẓm, *mutasallim* in the early 1820s, for instance, had collected the modest amount of 18,000 q. on top of the legal impositions.[105] Other *mutasallims* had been accused of imposing illegal charges on trade or other acts of injustice. The petitions addressed to the governor appear to have been directed more often against *mutasallims* who were either non-locals or who did not belong to the ʿAẓm faction.[106] But in the final years of ʿAẓm domination in the district, the *mutasallims* recruited from the family were increasingly the object of complaints. There might well have been a correlation between the growing opposition at home and the demise of their power on the provincial level.[107]

Increased demands and the benefits of injustice

Accusations of injustice and oppression, in particular when followed by an investigation, influenced the career of office-holders. In the best case it proved to be a temporary setback; in the worst case, it resulted in their execution. Faraj Aghâ had been dismissed to open the way for an

[104] He was the *wakîl*, agent, of Faraj Aghâ in the Hama district after the latter had been called to higher office in the 1840s. ʿUthmân Aghâ was a member of the *majlis* of Hama in 1850, and possibly earlier, see SMH 52, p. 222, 1 Rabîʿ II 1264; SMH 53, p. 158, 30 Dhû al-Ḥijja 1267

[105] SMH 43, p. 71, Rabîʿ II, 1239

[106] See, for example, SMH 46, p. 215, 20 Ramaḍân 1209 (ʿAlî Aghâ, serving under Jazzâr Pasha); SMH 46, p. 259, 13 Ramaḍân 1213 (ʿAbdallâh Aghâ al-Maḥmûd serving under Jazzâr Pasha) and, of course, Mullû Ismâʿîl

[107] For villagers of Qumḥâna complaining against Salîm Bey and his successor Sulaymân Bey, see SMH 43, p. 262, 13 Jumâdâ I 1237. Market gardeners complaining against ʿAbd al-Qâdir Bey, see SMH 43, p. 32, 7 Shaʿbân 1237 and p. 24, 10 Shaʿbân 1238; Silk traders complaining against ʿAbd al-Qâdir Bey, see SMH 43, p. 5, 2 Jumâdâ I 1238. Note that Ḥusayn Bey, *qâyimmaqâm* of Tripoli in 1821, was also accused of *ẓulm*, and that ʿAbdallâh Pasha had a reputation of being rapacious in Damascus.

investigation, but, in defiance of the findings, it was not long before he was re-appointed to Hama. The developments might indicate that the investigation formed a pretext for the imposition of a heavy fine on the *aghâ*, but at any rate, his superiors recognized that Faraj Aghâ possessed a number of valuable qualities. His two main errors had been that his policies had provoked unrest in Hama and that he had withheld money from the treasury and from his superiors. Some disciplinary action seemed certainly in place. But he had proved to be an able tax collector, a quality which could not be easily ignored at a time in which the financial needs of the empire were exceptionally high. The reorganization of the imperial armies by Sultan Mahmud II had led to a sudden and sharp increase of military expenditure in the late 1820s. In order to finance the military reforms, the sultan had enacted the imposition of high additional charges.

Shortly after Faraj Aghâ had been reinstalled as *mutasallim* in Hama, he received an order to levy no less than 252,631 q. from the town of Hama as a substitute tax to cover military expenses (*badal maṣârif al-ᶜaskar*). It was the largest single charge ever imposed on the town or the district at large.[108] In the province of Damascus the increased tax demands provoked serious opposition and eventually led to a revolt in the city of Damascus. The imposition of large additional sums on top of the regular taxes required the service of capable officials in the provinces. One of the more cynical findings of the inquiry into the financial dealings of Faraj Aghâ may have been that he had the capacity to enlarge the revenue. The initiation of the inquiry might well have been partly motivated by the urgent financial needs of the empire. Whatever the precise motivations were which led to the swift reinstatement of Faraj Aghâ, his return to office and further career demonstrate that the higher authorities of the state could not afford to ignore him. The material claims of the state were generally better served by governors who were inclined to use a wide range of instruments in order to maximize the revenue. They appropriated a considerable part of the wealth of the provinces, but by doing so they were able to perform their administrative duties better than others, and, what is more, they were able to honour the material claims of the central state.

[108] SMH 49, p. 364, 12 Ramaḍân 1245

Revenue sources; the conditions in the villages

By the turn of the nineteenth century, Hama had gained the reputation of a place of injustice and agony. According to an early twentieth-century religious sheikh of the town, the conduct of the horsemen was so rude that people reconstructed their front doors in order to prevent them from entering on horseback.[109] This might be a figure of speech, but few places appear to have been as plagued by oppressive rule as Hama was at the time. A chronicler alleges that during one month in the year 1803, no less than five *mutasallim*s served in Hama consecutively and that they were all brutal, bringing about the exodus of the majority of the population to Mount Lebanon and Tripoli.[110]

Villagers were extremely vulnerable in times of instability, when investment in agriculture dropped. They were not only visited by local officials who demanded payments on top of the regular charges, but also by tribesmen who demanded protection money (*khuwwa*) and bands of unemployed or fugitive horsemen. The pressure on the rural population had become acute and subsequently many left their villages. At the time, village desertion was usually explained by both Ottoman authorities and other observers as the negative effect of the heavy tax burden and the additional claims of the military. In 1788, for instance, the *qassâmiyya* was accused of terrorizing the peasantry, causing land and entire villages in the Hama area to be abandoned.[111] Other causes of impoverishment in the villages were also taken into account, like drought, plague, locusts, and *ᶜarab* incursions. Considerations of the market were rarely taken into account. In the late eighteenth and early nineteenth centuries, conditions seemed to have been set for a prolonged agricultural crisis; violent provincial factionalism combined with massive movements of troops following the invasion of Palestine by the troops of ᶜAlî Bey al-Kabîr, the French occupation of Egypt and coastal Palestine and the Wahhâbî take-over of the Hijaz induced many peasants to leave their villages for shorter and longer periods, in particular along the Sultanic Road which connected Anatolia with Egypt and the Hijaz. Until 1804 many troops passed through the area and usually camped for a day or two near Hama. The presence of the troops inspired awe in the population, because of their rude conduct.[112] In the early 1770s the

[109] Sâbûnî, *Târîkh*, p. 16
[110] Shihâb, Lubnân, p. 408; see also al-ᶜAbd, *Târîkh*, p. 82
[111] SMH 46, pp. 74–75, 15 Rabîᶜ I 1203
[112] SMH 43, p. 118, [Muḥarram 1217]

imperial troops passing through the Hama and Homs areas caused many to depart for the other places.[113] The massive movements of troops accelerated the process of land and village desertion. When in 1800 the officer in charge of the provisioning of the troops prepared a list of villages for the distribution of the expenses, it became evident that about 10 per cent of the villages of the Hama plain had very recently been evacuated by their inhabitants.[114] Tribal pressure added to the ordeal of the peasantry, but those parts of the district which were generally less exposed to the *ᶜarab*, like the Jabal Kalbiyya to the west of Hama, also suffered from a contraction of farming. For instance, one-third of the land of the Nuṣayrî village of Abû Qubays was taken out of production in 1785 because the locals were unable to pay the taxes resting on the land. They sold the land to a Christian moneylender from Hama for an amount that equaled their debt to the treasury.[115] The authorities were well aware of the financial needs of the peasantry and tax rates were occasionally lowered, for example in 1788 by Ibrâhîm Deli Pasha and in 1799 even by Jazzâr Pasha.[116]

By the beginning of the second decade of the nineteenth century provincial factionalism subsided, but several areas, in particular the areas of Hama and Homs, suffered from the effects of the changes in the migratory movements of the large ᶜAnaza tribes. In the early 1820s the revolt of ᶜAbdallâh Pasha of Acre generated another round of massive military manoeuvring. The decade was later troubled by drought, locusts, and plague, and once again the Hama area became the scene of *ᶜarab* incursions.

The records of the Hama court contain rich data on the state of the villages in these decades and data show that rural society was indeed to vulnerable to, above all, the movement of large armies and to military campaigns, but appeared less susceptible to increased financial demands. Table 7 shows that after the cessation of violent provincial factionalism the area under cultivation increased markedly, but the number of inhabited and cultivated places showed an increase only towards the late 1820s. Peasants were less inclined to take up farming in a deserted place and the increase of land under cultivation was due to the extension of the farmland belonging or adjacent to the larger villages. Among the villages which were impoverished and unable to meet the tax demands

113 Ibn al-Siddîq, *Gharâ'ib*, pp. 68–70

114 SMH 43, p. 89, 5 Rabîᶜ II 1215

115 SMH 46, p. 120, 15 Muḥarram 1200

116 SMH 46, pp. 74–75, 15 Rabîᶜ I 1203 and p. 384, 13 Shawwâl 1214

Table 7. The condition of the villages

A. Number of inhabited villages and cultivated farms

B. Number of villages and farms described as 'impoverished', in arrears or receiving tax exemptions

C. Number of recently deserted villages and farms

D. Number of *faddân*

Year	A	B	C	D
1800	116	?	11	1,500
1818	101	27	16	2,208
1829	110	29	4	2,350

Sources: SMH 43, p. 89, 5 Rabîᶜ II 1215; SMH 43, pp. 180–87, 7 Rabîᶜ I 1233; SMH 49, pp. 326–29, 23 Rabîᶜ I 1215; SMH 49, p. 443, 29 Rabîᶜ I 1247; SMH 49, p. 449, 15 Rajab 1247; SMH 49, p. 468, 20 Shaᶜbân 1247

made on them – about 25 per cent of the total number of villages – were most villages of the northern part of the district, the Aᶜlâ. The Aᶜlâ bordered on the triangle between Qalᶜat al-Madîq, Jisr al-Shughûr and Arîḥa, the refuge of rebel officers like Mullû Ismâᶜîl and the Mawâlî *ᶜarab*. The few villages to the west of the Sultanic Road, both to the north and south of Hama, on the edge of the desert, had difficulty to survive. Clearly, peasants were reluctant to take up farming in such exposed places and some villages remained deserted for most of the period, whereas some other villages which had been recently deserted in 1800 were only repopulated during the 1830s.

In the core agricultural area, the plain to the west of Hama, most new land been brought under the plough. The relatively high frequency of land disputes between neighbouring villages in this area reflects this expansion.[117] While there was land in abundance in the district at large, land had become scarce in some localities.

One of the tasks of the *mutasallim* was the preservation of the villages. In the 1820s numerous villagers received loans from the treasury, referred to as 'strength' (*quwwa*). In 1826 the sheikhs and elders of 35 villages received such a loan from Faraj Aghâ, which would have enabled them to purchase ploughing animals and other necessities of farming.[118] In other years such loans were made as well, the largest of

[117] See SMH 48, p. 47, p. 63, p. 100, p. 225, p. 276, p. 306 (all cases occurred in the period 1818–1821)

[118] SMH 49, p. 199, 1 Jumâdâ I 1242

which (3000 q.) was granted to the sizeable village of Talldû in 1822.[119] The *mutasallim* also supplied villages with seed from the *anbâr*, the state granary. In 1831 Faraj Aghâ distributed wheat and barley seeds to, again, 35 villages. The amount constituted roughly 50 per cent and 40 per cent of the total quantities of wheat and barley, respectively, collected as tax in the previous year.[120] It is evident that the conditions for agriculture improved during the 1810s and 1820s, but it remains difficult to assess the impact of tax pressure or other financial pressures, political instability, tribal pressure and natural calamities and epidemics. It seems safe to assume that with the subsidence of the violent provincial factionalism peasants felt reassured. Whatever harm the *ᶜarab* and Mullû Ismâᶜîl may have caused between 1811 and 1818, it seems not to have seriously affected sedentary Hama in a permanent way. The effects of the tribal pressure were felt, no doubt, but only profoundly in the northern part and eastern fringes of the district. Considering the heavy tax burden and the exactions, as well as the drought, the plague and *ᶜarab* incursions during the 1820s, rural society displayed a remarkable resilience, a resilience which could be turned to use or misuse by strong officials, like Faraj Aghâ. They were able to develop the agricultural resources, but also turned to urban resources in order to maximilize the revenue. The material claims of higher authorities were expressed through various means, including investigations, and they succeeded in draining from their wealth and in decreasing their power without destroying their material base.

Of course, the suffering of the village population finds no expression in Table 7. In the wake of the devastating plague and famine of 1826 and 1827, many villagers left their homes in order to escape from the tribes who were desperately looking for food. Most of them returned to their villages after the crisis had subsided, and received some support from the authorities to continue their life of hardship.[121] Even in better years, villagers had a meagre subsistence; often they had no choice but to reap some of the wheat barely ripened and hide it from the eyes of the *aghawât*, in cellars and caves; roasted and cooked, it was part of their poor diet.[122]

[119] SMH 43, p. 354, 20 Rabîᶜ I 1238

[120] SMH 49, p. 468, 20 Shaᶜbân 1247

[121] Apart from investigating the finances of Faraj Aghâ, Sulaymân Aghâ was to see to the return of peasants to their villages, SMH 49, p. 224, [Muḥarram] 1245

[122] Volney, *Voyages*, vol. 2, p. 379

8. The Egyptian Experience

The decade of Egyptian rule over Syria witnessed a remarkable increase of tax-income of the state. The maximization of the revenue greatly impressed the central authorities, but because the revenues were used to confront the authority of sultan, there was no escape from condemning the rebel pasha and to present his rule as 'unjust and oppressive'. In the popular experience, Egyptian rule was indeed conceived as possessing strong oppressive traits, albeit that in the early years the Egyptians gained some popularity among various communities, in particular among Christians and Druzes. The policies applied during the decade encompassed a mixture of new and traditional methods aimed at resolving some of the predicaments of the traditional state, most notably the inadequacy of the resources and the abuse of delegated power. Some of the newly initiated policies shocked the general public, in particular the disarmament and conscription campaigns. A number of more traditional tools were also applied, but on an unprecedented scale and in a systematic fashion, such as forced labour services and trade monopolies. Muḥammad ᶜAlî Pasha's regime in the Syrian provinces differed from those in Egypt, firstly, because his hold on Syria was never secure, and secondly, because Syria had to serve the needs of the Nile valley.

The old ambition

From the time Muḥammad ᶜAlî Pasha, the governor of Egypt, had taken up the task of restoring the Hijaz to Ottoman rule, the pasha dominated politics in Ottoman eastern Mediterranean and Red Sea regions. The annexation of the Syrian provinces in 1831–32 had been the realization of an old ambition of the governor of Egypt.[1] In the 1820s his influence grew very strong in southern Syria and the coastal areas, including Lebanon; in 1827 the judges of Damascus even started to present gifts to him in recognition of his dominant position.[2] Until the occupation by Egyptian troops, coastal Syria – the province of Sidon and its dependency, the province of Tripoli – remained in the hands of one of Jazzâr

[1] Fahmy, *All*, pp. 38–75; al-Sayyid Marsot, *Egypt*, p. 199

[2] Koury, *Province*, 185–86

Pasha's former *mamlûks*, ᶜAbdallâh Pasha, despite the difficulty he found in controlling various local factions. Contrary to the province of Damascus the containment of provincial factions proved difficult in coastal Syria; when the Porte moved against ᶜAbdallâh Pasha in 1821, the limitations on the capabilities of the central authority were revealed; ᶜAbdallâh Pasha refused to accept his dismissal, was declared a rebel and condemned to death, but through the good offices of Muḥammad ᶜAlî Pasha he was pardoned and re-appointed to Acre.[3] But the relation between the two pashas was not friendly. ᶜAbdallâh Pasha resisted encroachments upon his authority in the coastal areas, but Muḥammad ᶜAlî Pasha increasingly acted as the patron of some local strongmen like the emir of Mount Lebanon, Bashîr al-Shihâb II, and of Muṣṭafâ Aghâ Barbar of Tripoli. Both found refuge in Egypt during a crisis in their career and later resumed office in their areas of origin. The habit of seeking the hospitality and support of the master of Egypt dated back to the end of the first decade of the century. The most senior office-holder who escaped to Egypt had been Kunj Yûsuf Pasha.[4] Many more found their way to Egypt, including many Christians who had converted to Catholicism and evaded the anger and pressure put on them by the old Greek Orthodox church which had the support of the Ottoman authorities.[5] The Syrians of Egypt were to play a role of some importance during the decade of Egyptian rule over Syria.

In the late 1820s, Muḥammad ᶜAlî Pasha increased the pressure on ᶜAbdallâh Pasha to adopt a more cooperative attitude until finally the governor of Egypt was openly picking quarrels with his colleague in Acre. In the early 1820s, Muḥammad ᶜAlî Pasha had settled a debt of ᶜAbdallâh Pasha to the treasury. ᶜAbdallâh Pasha had failed to repay Muḥammad ᶜAlî Pasha. The governor of Egypt also accused his colleague in Acre of encouraging smuggling between Palestine and Egypt. Moreover, he accused him of welcoming Egyptian peasants who escaped conscription. A final insult had been the refusal of ᶜAbdallâh Pasha to supply Lebanese silkworms.[6] These quarrels served as the pretext to send in his army in November 1831. The decision to invade and occupy Syria constituted above all the outcome of a prolonged dispute with the

[3] See also p. 120

[4] See p. 101

[5] See on migration to Egypt, Philipp, *Syrians*.

[6] Fahmy, *All*, p. 41; Sâlim, *Ḥukm*, pp. 25–42; Shihâb, *Lubnân* 819–72; al-Sayyid Marsot, *Egypt*, p. 222; *Maḥfûẓât*, vol. 1, p. 94, p. 115, p. 119

central authorities on a compensation for the pasha's military efforts in protecting the Ottoman sultanate.

In the Syrian provinces the troops of Muḥammad ᶜAli Pasha of Egypt, commanded by his son Ibrâhîm Pasha, met with little resistance. Only ᶜAbdallâh Pasha of Acre offered resistance to the advance of the Egyptian troops, but then he had good reason to do so. It took the Egyptian army six months of siege before ᶜAbdallâh Pasha surrendered and opened the gates of Acre. ᶜAbdallâh Pasha was sent to Egypt. The siege of Acre was the only serious delay in the Egyptian advance caused by resistance. The reaction of local officials in most parts of Syria varied from open support of the Egyptian troops to quiescence, but a number of local *aghawât* retreated with non-local officials to areas that were under loyalist control. In June 1832, shortly after the fall of Acre, those in control of Damascus surrendered to Ibrâhîm Pasha after a short display of nominal resistance.[7] Many of the office-holders, as well as a number of *aghawât* and ulema who had been involved in the rebellion against Salîm Pasha, had left the city prior to the arrival of the Egyptian troops.[8] By the summer of 1832 the army of Muḥammad ᶜAlî Pasha, under the command of his son Ibrâhîm Pasha, had occupied the area to the south of the Tripoli-Homs line. Egyptian units had already reached the outskirts of Homs in spring – before the capture of Damascus – but failing supplies precluded a swift advance. Profiting from this delay, imperial troops built up their forces near Homs and Hama, supported by local units. In late July raids by vanguard units composed of the Egyptian beduin embarked on the final advance to the north. In a short battle, the imperial troops were defeated, suffering great losses in both men and equipment.[9] Within about a week's time the remainder of Syria was annexed to the realm of the governor of Egypt.

[7] *Maḥfûẓât*, vol. 2, p. 19

[8] See, on the revolt against Salîm Pasha, p. 110

[9] According to an Egyptian report 1500 Ottomans troops were either killed or wounded. See *Usûl*, vol. 2, pp. 15–16. In a document reproduced in *Mudhakkirât* pp. 54–55 this number is repeated. 2500 troops were taken captive. Shihâb writes (*Lubnân*, pp. 867) that the Ottoman troops left 4,000 tents, 4,000 pieces of artillery and abundant provisions to the Egyptians. See also Fahmy, *All*, p. 63

The end of an era ?

Egyptian rule in Syria is regularly depicted as a clear, if not radical departure from the preceding Ottoman administrative traditions.[10] Expressions of admiration for the efforts of the Egyptian authorities to transform the Syrian provinces are common, but so are concessions that these efforts were by and large ineffective. In this view Syrian society proved unable to absorb the new, and well-intended and beneficial Egyptian reforms. In the words of an Egyptian historian the region returned to '. . . a way of life permeated by rancour, fanaticism, contention, fighting and trouble...' after the withdrawal of the Egyptian troops.[11] Obviously, it is doubtful whether, at the time, the inhabitants of Syria would have agreed with later interpretations.

For several reasons the annexation of the Syrian provinces to the realm of Muḥammad ᶜAlî Pasha can be regarded as a turning point in the history of Syria. Firstly, after having acted as such for about half a century, the coastal stronghold of Acre ceased to function as the main political centre. After a siege of six months, the fortifications of the town were dismantled and the Egyptians re-established Damascus as the principle centre of administration. Acre was not to resume any position of political or economic strength. Secondly, with the occupation by the troops of the ambitious governor of Egypt, the Syrian provinces were placed on the agenda of the European powers. In particular the British, who had previously largely ignored these provinces, demonstrated a strong interest in the area after they had decided to support the Ottomans in their efforts to re-establish their control. It was to a

[10] This approach is best illustrated by the following quotation from Ma'oz (*Ottoman*, p. 12): 'The Egyptian occupation [. . .] put an end to a long period of confusion and backwardness, and opened a new era in Syrian history. Bold measures which were carried out by Ibrahim Pasha brought about a profound change in almost every aspect of the old life [. . .]'. In 1929 Sulaymân Abû ᶜIzz al-Dîn published his *Ibrâhîm Bâshâ fî Sûriyâ* in Beirut. However, the pioneering work on the Egyptian administration in Syria was conducted by Asᶜad Rustum, notably in his *Uṣûl* (1930–34), a collection of, predominantly, court documents and his *Maḥfûẓât* (1940–43), a calendar of state papers relating to Egyptian rule in Syria

[11] Sâlim, *Ḥukm*, p. 322. Hofman (*Administration*, p. 333) comes to a similar conclusion, but he and some others (for instance, Abir, *Local*) are more careful and pay attention to the difficulties the Egyptians encountered in the process of establishing their methods of administration. See on the histography on Muḥammad ᶜAlî Pasha, Fahmy, *All*, pp. 12–25 ff

considerable extent due to British policy that Muḥammad ʿAlî Pasha's hold over the Syrian provinces remained insecure and eventually became untenable. After the British had forced Muḥammad ʿAlî Pasha to renounce his claim on the Syrian provinces in 1841, British, as well as French, interference with the affairs of Syrian provinces, most notably in Lebanon, rapidly increased.

To what extent the nature of the Egyptian administration influenced future developments in the Syrian provinces is hard to assess, but in essence Egyptian rule in Syria did not differ markedly from the previous decades. The main difference between the Egyptian and the Ottoman regimes existed in that the capabilities of the Egyptian provincial state – in contemporary writing called *al-dawla al-Miṣriyya*[12] – exceeded those of the Ottoman (central) state. It should be realized that the rule of Muḥammad ʿAlî Pasha in Syria did not equal his rule in Egypt. Policies applied in the Syrian provinces were mostly based upon those implemented in Egypt earlier, but the Egyptian authorities did not put the Syrian provinces on an equal footing with the province of Egypt and from the outset they were well aware of at least a number of differences between Syrian and Egyptian society and the economy of the two areas. The Egyptian authorities regarded the newly acquired provinces as secondary to Egypt. The exploitation of the area was to serve the interests of the Egyptian state. This notion was not a nationalist concept, but the combination of a geographical orientation with the interests of the military household of Muḥammad ʿAlî Pasha, which was of a mixed, predominantly Albanian origin.[13] He recruited the key officials from his family and his hometown of Kavalla – in present-day Greece. Low-ranking and middle-ranking officers of the Egyptian army in the Syrian provinces were allowed to marry local girls, whereas the high-ranking officers were prohibited from entering into marriage with locals.[14] The insecure position of Egyptian rule in Syria also influenced Egyptian attitudes, as did the opposition of large segments of Syrian society to the strong coercive traits of the new administration.

The Egyptian regime in Syria differed from traditional Ottoman rule in a number of respects. The various military and para-military

[12] The term *dawla Miṣriyya* was also used in edicts emanating from the Egyptian government. See for example SMH 49, p. 543, [Rabîʿ I] 1248

[13] Hunter, *Egypt*, pp. 22–25; See, on his armies and their relation to the development of an 'Egyptian nation', Fahmy, *All*.

[14] *Maḥfûẓât*, vol. 3, p. 97. Soldiers were also prohibited from marrying locals, because their pay was insufficient to support a family.

organizations lost their near autonomy. Some were disbanded and others were integrated in the new military and police forces, but the disbanding and integration were not fully completed during the decade. The Egyptians made used of very traditional military formations, like beduin units and *deli*s. The more irregular local paramilitary formations, like the bands headed by rural chieftains, suffered greatly from the general disarmament of the population, but some were allowed to keep their arms, or were even furnished with better fighting equipment, like Druze and Christian militia of Lebanon, who were supportive of the Egyptians and instrumental in suppressing several revolts.

A second difference with the traditional regimes was the establishment of a far higher degree of control over local finances. Most vital in this operation was the abolishment of the system of the collection of fees for the support of office-holders.[15] Instead they were to receive a salary. The abolishment of several charges – in particular the *ᶜawâyid* – was presented as an act of benevolence, but the demands made upon the population at large increased sharply. In addition to increased fiscal claims, the Egyptians implemented conscription for the army and made extensive use of forced labour. Conscription for the insatiable Egyptian armies, usually preceded by disarmament of the local population, was generally considered to be a major outrage against the local values and sparked off a number of revolts.

Most of the changes from the rule of the preceding decades were not conceived as improvements, but some were received more favourably. The Egyptian authorities took drastic action to stimulate the rural economy. In order to improve the conditions in the countryside they invested in agriculture on a large scale. Vital for the well-being of the rural population was the achievement of an unprecedented degree of public security; the times what bands of fugitive military, highway men, or destitute beduin harassed villagers came to an end. In the urban centres, too, public order was upheld. Corruption, especially illegal material demands by office-holders, persisted at first but was by and large suppressed until the Egyptian state failed to make ends meet, but on the whole the demands of the regime remained more predictable and governed by law than in the previous years. A final breach with early principles concerns the emancipation of Christian and Jewish subjects who were treated on an equal footing with the traditionally privileged

[15] See, for example, two orders to that respect *Uṣul*, vol. 2, pp. 31–32 and pp. 35–36

Muslim subjects in most fields of the administration, although conversion rates to Islam in the Hama area fail to reflect this policy.[16] The Sunni Muslim majority – or at least its spokesmen – did not support the idea of the near equality of the law for, unbelievers.

Although the Egyptian regime differed from the traditional Ottoman regime in several, sometimes important aspects, the basic principle remained unchanged. Like the Ottoman state, the Egyptian provincial state represented the rule of a distinct household, which claimed absolute power and, consequently, the disposal of the entire revenue of its domains. The exploitation of the domains by Muḥammad ᶜAlî Pasha and his men followed by and large the traditional concept of the Circle of Justice, in which coercion, or force, and rendering justice complement each other in the process of revenue extraction. The keeping of a balance had proved to be problematic in the past, and in the course of the 1830s, particularly from 1834 onward, an increasing number of inhabitants of the Syrian provinces expressed their opposition to the Egyptian regime's claims on local resources. The response of the state was violent; where the traditional *ẓulm*, oppression, had been an attribute of the local agents of the state rather than the state itself, *ẓulm* now appeared to have become an official policy.

Disciplining Syrian society

The Egyptian occupation clearly impacted on local society, but it took society, in particular the local elite, some time to adapt or to remonstrate. At first the Egyptian authorities retained many of the local officials in office. Members of the traditional local elite largely filled the vacancies that had been created by the departure of office-holders who had fled with the defeated Ottoman troops. Only a small number of officials had been dismissed immediately, some of them because they had opposed the Egyptian advance. Others had to make place for locals who were rewarded for their support of the Egyptians. Of all local officials and strongmen who had welcomed the Egyptians some old factions in the area, formerly controlled by the governors of Acre, acted most openly and actively. The veteran strongman of Tripoli, Muṣṭafâ

[16] The number of registered converts to Islam in Hama during the years of Egyptian rule is congruent with that of the preceding and following periods: five Christians and one Jew (who might have been the last Jew of Hama, Aṣlân ibn Yaᶜqûb, see SMH 49, p. 445, 20 Jumâdâ II 1247) during 1824–1832; 6 Christians during 1833–1841; five Christians during 1842–1850.

Aghâ Barbar, was quick to embrace the rule of his former host and current patron. His close neighbour, Amîr Bashîr al-Shihâb of Mount Lebanon, also maintained close relations with the governor of Egypt since the early 1820s and from then rendered military services to his son Ibrâhîm Pasha in subjugating the population. Bashîr al-Shihâb was an associate of Aḥmad Bey, who had acted as the agent of Ibrâhîm Pasha in Damascus and was appointed deputy governor (*qâyimmaqâm*) of the city in 1832.[17] Aḥmad Bey was the adopted son of Kunj Yûsuf Pasha, the former governor of Damascus who had sought refuge with Muḥammad ᶜAlî Pasha in 1810 after his failure to check the Wahhâbî movement.

The Egyptian authorities were sceptical about the qualities of their local counterparts in Syria. The early experiences with local and provincial officials were on the whole unsatisfactory, because they failed to comply with the Egyptian standards of proficiency. Few of them had received a proper education or training, at least in the eyes of the Egyptians.[18] Egyptian functionaries, some of them of Syrian background, were sent for assistance and instruction, but only the central provincial institutions were served in this fashion. The Egyptian authorities were suspicious about the intentions of the local officials who had served under sultanic authority. The suspicion was undoubtedly mutual, also because the Syrians were generally well informed on the style of Muḥammad ᶜAlî's government in Egypt. One of the first acts of the new government was the prohibition of the imposition of levies on top of the regular taxes. Charges like the *ᶜawâyid* and *ᶜubûdiyya*, levied to cover the expenses of local office-holders, were abolished. In a letter to Muṣṭafâ Aghâ Barbar, Ibrâhîm Pasha explained this decision by pointing out to him that the multitude of existing taxes burdened the population to the extreme.[19] From now on all officials were to receive a salary from the state. It proved difficult to eradicate the old habits overnight, certainly during the transitional period in which the Egyptian authorities, both civil and military, faced serious shortages in cash and kind and were unable to pay (full) salaries.

The popular reaction to the advent of the Egyptian rule ranged from

[17] *Mudhakkirât*, p. 54

[18] Ḥannâ Baḥrî, for example, complained on several occasions to Muḥammad ᶜAlî Pasha about the shortage of skilled functionaries Sâlim, *Ḥukm*, pp. 74–75

[19] The order from Ibrâhîm Pasha to Muṣṭafâ Aghâ Barbar, dated 22 Rabîᶜ II 1248, is reproduced in Khûrî, *Barbar*, p. 258. See also SMH 49, p. 543, [Rabîᶜ I] 1248. See also Sâlim, *Ḥukm*, p. 111

strong suspicion due to the pasha's reputation, to careful favourable acceptance following some of the first policy measures. During the first two years of Egyptian rule, Syria witnessed an unprecedented degree of public security, which stimulated the economy and the general sense of well-being. The inflationary effects of the enormous spending of the army and the sudden increase in the demand for local, both agricultural and industrial, products did not as yet affect the population at large because job opportunities were ample and wages and prices for agricultural products high.[20] During the first two years no radical reforms were implemented. Some were initiated, but these were largely ignored by the local office-holders. The traditional system of exploitation still functioned in much the same way as it had done for decades. The relative prosperity of the early 1830s might have blunted the sharp edges of the system. Moreover, many officials showed some moderation in their demands on the population, because of the reputation of Muḥammad ᶜAlî Pasha's rigid handling of those who collected more than the legal share.

In the first years, the Egyptian authorities faced several major problems in establishing their rule, in particular huge cash deficits and failing supplies of their troops. They had great difficulty in organizing the revenue collection, with the result that the amounts of revenue which reached the treasury were small. In the beginning of 1833 the Egyptian treasury was virtually empty.[21] Only after the signing of the Kütahya treaty (8 April 1833), which legalized, at least for the time being, Muḥammad ᶜAlî Pasha's hold on Syria, the Egyptian authorities pressed their claims upon the local administration and on the population at large. With the assistance of troops which had returned from Anatolia they established a strict control over the finances of the provinces and were quick to react upon complaints brought by the population against local officials who continued to levy *ᶜawâyid* and other abolished charges. A considerable number of them were dismissed after the charge of injustice against them had been verified. The most famous victim of this policy was Muṣṭafâ Aghâ Barbar, whose remarkably long career ended with his dismissal and arrest in October of 1833.[22] A large

[20] See, for the Syrian economy under Egyptian rule Owen, *World*, pp. 76–80; Abir, *Local*, p. 306

[21] In some areas nothing appears to have been remitted to the treasury in 1832, see Abir, *Local*, p. 305

[22] Khûrî, *Barbar*, pp. 360–70; *Maḥfûẓât*, vol. 2, p. 345. Muṣṭafâ Aghâ Barbar died in 1835.

number of local office-holders followed the same fate all over Syria, in particular leading members of the once powerful local – urban and rural – *aghawât* families.[23]

The actions against corrupt officials met with popular approval, but other policies met with widespread opposition. The imposition of high tax rates, the ban on the possession of arms and the actual implementation of conscription for the army, were all received with anxiety and hostility. In many areas the traditional, mainly military, local leadership was able to mobilize popular support for their defence against the imposition of a stricter centralized control. In 1834 numerous smaller and larger revolts erupted especially in Palestine and areas to the south of Damascus. Local officials who had been recently dismissed played an important role in the rebellion against Egyptian rule in Palestine. The rebellion, or rather the multitude of smaller revolts following the lack of co-ordination between the rebel chiefs, was brutally crushed.[24] Clans in the Nuṣayrî Mountains also confronted Egyptian officials and troops who attempted to disarm them. They even raided the coastal town of Latakia. With great difficulty and the help of troops of Bashîr al-Shihâb from Lebanon, the revolt was suppressed.[25]

The Egyptians maintained a large standing army in Syria after the suppression of the revolts and coercion became the dominant feature of Egyptian rule. Instances of violent and arbitrary actions by Egyptian troops increased, in particular during conscription campaigns. The conscription constituted by far the most unpopular innovation and people resorted to almost every means to escape from it; many offered bribes in the hope to have their sons excluded, others even resorted to self-mutilation. Many went into hiding in hilly or mountainous areas or escaped to the ᶜ*arab* tribes in the desert or to areas under Ottoman control. Not before long, fathers were forced to follow their sons in hiding or exile, because Egyptian troops increasingly used torture in their attempt to discover the whereabouts of fugitive conscripts. In the late 1830s, when Muḥammad ᶜAlî Pasha was preparing for another battle with the sultan, the conditions became worse. Apart from the young men, the army carried off huge numbers of pack animals from the villages, as well as food and fodder. Villagers were hardly ever compensated. By the late 1830s bribing had become one of the few

23 See, for the arrest in areas in between Tripoli and Hama, *Ḥurûb*, p. 42

24 Abir, *Local*, pp. 309–10

25 *Maḥfûẓât*, vol. 2, p. 432 onward; Ṣâyikh, *Muqtarab*, f. 61–63 and 78; *Âthâr*, vol. 2, f. 35–38

relatively secure options to protect one's family, animals and crops.[26] The heavy demands of the Egyptians also caused some of their earlier allies to turn against them and take up arms, especially in Lebanon.

Local rule under the Egyptians

Damascus was re-established as the political centre of a united Syria, comprising the former provinces of Damascus, Sidon (Acre), Tripoli and Aleppo. Serving as the centre of this new entity, Damascus became the seat of senior Egyptian officials and their aids, including Syrians who had migrated to Egypt earlier or their sons. Apart from Aḥmad Bey, who was appointed deputy governor, Ḥannâ Baḥrî, the son of Kunj Yûsuf Pasha's secretary ʿAbbûd Baḥrî who had escaped with him to Cairo, came to prominence. He had made his career in Cairo when the Egyptian troops invaded Syria and headed the influential financial department in Damascus from 1832 onward. Some Damascene *aghawât* had established relations with the Egyptians prior to the occupation of Damascus and, in reward for their constructive stance, were appointed to senior provincial offices, often to be dismissed within a short period. Others, including *aghawât* of the Maydân and some ulema who had ruled the city since the revolt of 1831, had retreated to areas under Ottoman control. Most were allowed to return to Damascus in 1833, but a few were no longer welcome in their city.[27] The ʿAẓms, albeit related by marriage to the new governor of the united provinces of Syria, the 'Egyptian' Muḥammad Sharîf Pasha, did not belong to the small group of Syrians who had a intimate relationship with Muḥammad ʿAlî Pasha's extended household. However, they were able to obtain positions of local significance in the prominent consultative councils which replaced the traditional *dîwân*.[28] The Murâdî family retained its position as the dominant family of ulema.

According to a popular tradition, the commander of the Egyptian, troops, Ibrâhîm Pasha, spent the night in the *sarâyâ* of Hama after the town had been captured by his troops in late July of 1832. The loud moaning noise of the huge waterwheels in the ʿÂṣî River near the buildings kept him from sleeping and he ordered his men to silence the

[26] See for a description of the coercive traits of Egyptian rule, Ṣâyikh, *Muqtarab*, f. 78–84; *Mudhakkirât*, pp. 76–79; Ṣâbûnî, *Hama*, p. 85

[27] *Maḥfûẓât*, vol. 2, p. 338

[28] Some contemporaries believed Aḥmad Bey to be a member of the ʿAẓm family. See *Ḥurûb*, p. 16

wheel, which they did. Normally, these famous wheels, and symbol of the town of Hama, were only stopped when they needed repair. The lamentations of the waterwheels had inspired many a poet,[29] but the son of the pasha of Egypt did not always respect established reputations.

The *mutasallim* of Hama, Faraj Aghâ, was maintained until November 1832, when he was replaced by Rashîd Aghâ al-Shâmlî. The Egyptian authorities were suspicious of his position of strength because of his control over the *ᶜarab* tribes in the area. Another reason for his dismissal sounds more familiar: '. . . he was indebted to the population which was most fearful of his infringements upon their rights and of his severity'.[30] His successor, Rashîd Aghâ, was a cousin of ᶜAbd al-Ghanî Aghâ al-Shâmlî, who had served briefly as *mutasallim* of Hama in 1829 after Faraj Aghâ had been suspended following accusations of extortion.[31] The Shâmlî family belonged to the most influential *aghawât* of the Maydân quarter of Damascus. Rashîd Aghâ had figured prominently during the revolt of 1831 in Damascus against the Ottoman governor, Salîm Pasha, and established a good relation with the Egyptians and their agents during the long siege of Acre.[32] Rashîd Aghâ did not remain in office in Hama for long. In June of 1833, he was replaced by a local Kurdish *aghâ*, ᶜAbdallâh Aghâ Ṭayfûr. Rashîd Aghâ had been accused and found guilty of exacting money from sixteen village sheikhs, four local tax farmers in the western parts of the district as well as from one tribal sheikh. The Damascene aghâ died shortly afterwards and his victims were compensated from his inheritance. The compensations amounted to 27,281 q. The scribe of the local treasury had audited Rashîd Aghâ's books and had established that he owed another 44,366 q. to the treasury.[33] Clearly, Rashîd Aghâ al-Shâmlî had not been the model *mutasallim* the Egyptian authorities envisaged.

Faraj Aghâ returned to the office in Hama in 1834 despite the hesitations on the part of the Egyptian authorities. His reappointment may well have been motivated by the strong opposition to Egyptian

[29] See, for example, the lines of sheikh ᶜAbd al-Ghanî al-Nâbulsî on the 'weeping wheels', *Ḥaqîqa*, p. 48

[30] Cited from a document dated 2 Jumâdâ I 1248, in Sâlim, *Ḥukm*, pp. 67–68. See also *Maḥfûẓât*, vol. 2, p. 154, n. 2106

[31] See p. 178

[32] *Maḥfûẓât*, vol. 1, pp. 151–53, pp. 278–79

[33] SMH 49, p. 22 Rajab 1249 and p. 570, 5 Dhû al-Ḥijja 1249. The letter of appointment of ᶜAbdallâh Aghâ Ṭayfûr, dated 25 Ṣafar 1249 is reproduced in Rustum, *Uṣûl*, vol. 2, pp. 71–72

reform policies which surfaced that year in many areas. During the revolts the ᶜAnaza tribes had taken the opportunity to resist attempts by the Egyptians to limit their migratory range and to deny them access to pastures close to the cultivated areas. The incidence of robberies committed by ᶜAnaza tribesmen in the Hama area worried Ibrâhîm Pasha who was striving for the forced settlement of the tribes.[34] In 1835, after the pacification of most of Syria, including the steppe and desert, Faraj Aghâ was again succeeded by ᶜAbdallâh Aghâ Ṭayfûr. In 1837 a new functionary was appointed who ranked above the *mutasallim*, namely the *qâyimmaqâm*, who acted as the deputy of the governor general of Syria in the district, having both civilian and military duties. The *mutasallim* was relieved from military duties and his function was restricted to the civil affairs of the town only. For most districts in Syria the *qâyimmaqâm* was recruited from the Egyptian military,[35] but in the district of Hama, ᶜÂrif Efendi Jâbirîzade, a member of an influential sharifian family of Aleppo served in this capacity.[36] He was the first governor of the district of Hama who was not an *aghâ* or bey, although the *sharîf*s of Aleppo had long since functioned as a local para-military force. Faraj Aghâ remained a dominant actor in the politics of Hama and, following a petition in his favour by the local elite, he was again called upon in a time of insecurity that accompanied the evacuation of the Egyptian troops and the transition of power from Muḥammad ᶜAlî Pasha to the authority of the new Ottoman sultan, Abdülmecid.[37]

The composition of the local elite, the *aᶜyân* did not undergo significant changes during the decade of Egyptian rule. The judge *qâḍî*, *muftî*, and *naqîb* continued to be recruited from the Kaylânî family. Contrary to the years preceding the Egyptian occupation, no attempts appear to have been made to replace candidates from this family by others.[38] The jurisdiction of the judge was restricted and the

[34] *Maḥfûẓât*, vol. 2, p. 427

[35] Hofman, *Administration*, p. 325

[36] SMH 51, pp. 206–07, 17 Rabîᶜ I 1256

[37] See, for the letter of appointment, dated 3 Shawwâl 1256, *Uṣûl*, vol. 5, pp. 237–38. See also SMH 51, p. 277, 24 Dhû al-Ḥijja 1256 and p. 297, 7 Muḥarram 1257

[38] Four members of the Kaylânî family acted as *qâḍî* during the 1830s; Sharaf al-Dîn Efendi, ᶜAbd al-Qâdir Efendi, Aḥmad Efendi and Muḥammad Salîm Efendi. ᶜAbd al-Qâdir Efendi also acted for some time as *naqîb*, and was succeeded by Muḥammad Ṭâhir Efendi after his death. The office of *muftî* was throughout the 1830s occupied by Muḥammad ᶜAlî Efendi Kaylânîzade.

formal interference of the judge in affairs outside of the religious law became minimal, but the creation of a local council (*majlis al-shûrâ*) in all towns of Syria which numbered 2,000 inhabitants or more, served as an additional platform of *aᶜyân* activity. The council was modelled on the traditional *dîwân* of the provincial capitals. The new council was not granted more extensive powers than those of its predecessor, but it acted in a similar, servile way.[39] The recruitment of the appointees for the council largely followed the traditional make-up of the elite of Hama. The ᶜAẓm and Kaylânî families dominated and were each represented by at least two members, among them the then patriarch Ḥusayn Bey al-ᶜAẓm and Muḥammad ᶜAlî Efendi al-Kaylânî, the *muftî*. Others who were appointed to the council included the highly regarded religious sheikh, Muṣṭafâ Efendi al-ᶜAlwânî, and Khalîl Aghâ al-Jijaklî.[40] Through the combination of offices, the Kaylânî family preserved the political dominance that the family had acquired during the 1820s. Muḥammad ᶜAlî Efendi al-Kaylânî figured most prominently among the *aᶜyân* of Hama until his dismissal 1845 following charges of corruption.[41]

The maximalization of the revenue

In 1831 Damascus revolted against the increased tax demands. The revolt influenced the timing of the invasion by the Egyptian army. The material claims of the central Ottoman authorities were to be dwarfed by excessive claims of Muḥammad ᶜAlî Pasha. During the first year, the Egyptian authorities failed to collect a large share of the taxes, but from mid-1833 onwards they started to reorganize the fiscal regime of Syria and by the end of the year they had sufficient troops at hand to compel people to pay. The Egyptians abolished a number charges, but in the late summer of 1833 they introduced the *farda*, a progressive poll tax on

[39] Hofman, *Administration*, pp. 330–33

[40] The Hama records contain no complete list of the membership of the *majlis*. Only occasionally reference is made to the membership of the *majlis* in *ḥujja*s, in which members or their representatives acted as witnesses, see *Uṣûl*, vol. 3, pp. 8–9; SMH 51, p. 99, 20 Muḥarram 1253; p. 145, 15 Rabîᶜ I 1253; p. 149, end Rabîᶜ II 1253; p. 161, 17 Ramaḍân 1254; p. 156, 21 Dhû al-Ḥijja 1255. Normally, Christians were granted membership as well, but no reference was found to their membership.

[41] See for a biography of Muḥammad ᶜAlî Efendi, Jundî, *Aᶜlâm*, vol. 2, pp. 37–38

male adults. In Syria, the rates of this tax exceeded those in Egypt.[42] The imposition of the *farda* led to grievances among the Muslim establishment because the tax resembled the *jizya*, the discriminatory tax payable by non-Muslim subjects.[43] Many considered it to be an outrage against the community of the faithful and the tax became the most infamous imposition of the decade. However, the magnitude of the amounts of *farda* collected was relatively small, at least when compared to some other impositions. In 1839 the amount of *farda* collected in the Hama district constituted about 6 per cent of the total revenue.[44]

The maximalization of the revenue existed above all in the imposition of much higher rates of some existing taxes. Not only were the rates of some 'old' taxes increased, some old designations – for instance the *iʿâna* – came to cover what were in fact new impositions. In the Hama district the *iʿâna* had figured previously as a relatively moderate charge to finance the postal resting house and rested upon the quarters of the town of Hama only. Under the Egyptians the *iʿâna* was transformed into a tax on property both in the towns and the villages and also covered rights payable at the transaction of real estate. By the time of the Egyptian evacuation, the *iʿâna* figured as the largest single imposition resting upon the district and might have amounted to about 900,000 q.[45] The rates of the *iʿâna* resting upon urban properties exceeded the *iʿâna* liabilities in the villages, because the rates payable by the villages had been lowered in 1836 at the expense of the urban tax payer.[46] Figures for

[42] *Maḥfûẓât*, vol. 2, p. 344

[43] According to Sâlim the *farda* had already been introduced by the Ottomans, but not in Syria. See *Ḥukm*, p. 114. Ṣâyigh writes that a tax similar to the *farda* already existed. See *Muqtarab*, f. 77. The *farda* was abolished by the Ottomans in 1841, because it was considered *bidʿa*. See SMH 51, p 425, 3 Jumâdâ I 1257

[44] 84,861 q. of a total revenue of 5,269,824 q. see F.O.195/196, n. 73, Damascus, 5 October 1842

[45] The Ottoman authorities claimed that the amount of *iʿâna* they imposed on the district following the Egyptian evacuation, namely 452,048 q., constituted half of the amount levied in the previous year (by the Egyptians), see SMH 51, p. 425, 3 Jumâdâ I 1257. See, on the *iʿâna* Sâlim, *Ḥukm*, pp. 115–16. See, on the different use of the *iʿâna* in the mid 1840s, Rafeq, *Land*.

[46] *Maḥfûẓât*, vol. 3, p. 165. The large village of Laṭmîn had been earmarked for the moderate amount of 720 q. of *iʿâna* in 1840. See Rustum, *Uṣûl*, vol. 4, p. 203

Table 8. Tax increase during Egyptian rule

	1831/2	1839/40	Increase (per cent)
I. Rural			
Revenue villages	372,283	662,736	79
Cotton villages	27,167	33,300	22
Fixed amount villages	51,905	166,225	223
Turcoman villages	103,395	195,087	89
Jabal Gharbî	140,423	327,508	133
Tax farms	510,665	1,131,086	121
ᶜ*arab* tribes	111,848	144,787	30
II. Urban			
craft organizations	71,683	71,735	0.07
urban tax farms	157,503	326,844	107
III. Other			
farda		84,861	
*i*ᶜ*âna* (estimate)		900,000	
other		510,074	
TOTAL	1,546,872	4,554,766	195%

Sources: SMH 51, pp. 316-17, [1257] and pp. 425-26, 3 Jumâdâ I 1257

the amounts of the proportional agricultural (*qism*) collected in the years concerned are uncertain, but the amounts and cash value may have increased at a similar rate and may have tripled by the year 1840.[47] The

[47] No figures exist for the year 1831/32, therefore the figure for 1829 is used 1840

quatities	cash value	quatities	cash value estimate
wheat 320 *makkûk*	= 76,800	1076 *ardabb/makkûk*	= 258,240
barley 163 *makkûk*	= 20,864	558.5 *ardabb/makkûk*	= 71,488
dura 47.5 *makkûk*	= 6,840	35 *ardabb/makkûk*	= 5,040
kirsinna 24 *makkûk*	= 4,224		
Total	108,728		339,808

The cash value figures for 1840 should be handle with the greatest caution. The amounts of grains collected in 1840 are derived from a synopsis prepared by the local treasury (SMH 51, pp. 316–17, [1257]). In this synopsis no official

total tax income of the district in the previous fiscal year was even slightly higher and exceeded 5 million q.[48]

The increase of the taxes payable by the villages corresponds partly to the substantial expansion of land under cultivation (see below). It is of interest that the Egyptian authorities abandoned the tradition of treating the 'fixed amount' (*maqṭûʿ*) villages with leniency. The tax demands made upon these villages were more than tripled. In the case of the cash revenue, inflation should of course be taken into account. Unfortunately there are no figures on the rate of inflation during the 1830s. Given the shortage of coins, it seems unlikely that all revenue entered in the books in cash had actually been collected in cash. Moreover, it was the policy of the Egyptians to demand payment in kind when the market prices of cereals were high.[49] Thus the government profited from the difference between official and market prices. The synopsis from which most of the figures presented in Table 8 are derived, was prepared in order to facilitate the assessment of the taxes by Ottoman officials after the Egyptians had evacuated the Syrian provinces. The authorities were deeply impressed by the fiscal efforts of the Egyptians, not only because the revenue had increased, but also because a much larger share was remitted to the treasury. Only about half of the amount for 1831/32 consisted of taxes which were directly remitted to the treasury, although a substantial part of the remainder found its way to the imperial centre by way of 'gifts'. The sum for 1840 was remitted to the treasury in its entirety. The system of tax farming had not been replaced by direct collecting in the case of most taxes, but the control over the tax farmers had

price is given. For lack of an alternative the official prices of 1829 have been used for 1840. The *ardabb* used in the synopsis of the treasury of Hama for 1840 did not correspond to the use of this Egyptian measure, but equaled the traditional local *makkûk*. It was not unusual for a 'foreign' measure to be adopted, or forced upon a locality, while the actual measure remained unchanged (see for example Mundy, *Shareholders*, p. 224). Other products collected in kind, like silk, soap, cheese, animal fat and sheepskins, have been excluded because of the absence of figures prior to 1840. The quantities were, at any rate, marginal.

[48] According to a synopsis of the tax registers of Damascus. See F.O. 195/196, n. 73, Damascus, 5 October 1842. Contrary to the synopsis prepared by the local treasury of Hama (SMH 51, p. 316–37, [1257]) the synopsis derived from the provincial tax registers gives no information on the various components of the revenue, except for the *farda*.

[49] Sâlim, *Ḥukm*, p. 112

been tightened and Egyptian troops regularly accompanied them when collecting the taxes. Abuses on the part of the tax farmer occurred, but these abuses were largely at the expense of villagers, tribesmen and others, and not at the expense of the treasury.[50] Jealous of the income derived from the Syrian provinces and the discipline imposed on tax farmers during the 1830s, the Ottomans attempted to achieve similar results. The immense governmental expenditure to which the Egyptians had committed themselves was disregarded. The part of the revenue of the provinces of Damascus, Sidon and Tripoli that reached the treasury had dropped by 42 per cent in 1842. The income of the treasury from the district of Hama showed a decrease of 38 per cent.[51] It is uncertain whether the net proceeds dropped correspondingly, since governmental spending is most likely to have decreased in the first years after the evacuation.[52]

Agricultural and tribal policies

The imposition of high tax rates and strict control over the collection and farming of taxes were not the only instruments used by the Egyptian authorities to maximalize the revenue. In their economic policies they aimed to augment, in particular, the agricultural production, basically in order to feed the Egyptian armies and industries. The attempts by the Egyptian government to create an independent industrial base distinguished the regime from the central Ottoman government, but the Egyptian economic policies did not differ from the traditional Ottoman economic concepts, in the sense that the state continued to occupy a central position, both as regulator and beneficiary of the economic activities. Industrial and agricultural production served the institutions of the state, rather than the contrary which was increasingly the case in Western Europe.

By combining incentive with coercion, the Egyptian government succeeded in expanding agriculture in the Syrian provinces, both in the

[50] Tax farmers often failed to compensate villagers for food and fodder, and occasionally imposed illegal charges. See *Maḥfûẓât*, vol. 3, p. 121; Sâlim, *Ḥukm*, pp. 118–19

[51] See, for the tax figures F.O. 195/196, n. 73, Damascus, 5 October 1842

[52] In 1842 in southern Palestine (districts of Jerusalem, Gaza, Yafa, Hebron, Ramla and Lidd) the net proceeds were expected to be no less than 75 per cent of the total revenue of nearly 7 million q. See F.O. 195/196, n. 56, Damascus, 20 July 1842. However, the actual revenue from these districts only amounted to about 4 million q. See F.O. 195/196, n. 73, Damascus, 5 October 1842

interior and the coastal areas. The most commonly applied measures to stimulate agricultural production included tax exemptions, the provision of capital to village communities and forced settlement or resettlement. All of these were traditional means, but contrary to the preceding period they were now being used more systematically and extensively. Although some attempts were made to introduce new crops and cropping techniques, most peasants, and definitely those producing cereals, continued to work their fields and process their crops in the same fashion as the previous generations. Not only did the methods and means of production remain unchanged, the control over these means showed no marked alterations either. Most agricultural land remained state-owned and the peasants continued to enjoy usufructuary rights. They continued to depend on capital provided by either the state or by well-to-do individuals. The main difference with the preceding decades was that fewer infringements on the rights of the state and, to an extent, of the peasantry occurred.

The protection of public order constituted a precondition for the expansion of agriculture. The generally well disciplined military enforced and guaranteed an unprecedented degree of public security. Highway robbery, which had been endemic, disappeared from most areas, except during some of the revolts in 1834. The tribal policies of the Egyptian government were aimed at establishing favourable conditions for agriculture in the transitional zone and adjacent fertile and well watered land that had been used for herding for ages. In the Aleppo and Hama areas, the ᶜAnaza continued to dominate the local tribes and villages in the transitional zone during the first two years of Egyptian rule, but later Egyptian troops withheld access of the larger tribes and their herds to grazing land in the vicinity of cultivation. Furthermore, they denied the larger *ᶜarab* tribes the, often self-acclaimed, right to levy protection money (*khuwwa*) from subordinate tribes and villages. The Egyptian authorities were by and large successful in containing the ᶜAnaza and other militant tribes.[53] The privileges enjoyed by the tribes who controlled tracks of the Sultanic Road between Damascus to the Hijaz were abolished.[54]

When in 1834 numerous revolts erupted in the Syrian provinces, the ᶜAnaza were quick to join. Several military campaigns were directed

[53] See, for tribal policies in general, Sâlim, *Ḥukm*, pp. 216–19 and for the Aleppo area, N. Lewis, *Nomads*, p. 38–39

[54] The payment of *ṣurra* to the Wuld ᶜAlî and the Banî Ṣakhr was stopped, see *Maḥfûẓât*, vol. 2, p. 383

against the tribes. Additional ᶜ*arab* forces were sent from Egypt and also the emir of the Mawâlî – and head of the tribes of Hama – participated in the campaigns. The employment of ᶜ*arab* forces was, of course, not unique and it is of interest that the forces of the Mawâlî emir, Muḥammad Khurfân, rendered vital police services in the steppe and desert. The Mawâlî chief was one of the principal provincial officers during the 1830s. He may not have had as autonomous a position as his predecessors once occupied, but his prominence in the military affairs of the Syrian interior reflects the revival of the Mawâlî at the expense of those who had pushed them to the margins of the Syrian desert, the ᶜAnaza tribes.[55] In late 1834 the migratory movements of the ᶜAnaza tribes were seriously restricted and they were prevented from collecting protection money. Violent tribal incidents became rare, although ᶜAnaza tribesmen raided an encampment of the Banî Khâlid and the Juhma tribes near Hama in 1837.[56] But normally the ᶜAnaza kept aloof, also because Hama served as one of the major garrison towns and occupied a strategic position in the almost perpetual movements of troops.

Measures to induce people to take up farming in (partly) abandoned places met with some success, but it was compulsory sedentarization of nomadic tribesmen and resettlement of peasants that supplied the necessary additional agricultural labour. The Egyptians induced or forced tribesmen to take up farming, but this policy only succeeded when they belonged to smaller, predominantly sheep rearing tribes.[57] Peasants from well-established villages were also compelled to settle in long abandoned places closer to or in the steppe, sometimes at gunpoint. Again others were forced to return to their recently deserted or impoverished village of origin, a neither new, nor undisputed measure.[58] As in the past, the settlers were provided with seeds, ploughs and ploughing animals and granted tax exemptions. Some took the opportunity to take possession of villages which were neither deserted,

[55] SMH 49, p. 569, 2 Dhû al-Ḥijja 1249; *Maḥfûẓât*, vol. 2, p. 427, n. 3564 and 3568, and vol. 3, p. 98, n. 4478. In the *Maḥfûẓât* the *amîr* Muḥammad Aghâ, later Bey, Khurfân, is referred to as Muḥammad '*aghat khaftân* (uncertain spelling) and head of the tribes of Hama'. See vol. 4, p. 82, n. 5836/10. *Aghat khaftân* may have been a title (Officer of the Robe), or it simply may have been a misspelling of his name. See also SMH 51, p. 44, 7 Shaᶜbân 1252

[56] SMH 50, p. 68, [Ṣafar 1253]

[57] For instance, in the villages of al-Jannân and ᶜIzz al-Dîn, both to the south of Hama, ᶜ*arab* settled, SMH 51, p. 156, 28 Shaᶜbân 1254

[58] See p. 157

nor assigned to them, among them the Danâdisha of the Tellkalakh area.[59] Forced investment of capital in agriculture constituted another instrument to stimulate the rural economy. More affluent Syrians were sometimes obliged to take an interest in the village economy. In the Hama area the families which entertained the strongest relations with the villages, in particular the ᶜAẓm, Kaylânî and Jijaklî families, continued to invest in the old villages, but were hardly engaged with the repopulated villages. The local *aghâ* who acted as *mutasallim* for several years during the decade, ᶜAbdallâh Aghâ Ṭayfûr also opted for the more secure investments in some large and well-established villages.[60] Their apparent reluctance to invest in these villages might well have been motivated by the insecure position of Egyptian rule. Surprisingly, the person who seems to have invested most in the (re-)cultivation of wasteland of Hama was the Mawâlî chief Muḥammad Khurfân Bey. Both Faraj Aghâ and his trustee ᶜUthmân Aghâ, too, were financially involved in repopulating villages, sometimes as partners of Muḥammad Khurfân Bey. In most of these villages to the east of the town the new settlers were *ᶜarab* of the Mawâlî, Nuᶜaym and ᶜUqaydât tribes.[61] However, the main drive for the expansion of agriculture came from the state itself.

Towards the end of Egyptian rule the area under cultivation in the Hama area showed an increase of no less than 60 per cent compared to 1831. The highest increase occurred in the area to the immediate south of the town.[62] When the current shortages of the human and animal labour as well as the high tax pressure are taken into consideration, this extension was indeed a great achievement. The conscription and the extensive use of forced labour constituted a heavy drain on the agricultural labour resources. The construction of large army barracks in Hama required the deployment of so many villagers that the then *mutasallim*, Faraj Aghâ, alarmed the authorities in Damascus, informing them that the village fields were being neglected.[63] The transport of the

[59] Sâlim, *Ḥukm*, pp. 145–46

[60] SMH 51, p. 365, [1257] and p. 439, 19 Jumâdâ II 1257. The villages involved are Kafr Buhum, Talldhahab, Talldû and Ḥalfâyâ

[61] SMH 51, p. 33, 9 Rajab 1252 (Talldara); p. 156, 28 Shawwâl 1254 (ᶜIzz al-Dîn, Abû Imâma); p. 165, [Shawwâl 1254] (al-Khuṣaymiyya); p. 167, 29 Shawwâl 1254 (Talldara). Muḥammad Khurfân also leased a large track of uncultivated *waqf* land of the village al-Jâjiyya, SMH 51, 44, 27 Shaᶜbân 1252

[62] SMH 51, pp. 316–317, [Rabîᶜ I] 1257

[63] *Uṣûl*, vol. 3, p. 3

harvest constituted an additional problem. The shortage of pack animals often caused the loss of large quantities of cereals, which were left on the threshing floor for too long.[64] During the last years of Egyptian rule the army appropriated high numbers of pack animals, rendering the transport of the crops even more problematic. At this time the movements of the Fadʿân, Ṣibaʿa and other large tribes in the ʿAnaza disquieted the Egyptian authorities and a new campaign was initiated.[65]

The contribution to the increase of the acreage and the revenue by the repopulated villages should not be exaggerated. Much of the expansion happened in those parts of the district where relatively large village communities existed and where more distant fields were brought under cultivation. In the Hama area approximately twenty ruined villages, including Salamiyya, were reoccupied, but – like elsewhere in the Syrian interior – most of these were small. It often concerned villages, which had been out of production for most of the Ottoman period or longer, but some had been deserted as recently as the late eighteenth century.[66] The newly established village communities proved to be fragile. The settlers, certainly those who had been forced to settle, were not nearly as devoted to farming in the difficult places. Many abandoned the newly cultivated land and returned home as soon as the Egyptians started leaving Syria. Another group of farmers of new fields, the *ʿarab* tribesmen adapted rather smoothly to the pastoralist lifestyle and most of them vacated the villages in the steppe in the early 1840s. Very few of the repopulated villages survived the 1840s, with the exception of some located close to Hama.[67] The Egyptian episode had not been a watershed in the history of inland Syria. For some years tribal pressure in the transitional zone had decreased, largely due to military efforts. However, the impact of the tribal shifts, which had started somewhere in the seventeenth century, continued to be felt well into the second half of the nineteenth century. It may have been primarily external forces which obliged Muḥammad ʿAlî Pasha to retreat, but many of the policies of the Egyptian regime in the Syrian provinces fell

[64] *Maḥfûẓât*, vol. 3, p. 121

[65] *Maḥfûẓât*, vol. 4, p. 50, 75 and 177

[66] Apart from Salamiyya, Talldara, Taqsîs, ʿAyn al-Bâd, ʿIzz al-Dîn, Abû Imâma, and al-ʿUshr were repopulated

[67] For instance, Taqsîs, situated on, bank of the ʿÂṣî River to the south of Hama, close to Murayj al-Durr. This village had been deserted in the closing years of the eighteenth century.

short of his expectations. In particular, the dilemma of inadequate resources was far from being solved. The systematic coercion of the Egyptian regime was far more expensive than the more arbitrary application of coercion, which characterized traditional Ottoman rule in Syria.

Conclusions

"We examined the registers and found excessive increases and illegal impositions which the people were unable to bear [. . .]. We abolish and nullify categorically all *maẓâlim* and toilsome liabilities; firstly the forced sale of cereals (to the army) for less than half of their value; secondly, the forced labour of drought animals and their acquisition without any proper compensation; subsequently, the [state patronage of] wine houses and other recent departures from law; and the confiscation of houses against the will of their owners, and all other inconveniences that the population had to endure [. . .]. From now on [. . .]. There will be no violations, no injustice, no perfidy, no intimidation, no oppression, in whatever way. We will treat the district of Hama with compassion and [. . .] impose half of the land tax of last year and half of the property tax [. . .]. The greatest compassion [of the splendid sultanate] is the lifting of these illegal impositions from the population (flock) and the salvation from these heavy burdens resting upon you [. . .]. All of you rush out to praise and thank [. . .] and graze on the pastures of the Sublime Court . . ."[1]

On their return to the Syrian provinces, the Ottoman authorities found a society which had suffered greatly from heavy fiscal, labour and war demands. Moreover, some time-honoured traditions had been questioned by the Egyptian authorities, like the legal inequality of non-Muslims and the taboo on the consumption of wine. Apart from these religiously sensitive issues, which were treated with circumspection by the Egyptians, more open and resolute breaches of tradition had been enforced upon the population. Above all the disarmament, which combined with the conscription of young men into the army, confronted Syrian society with the absolute claims of the modern state.

In the above order, dealing with the new fiscal regime for the Hama district, no mention is made of disarmament or conscription, but the order demonstrates clearly that the authorities were well aware of – at

[1] A fragment from an Ottoman order on the tax allotment for the Hama district after the evacuation of Egyptian troops, SMH 51, 3 Jumâdâ 1257, p. 426–8

least some of – the misgivings of the population. They, however, remained quiet on some of the major issues (disarmament, conscription, and emancipation of non-Muslims) but elaborated on many of the Egyptian reforms, in particular fiscal policies.

The political vocabulary of the order does not indicate that times were rapidly changing. The patriarchal and pastoral image of the sultanate which provides protection and grazing for the flocks, the subjects, reflects the pertinence of traditional Ottoman ideology. The two fundamental dilemmas of the traditional state, namely the recurrent inadequacy of the resources and the centrifugal effects of the delegation of power, had shaped Ottoman ideology. In Ottoman political theory these two problems were not insoluble, but the dangers they posed were clearly understood. The Ottoman solution held that the sultan and the servile military class, the *askeri*, created the conditions in which the subject population could prosper. In return, the subjects produced the wealth which enabled the sultan and the military to continue protecting the subjects. The sultan wielded absolute power and guaranteed the reign of justice – injustice being defined as the abuse of (delegated) power. This Circle of Justice defined the relations of power and exploitation in the empire. Evidently, the ideal proved difficult to uphold. In Ottoman political thinking the inadequacy of the resources, i.e. revenue problems, did not constitute an economic problem, but a political one. The solution was to be found in the restoration of justice, in the re-establishment and maintenance of the proper relations of power.

Delegation of power

The central Ottoman authority applied a variety of policy instruments aimed at the maintenance or strengthening of the dependency of provincial office-holders on the imperial centre. These policies included the rotation of the senior offices, the separation of powers and, at times, arbitrary intervention. Nonetheless, extensive powers continued to be delegated to the office-holders, in particular to the provincial governors, who in their turn delegated power to their representatives on the local level, like the *mutasallim*, the deputy governor in the districts. The delegation of considerable powers facilitated the exploitation of the province and enabled the office-holders to provide vital services, the most important being the collection of revenue, the protection of production and, in the case of inland Syria, the organization of the annual pilgrimage to Mecca. These extensive powers enabled the office-holders to tap sources in addition to the regular revenue. The responsibility of the state for the protection of the productive units and the distribution of the products provided the office-holders with the opportunity to engage in commercial enterprise and to enlarge their own income. Complaints against economic policies of governors, in particular against monopolistic measures and hoarding, curbed their freedom of action. Some of these policies were backed by normal practice and tradition rather than by law or sultanic approval. Office-holders in the provinces also applied various methods of income derivation which were explicitly denounced by the central authority, for instance the imposition of higher rates of existing taxes or the introduction of new charges. Blatantly coercive methods, like various techniques of outright extortion, were not uncommon, but excessive violent patterns of rule were less frequent than the episodes of Jazzâr Pasha and, perhaps, Muḥammad ᶜAlî Pasha suggest.

The provincial office-holders were caught in a budgetary net. The extraction of additional income was a necessity, because the official allocation of revenue was well below the actual expenses incurred by the governors and their inferiors. The central authority was most reluctant to concede that the allocation of revenue failed to cover the expenditure. From the point of view of the central authority, the policy of denying adequate regular funds to its servants in the provinces had two major advantages. Firstly, the handling of provincial and local budget deficits was left to the office-holders in the province. Secondly, the additional income derivation was not fully sanctioned, and consequently could serve as a pretext for the central authority to intervene and press its political and material claims. The method derived its relative efficiency from the strong dependency of office-holders on the powers which were delegated to them. The delegation could be terminated at will, and the office-holders were well aware of that danger.

From the point of view of the central authority the disadvantages of the system were also obvious. The deficiency of the mechanism of control offered office-holders the opportunity for manipulation and the actual or potential revenue of the province remained obscure. Consequently, the central authority showed a high degree of suspicion. The system facilitated the inclusion of local elements, the *aᶜyân*, in the ruling class. Moreover, non-local nominees also exploited the system and were at times able to create a strong local power base. Some local power groups even acquired a dynastic quality, like the military households of the ᶜAẓm family and that of Jazzâr Pasha and his *mamlûk* predecessors. On the one hand, these households had better resources and were more able to honour the material claims of the state and to perform vital services. Hence they were difficult to ignore. On the other hand, they had the capacity to act independently. The formation of independent power bases posed a danger to the absolute power of the sultan, although open challenges to the position of the sultan were rare and seldomly successful.

The predicament of the delegation of power was not solved. The limitations imposed on the function of office-holders failed to prevent the creation of self-reliant power groups. The rotation of the senior offices, for instance, helped to strengthen the dependency of the candidates on the imperial centre, but the use of this instrument of containment proved to be hazardous during the period of 1785–1812 in the Syrian provinces. It stimulated provincial rivalry to the extent that provincial rule became highly oppressive and violent. Local power became fragmented and proved difficult to control. Eventually, the participants exhausted their resources and their ability to act independently diminished. The demise of the inland provincial households gave way to a change in the recruitment pattern of the governors of Damascus in the second decade of the nineteenth century.

By that time the province of Damascus had lost its prominent position in the wider region. In the closing decades of the eighteenth century, with the emergence of the *mamlûk* household of Jazzâr Pasha of Acre, the political centre of gravity had already shifted from the Syrian interior to the coastal area. The rise of Egypt as a regional power further contributed to the relative marginalization of inland Syria. But the governorship of Damascus continued to play an important role in the regional politics. Jazzâr Pasha desperately attempted to annex Damascus to his dynastic realm and never succeeded. In fact, the central authority used the governorship of Damascus in its efforts to establish a higher degree of control over the strongman of Acre and his heirs.

Moreover, the province of Damascus remained of great strategic importance. The organization of the pilgrimage was the responsibility of the governor of Damascus and added to the prestige of the office. Access to the holy places had become highly problematic in the early 19th century when the Wahhâbî forces occupied the Hijaz, until Muḥammad ᶜAlî Pasha, the governor of Egypt, re-established Ottoman rule over the holy cities of Islam in 1812. The way the central authority utilized the governor of Egypt's abilities would prove to be highly precarious.

However, for the time being, the formation of this competing centre of power in the empire allowed the central state to appoint its nominees to the province of Damascus; the era of the ᶜAẓm household and related factions had come to a definite end.

Coercion and abuse of power

The Ottoman ruling class was called *askeri*, military; coercion played a crucial role on most levels of administration. When and where other policy measures failed, the use of force constituted the familiar remedy. The military constituted the dominant group in the provincial and local administration. The other main group of office-holders, those who derived their position from religious learning, clearly wielded less power. However, the military were in more vulnerable position, due to their strong reliance on delegated power. The career of a military office-holder could end abruptly with his execution or death on the battlefield. Some *aghawât* were able to make a quick career and establish themselves firmly in the administration. The more illustrious examples are the soldiers who achieved the status of pasha. No less than five of the six governors of Damascus who served during the period of 1785–1812 had started their career as soldiers. But this was also the period in which the soldier's occupation, violence, proved to be high-risk.

The religious office-holders occupied a more secure position, because they derived their authority, or at least a considerable part of it, from a different source. They were the custodians of the Islamic tradition, and by extension of the local values. Moreover, the sultanic claim that its authority was God-given gave the religious establishment legitimating power. The Ottomans did not rule without a degree of consent. Consequently, the religious *aᶜyân* were less exposed to coercive action than any other group in the empire. The vicissitudes of members of the two most prominent families of the town of Hama, the ᶜAẓm and Kaylânî, clearly demonstrate that the *aghawât* of the ᶜAẓm were more exposed to changes in the relations of power in the province or the empire at large, when compared to the Kaylânî ulema. The brutal treatment of several Damascene ulema by Jazzâr Pasha was exceptional and contributed to his reputation as extremely oppressive. However, it did demonstrate that in the end the sword wielded more power than the book.

Coercion may have been a reasonably effective policy, but in traditional Ottoman rule it had a marked arbitrary aspect. This may be explained from the lack of co-ordination and the failing mechanisms of control. Arbitrariness may be an efficient instrument of coercion, however, it is difficult to combine with legitimization. In the late eighteenth and early nineteenth centuries this deficiency in the system became painfully manifest. The services of specialists of violence, like Jazzâr Pasha and Mullâ Ismâᶜîl, were in high demand, but they proved to be difficult to contain.

When applied in a concerted and consistent manner, coercion appeared to be a sound solution for the dilemma of the delegation of power, as was demonstrated in the decade of Egyptian rule over Syria. It was only during these years that coercion acquired a high degree of predictability. Coercion became much more persuasive; disarmament and massive employment of troops all over the provinces made the population more vulnerable, while conscription for the army made local society part of the coercion complex. In this sense, Egyptian rule may be called modern, but in the perception of the majority of the Syrian population this feature of Egyptian rule constituted the ultimate manifestation of injustice.

Resources

Coercion was an expensive policy instrument. Governors like Jazzâr Pasha, Kunj Yûsuf Pasha and others invested heavily in the military and by doing so exhausted their means. The fragmentation of power and the extremely violent application of coercive measures around 1800 impacted upon both the rural and urban economy. The village economy of the Syrian interior had been under strong tribal pressure for some time, due to the displacement of Mawâlî and other ᶜ*arab* tribes, but land and village desertion was caused primarily by the over-exploitation of the peasantry, to the extent that their subsistence was endangered. Significantly, village desertion occurred as well in areas which were less, or not, exposed to tribal pressure. Moreover, even a number of provincial towns suffered from population flight caused by episodes of extreme oppressive rule, for instance Hama and Acre. With the subsidence of violent provincial factionalism the village economy recovered and showed a remarkable endurance, at least in the district of Hama, during the second decade of the nineteenth century, notwithstanding the arrival of the large ᶜAnaza tribes. However, this is not to say that the resources became adequate; on the contrary, in the course of the 1820's in the wake of wars and military reform the financial needs of the empire sharply increased.

The military spending by Jazzâr Pasha and was minute in comparison to by that of Muḥammad ᶜAlî Pasha. The governor of Egypt may have solved the problem of the delegation of power, but he was unable to find a solution for the inadequacy of the resources. The occupation of the Syrian provinces in 1831–2, although intended as such, did not resolve his material predicament. Of course, a number of complications frustrated his efforts, in particular the unwillingness of the major European power, Great Britain, to allow the formation of a new Muslim empire and certainly one which attempted to create its own industrial base. However, apart from the ill-fated encounter with the major capitalist power, the Egyptian regime's policies of exploitation were in line with the traditional Ottoman economic concepts in which the state was both the regulator and beneficiary of the economic activities. Coercion played a prominent role in the economic policies of the Egyptian regime. In addition to forced settlement and labour services, the coercive traits manifested themselves in the conscription for the army, which constituted a further drain on the resources of Syrian society. In the end, the Egyptians resorted to force in order to solve revenue problems. This traditional mechanism further contributed to the perception of the regime as highly unjust.

Nevertheless, in the light of the Ottoman ideal of the Circle of Equity, the efforts of the Egyptian regime in Syria were quite remarkable. This achievement was acknowledged in the imperial centre. Not only proper relations of power were established, but the subjects prospered as well, in the sense that they produced considerable wealth compared to the previous periods. By the late eighteenth century, the Circle had been broken. The conduct of the military had caused massive village desertion. Tribal pressure had aggravated the predicament of a sedentary, agricultural society. With the cessation of violent factionalism during the second and third decades of the nineteenth century the condition of the villages of the Syrian interior improved, but the rural economy remained fragile. In contrast, during the decade of Egyptian rule the area under cultivation increased significantly and even some *ᶜarab* committed themselves to settled farming. However, from the point of view of the central authority, the Circle was not complete. It lacked the legitimacy of that vital chain of God-given sultanic authority, and hence Egyptian rule could, indeed, only be regarded as unjust.

Glossary

ᶜâda	local custom, customary law
aghâ	military title (commander, lord)
aghawât	plural of *aghâ*
akâbir	dignitaries
amîn al-fatâwâ	record keeper of *fatwâs*
amîr	title (emir, prince, lord)
amîr al-bâdiya	Lord of the Desert
amîr al-ḥajj	commander of the pilgrimage
amwâl	see *mâl*
anbâr	granary
anbarjî	keeper of the granary
ᶜarab	Arabic speaking pastoralists, beduin
arbâb al-fasâd	corrupt officials, rebels
arḍ	arable field
ᶜashâyir al-dâyira	local *ᶜarab* tribes
ᶜashîra	kinship group, tribe
askeri	Ottoman ruling class
atbâᶜ	following, clients
ᶜawâyid	levies for the support of office-holders
awlâd al-ᶜarab	urban Arab
ayanlik	
aᶜyân	notables (participating in local government)
bâdiya	desert, wasteland
başbuğ al-jarda	commander of the *jarda*
bashâyir	good tidings, tax (*takâlîf*)
bey	military title
bey-i büyük	head of the Turcoman *aghawât*
buyuruldu	edict
dalâtiyya	see *deli*
dawlat Dimashq	local janissaries (Damascus)
dawlat al-qalᶜa	imperial janissaries (Damascus)
dâyira	migratory cycle

deli	cavalryman, auxiliary
delibaşı	commander of *deli* forces
devlet	state, dynastic rule
dîwân	council
dizdar	commander of a fortress, see *muḥâfiẓ*
efendi	honourary title for ulema
faddân	land measure
fâ'id	interest (on loans)
fatwâ	legal opinion (see *muftî* and *iftâ'*)
garib yiğit	cavalry, janissaries
garib yiğit ağası	commander of the cavalry
ḥaḍar	sedentary society
ḥajj	yearly pilgrimage to Mecca
ḥâkim	ruler, judge
ḥâkim al-sharᶜ	see *qâḍî*
hâkim al-ᶜurf	governor
hudud (ḥudûd)	Bounds
ḥujja	judicial or noterized deed
iᶜâna	support, tax on real estate
ᶜîdiyya	gift, tax (*takâlîf*)
iftâ'	jurisconsultancy
iḥtisâb	market inspection, market dues
jamâᶜa	following
jarda	troops carrying provisions to the *ḥajj* convoy
kapikulu	imperial janissaries
kâtib	scribe
kâtib khazîna	scribe of treasury
kâtib sancak	district scribe
khân	
khazîna ᶜâmira	treasury
khuwwa	protection money
maḥkama	religious court
majlis al-sharᶜ	*maḥkama*
mâl	tax, payment
mâl kayânis	church tax
mâl muwassaṭa	tax, payment to the Mawâlî chief

mâl qaṣṣâbkhâna	slaughterhouse rights
malikane	leasehold for life, tax farm
mamlûk	white male slave-soldier
manzilkhâna	(postal) resthouse
mashâyikh	plural of *shaykh*
mashâyikh al-ḥajj	religious dignitaries accompaning the *ḥajj*
mazraᶜa	farm, semi-permanent agricultural settlement
mirahur	master of the horse
mîr	see *amîr*, Ismâᶜîlî chief
mîrî	state-owned, tax
mirmiran	governor-general
muᶜallim	title, Christian office-holder
muftî	jurisconsult
muḥâfiẓ	watchman, janissaries manning fortresses
muḥaṣṣil	tax collector in chief
müjdeci başı	chief emissary
muqaddam	title, Nuṣayrî chief
muqâṭaᶜa	tax farm
murattabât	impositions
murattabât Ḥijâziyya	equivalent to takâlîf
mutasallim	district governor or deputy governor
mutawallî	administrator of *waqf* estates
naqîb al-ashrâf	head of the descendants of the prophet
niẓâm	standing army
odabaşı	commander of the barracks, janissary
qabîqûl	imperial janissaries
qaḍâ'	jurisdiction of the *qâḍî*
qâḍî	judge
qaṣṣâbkhâna	slaughterhouse
qassâmiyya	collectors of the *qism*
qâyimmaqâm	deputy governor
qûl	see *qabîqûl*
reaya	subject classes
rusûmât	duties on importsn
sakabaşı	official in charge of water supply to pilgrims
salâmiyya	safe arrival, tax (*takâlîf*)
ṣalyân	yearly payment, tax

samniyya	tax on (the sale of) animal fat
sancak	district
sarâyâ	headquarter of the mutasallim
ṣarr	payments to tribes (*ḥajj*)
ṣarrâf	cashier of the treasury
serkerder	military title, head of the Mawâlî tribes
shâhid	witness, see also *shuhûd al-ḥâl*
sharᶜ	Islamic law
shawâyâ	sheep rearing *ᶜarab*
shaykh	title, sheikh, head, religious dignitary
shaykh al-islam	supreme *muftî*
shaykh al-sajjâda	head of a religious order
shuhûd al-ḥâl	witnesses assenting a *ḥujja*
sijill	register
sûq	market
ṣurra	see *ṣarr*
sürre	payments to the dignitaries and poor of Mecca
sürre emini	official in charge of the *sürre*
tâjir	merchant
takâlîf	taxes to cover expenses of the *ḥajj*
taṣarruf	right to usufruct
tüfenkçi	musketeer
tüfenkçi başı	commander of the musketeers
tujjâr	plural of *tâjir*
umarâ'	plural *amîr*
ᶜurf	sultanic law
wakîl al-kharj	superintendent of expenditures
wâlî	governor-general
waqf	religious or family foundation
waqfiyya	charter of a *waqf*
wâqif	founder of a *waqf*
ẓulm	injustice, oppression
zûr	irrigated field

Annex 1

ᶜ*Arab* tribes in 1245

1. ᶜ*ashâyir dâyirat Ḥamâ:* the tribes of the local cycle
(following the order of entry in the tax tabulation)

source: SMH 49, p. 250-2, dated 1245 and p. 326-9, 23 Rabîᶜ I 1245

A: tax payments to the treasury entered in cash (q.)
B: exactions by Faraj Aghâ and his retinue (q.)

tribe	A	B
Banî Khâlid	5700	7132
Nuᶜaym	6100	7754
Bashâkim	4050	9715
Ṭûqân	2050	3830
ᶜUqaydât	2250	9650
Banî ᶜIzz incl. Mashârifa	2850	6302
Fawâᶜira	3250	4955
Zurayq	2750	3350
Maᶜâqîr	2650	1380
Abû Ṣalîba	1150	2330
Kharâshin	2050	4240
Ḥuwayziyya	1850	2065
Shaqar	1150	-
Nabîṭ	2175	60
Ruṭûb	1300	1720
Abû Ḥayya	1850	1715
Ḥazûmîn	1400	2475
Shukr	1300	1410
Shaᶜar	1050	-
Ḥawârîn	600	145
Abû ᶜÂṣî	475	-
Shatîḥât	350	235
ᶜUwayshât	300	-
ᶜIzz al-Dîn	1400	3960

2. Other tribes frequenting the Hama area

Khuṭabâ	-	655
Jumlân	-	7150
Abû Ḥusayn	-	500
Jamâjima	-	-
Turkî	-	-
Ḥasana	-	-
Sibaᶜa	-	-
Fadᶜân	-	-
	51,400	82,728

The tribes were liable to the proportional *aᶜdâd ghanam*, as well as to several smaller impositions, like the *samniyya* (tax on animal fat), *kiṣlak* (winter camping fee) and *qayẓiyya* (summer camping fee).

Annex 2

The *ḥâṣil* villages in 1245
(following the order of entry in the tax tabulation)

source: SMH 49, p. 250-2, dated 1245 and p. 326-9, 23 Rabîʿ I 1245

A: village name
B: village size in number of *faddân*
number of *faddân mashâyikh** in between brackets
C: cash payment to the treasury (*mâl faddân*)
D: exactions by Faraj Aghâ and his retinue

A	B	C	D
1. Maʿardas	27 (3)	1,320	4,720
2. Mûrik	23 (3)	1,100	1,312
3. Kafr Zaytî	47 (4)	4,730	4,634
4. Khaṭâb	55 (4)	5,610	2,910
5. Ṭayyibat al-Aʿlâ	65 (4)	6,380	4,850
6. Laṭmîn	84 (6)	8,250	4,903
7. Kurnâz	29 (2)	2,970	450
8. Ṣûrân	24 (3)	1,155	4,390
9. Shayzar	25 (2)	2,530	6,897
10. Talîl	20 (2)	1,980	2,411
11. Mḥarda	46 (3)	4,730	13,250
12. Kafr Buhum	72 (4)	7,480	10,936
13. Aṣîla	18	1,980	-
14. Ḥalfâyâ	44 (4)	4,400	4,446
15. Akrâd Ibrâhîm	50 (2)	5,280	2,127
16. Kâzû	25 (2)	2,530	-
17. Albiyya	58 (2)	6,160	-
18. Maʿrîn	25 (2)	2,530	350
19. Umm Qanṭara	8	880	-
20. Îghûr al-Gharbî	30 (2)	3,080	5,160
21. Abû al-Rubayṣ	10 (1)	880	-
22. Ḥarbinafsa	29 (1)	2,970	1,160
23. Sîghâtâ	18 (1)	1,870	-

24. Kafr Qadḥ	11	1,210	1,150
25. Tall Sakkîn	10	990	245
26. al-Shîḥâ	18	1,980	1,403
27. Akrâd al-Dayâsina	20	2,200	2,080
28. Kafr al-Ṭûn	30 (2)	3,080	1,480
29. Qumḥâna	67 (4)	6,600	4,400
30. Ṭayyibat al-Gharbî	33 (1)	3,190	6,840
31. Taqḍîn	10	770	313
32. Bsîrîn	12 (1)	1,210	878
33. al-Julma	8	880	330
34. Miṣîn	11 (1)	1,100	-
35. Kafr ᶜAmîm	8 (1)	770	-
36. Ḥayâlîn	8	880	645
37. Dayr al-Firdîs	25 (1)	2,640	718
38. Talldû	86 (3)	9,130	35,350
39. Tîzîn	46 (2)	4,840	4,725
40. Naqârina	19 (1)	1,980	1,435
41. al-Rabîᶜa	41 (3)	4,180	-
42. al-Khâlidiyya	8	880	-
43. Maᶜarzâf	15 (1)	1,540	1,480
44. Tarîmsa	4	440	70
45. Ṣahriyya	18	1,980	-
46. al-Raqîṭa	19 (1)	1,980	1,815
47. al-Mughayyar	12 (1)	1,210	300
48. ᶜAmûrîn	10 (1)	990	420
49. al-ᶜUwayna	17 (2)	1,650	-
50. Kafr Lâhâ	80 (3)	8,470	28,291
51. al-Majdal	8	880	-
52. Talldhahab	65 (2)	6,930	17,563
53. Dîmû	17	1,870	1,210
54. Qîrâtâ	7	770	-
55. Arza	5	550	-
56. Kafr Nabûda	16 (2)	1,540	190
57. Arḍ al-Hâmid	12 (1)	1,210	80
58. Arḍ al-Bâd	(1)	880	-
59. Arḍ Ḥasaniyyât	10 (1)	990	60
60. Zalâqiyyât	7 (1)	660	-
61. (Arḍ) Jabrîn	10 (1)	990	-
62. Iyyû	6	660	-
63. Burnâ	16 (2)	1,540	-
64. Daᶜnân	10	1,100	-
65. Samᶜalîl	14 (1)	1,430	-
66. al-Tuwaym	8 (2)	660	-

67. al-ᶜJarniyya	6 (1)	550	-
68. al-ᶜArîḍ	6	330	520
69. Kafr Yahûd	4	220	405
70. Tall Milḥ	10	450	148
71. Ṣalbâ	6	150	-
72. Basqilla	7 (1)	300	-
73. al-ᶜAshârina	18	1,980	-

* No taxes rested upon the *faddân mashâyikh.* The yields of this land served as a compensation for the expenses of the village sheikh.

Annex 3

Maqtu^{c} villages and farms
(following the order of entry in the tax tabulation)

source: SMH 49, p. 250-2, dated 1245 and p. 326-9, 23 Rabî^{c} I 1245

A: village or farm
B: number of *faddân*
(*faddân mashâyikh*)
C: *mîrî*
D: *mâl faddân*
E: exactions by Faraj Aghâ and his retinue

A	B	C	D	E
1. Kafr Nân	20 (1)	115	1900	-
2. Kîsîn	16 (1)	300	1500	80
Ma^{c}ar Jafna				
3. Qa^{c}ya	7 (1)	103	600	260
4. Jadrîn	10	206	700	62
5. Kafr Lâm	13	412	1300	
6. Dayr Sunbul	3.5	100	350	
7. al-Maw^{c}a	10 (2)	500	800	
8. Dayr al-Ṣalib	50 (3)	928	4700	1601
Rab^{c}û				
Jarrâda				
9. Bîsîn	26 (2)	257	2400	1100
10. Dayr Ḥuwayt	14 (1)	100	1300	150
11. Umm al-Ṭuyûr	20 (2)	154	1800	470
12. Ḥuwayr	10 (1)	175	900	-
Baḥra				
13. Balîn	5	175	500	140
Bajja				
14. Squlaybiyya	12 (1)	100	1100	-
15. al-Jaf^{c}a	5 (1)	?	400	-
		3,625	20,250	3,863

Annex 4

Turcoman villages
(following the order of entry in the tax tabulation)

source: SMH 49, p. 250-2, dated 1245 and p. 326-9, 23 Rabîᶜ I 1245

A: village/tribe*
B: number of *faddân*
(*faddân mashâyikh*)
C: *mâl faddân*
D: exactions by Faraj Aghâ and his retinue

A	B	C	D
1. al-Bayâḍiyya	19 (1)	4,050	1,350
2. al-Bakmashliyya	13 (1)	2,700	854
3. al-Tumkhurliyya*	51 (4)	10,575	1,609
Ṭillif			
al-Madḥ	-		
Maṭar al-Khûla	-		
4. Qirra Khalîliyya*	49 (3)	10,350	7,380
ᶜAqrab			
Ik'ûna	-		
5. Qirra Dûkar	14 (2)	2,250	1,138
6. Âq Dûkar	16 (1)	3,375	-
7. al-Qanqaliyya	15 (1)	3,150	-
8. al-Sharqaliyya	12 (2)	2,250	-
9. Jarjîsiyya	21 (1)	4,500	397
10. al-ᶜAlbiyya*	37 (2)	7,000	-
al-Jumqaliyya	-		
Barâq	-		
11. al-Jalîqaliyya*	36 (4)	7,200	800
Murayj al-Durr			
Ighûr al-ᶜÂṣî	-		
12. Bîrîn	11	2,200	840
13. al-Suwayda	10	2,700	-
14. Qarṭal	8	-	
		45,232	14,368

Annex 5

Jabal al-Gharbî in 1245
(following the order of entry in the tax tabulation)

source: SMH 49, p. 250-2, dated 1245 and p. 326-9, 23 Rabîᶜ I 1245

A: village
B: *takâlîf* in reduced rates
(*takâlîf* in 1233)
C: exactions by Faraj Aghâ and his retinue

A	B	C
1. Nîşâf	7,250 (9,250)	14,969
Al-Ḥaydariyya		
2. Fâḥil	7,250 (9,250)	11,200
3. Kafr Kamra	7,250 (9,250)	14,969
4. Maryamîn	7,250 (8,865)	6,110
(Qîrâṭâ)		
Qurmuş	4,580	
Bazza		
5. Bᶜamra	3,625 (4,625)	3,080
6. Bshînîn	3,625 (4,625)	5,100
7. Khirbat al-Qabû	3,625 (4,625)	5,100
8. Qaşrâyâ	2,352 (3,468)	
9. Khanîzîr	906 (1,156)	3,080
10. ᶜAkâkîr	1,812 (2,312)	3,080
11. al-Shanniyya	1,273 (1,541)	1,550
12. Tansâ	906 (1,156)	
	47,125	72,818
mîrî	17,158	
tot.	64,283	

Annex 6

Quṭuniyyât villages

source: SMH 49, p. 250-2, dated 1245 and p. 326-9, 23 Rabîᶜ I 1245

A: villages
B: number of *faddân*
(faddân mashâyikh)
C: *mâl faddân*
D: exactions by Faraj Aghâ and his retinue

A	B	C	D
1. al-Ḍâhiriyya	22 (2)	4950	-
2. al-Dajâjiyya	20 (2)	4500	510
3. Sarîḥîn	19 (2)	4275	2139

Bibliography

Documents

CE: Correspondance avec les Echelles, Beyrouth, carton 44, 53, 132 and 142, Les Archives Diplomatiques de Nantes (ADN), Nantes

FO: Foreign Office,, series 195, Public Record Office, Kew

SMH: Sijillât al-Maḥkama al-Sharʿiyya, Ḥamâ, vols. 43, 46, 48-53, 57. Markaz al-Wathâ'iq al-Târîkhiyya Centre for Historical Documentation), Damascus

Chronicles, documents and travel accounts

al-ʿAbd, Ḥ. A., *Târîkh Ḥasan Aghâ al-ʿAbd.* ed. Y.J. Nuʿaysa, Damascus 1979

Athâr al-ḥiqab fî Ladhiqiyyat al-ʿArab, 3 vols., private collection, Latakia (Syria), unfinished and undated manuscript [prob. 1882]

ʿAwra, Ibrâhîm, *Târîkh Sulaymân Pasha al-ʿÂdil*, ed Qustantîn al-Khûrî, Beirut 1936

al-Baṣrî, ʿUthmân, *Mukhtaṣar Târîkh ʿUthmân ibn Ṣanad al-Baṣrî*, ed. Amîn Hasan, Bombay 1887

Brown, W.G., *Travels in Africa, Egypt, and Syria, from 1792 to 1798*, London 1806

Buckingham, J.S., *Travels among the Arab tribes inhabiting the countries east of Syria and Palestine*, London 1825

al-Budayrî, al-Ḥallâq, A., *Ḥawâdith Dimashq al-Yawmiyya.* ed. A.ʿI. ʿAbd al-Karîm, Cairo 1959

Burayk, al-Khûrî, M., *Târîkh al-Sham.* ed. A.Gh. Sabânû, Damascus 1982

Burckhardt, J.L., *Travels in Syria and the Holy Land*, London 1822

-, *Notes on the bedouins and Wahabys*, 2 vols., London 1831

de Corancez, L.A., *Histoire des Wahabis, Depuis Leur Origine Jusqu'à la Fin de 1809*, Paris 1810

Dahlân, Aḥmad, *Khulâṣat al-Kalâm fî Bayyân Umarâ'al-Balad al-Ḥarâm*, ed Ishik Kitabevi, Istanbul 1980

al-Dimashqî, M., *Târîkh Ḥawâdith al-Shâm wa-Lubnân*, ed. A.GH. Sabânû, Damascus 1982

al-Jabartî, ʿAbd al-Rahmân, *ʿAjâ'ib al-Athâr fî al-Tarâjim wa-l-Akhbâr*, ed. H.M. Jawhar, U. al-Dasûqî and I Sâlim, 7 vols, Cairo, 1958-1967

al-Jumayma, ʿA.-M., *al-Jays al-Miṣrî wa-Fataḥ ʿAkkâ*, 1831-1832, Cairo 1987

Ibn Khaldûn, *The Muqaddimah*, trans. F. Rosenthal, 3 vols., Princeton 1958

Ibn al-Siddîq, Ḥ, *Gharâ'ib al-Bidâ'iᶜ wa-l-ᶜAjâ'ib al-Waqâ'iᶜ*, ed. Y. Nuᶜaysa, Damascus nd

al-Khûrî, I.T., *Muṣṭafâ Aghâ Barbar, Ḥâkim Ṭarâblus wa-l-Lâdhiqiyya*, Tripoli 1985

al-Maḥfûẓât al-Malakiyya al-Miṣriyya. Bayân bi-Wathâ'iq al-Shâm, ed. A. Rustum, 4 vols., Beirut 1940-1943

al-Makkî, M., *Târîkh Ḥimṣ, Yawmiyyât*, ed. ᶜU.N. ᶜUmar, Damascus 1987

Mishâqa, M., *Kitâb Mashhad al-ᶜAyân bi-Hawâdith Sûriyâ wa-Lubnân*, ed. M.Kh. ᶜAbdû and A.H. Shakhâshîr, Cairo 1908

Mudhakkirât târîkhiyya ᶜan Ḥamlat Ibrâhîm Bâshâ ᶜalâ Sûriyâ. ed. A.Gh. Sabûnî, Damascus n.d.

al-Munayyir, Ḥ, *al-Durr al-Marsûf fî Târîkh al-Shûf*, Beirut 1984

al-Murâdî, M.Kh. *Silk al-Durar fî Aᶜyân al-Qarn al-Thânî ᶜAshar*, 4 vols., Bulaq 1301 A.H.

al-Nâbulsî, ᶜA.-Gh., *Kitâb ᶜAlam al-Milâḥa fî ᶜIlm al-fIlâḥa*, n.ed., Beyrout 1979

-, *al-Ḥaqîqa wa-l-Majâz fî al-Riḥla ilâ Bilâd al-Shâm wa-Miṣr wa-l-Ḥijâz*, ed. A.ᶜA.M. Huraydî, n.p., 1987

Pockocke, R., *A Description of the East and some other Countries*, 3 vols., London 1745

Robinson, E. and Smith, E., *Biblical Researches in Palestine. A journal of travels in the year 1838*, 3 vols., London 1841

Russell, A., *The Natural History of Aleppo*, London 1794

al-Ṣâbûnî, M., *Târîkh Hamâ*, n.ed., Ḥamâ, n.d.

al-Sâyigh, Fatḥ Allah, *Al-Muqtarab fî Ḥawâdith al-Ḥaḍar wa-l-ᶜArab*, Latakia 1843, Fonds arabe 1658, Bibliothèque Nationale, Paris

Seetzen, U.J., *Reisen durch Syrien, Palästina, Phönicien, die Transjordan-Länder, Arabia Petraea und Unter-Aegypten*, 3 vols., Berlin, 1854

al-Shaṭṭî, M.J. *Rawḍ al-Bashar fî Aᶜyân Dimashq fî al-Qarn al-Thâlith ᶜAshar*, Damascus 1972

al-Shihâb, Ḥ.A., *Lubnân fî ᶜAhd al-Umarâ' al-Shihâbiyyîn*, 3 vols., ed. A. Rustum and F.E. al-Bustânî, Beirut 1984

Usûl al-ᶜArabiyya li-Târîkh Sûriyya fî ᶜAhd Muḥammad ᶜAlî Bâshâ, ed. A. Rustum, 5 vols., Beirut 1930-1933

Wathâ'iq Muqaddisiyyah Târîkhiyya, vol. 3, ed. al-ᶜAsalî K.J., ᶜAmmân 1989

Volney C.-F., *Voyage en Égypte et en Syrie, pendant les années 1783, 1784 et 1785: suivi de considérations sur la guerre des Russes et des Turks*, 2 vols. Paris 1792

Monographies and articles

ᶜAbd al-Munᶜim, Ḥ., *Dîwân al-Maẓâlim*, Beirut 1981

ᶜAbd al-Rahîm, ᶜA.ᶜA., *al-Rîf al-Miṣrî fî al-qarn al-thâmin ᶜashar*, Cairo 1986

Abdel Nour, A., "Traits et conflicts du monde rurale Syrien au XVIIIe siècle d'après les *fatwa* de Ḥâmid al-ᶜImâdî", *Mélanges de l'Université Saint-Joseph*, 50 (1984), p. 71-84

Abou-El-Haj, R.A., *Formation of the Modern State. The Ottoman Empire, Sixteenth to Eighteenth Centuries*, Albanu 1991

Abu Husayn, A.R., *Provincial leaderships in Syria, 1575-1650.* Beirut 1985

Abu-Manneh, B., "The Husaynis: the rise of a notable family in 18th century Palestine", in Kushner (ed.), p. 94-107

al-ᶜAẓm, ᶜA.-Q., *al-Usra al-ᶜAẓmiyya*, Damascus 1960

Azmeh A. al-, *Muslim Kingship: Power and the Sacred in Muslim, Christian and Pagan Polities*, London 1997

Aladdin, B., "Deux Fatwâ-s du Šayḫ ᶜAbd al-Ġanî al-Nâbulsî (1143/1731). Présentation et édition critique", *Bulletin d'Études Orientales* 39-40 (1987-88), p. 9-37

Anderlind, L., "Ackerbau und Thierzucht in Syrien, insbesondere in Palästina", *Zeitschrift des deutchen Palästina-Vereins* 9 (1886), p. 1-73

Asᶜad, M.ᶜI., *Târîkh Ḥimṣ*, 2 vol., Homs 1984

Baer, G., "The administrative, economic and social functions of Turkish guilds", *International Journal of Middle East Studies* 1 (1970), p. 28-50

-, *Fellah and Townsman in the Middle East. Studies in Social History*, London, 1982

-, "Jerusalem's families of notables and the wakf in the early 19th Century", in Kushner (ed.), p. 109-122

Bakhit, M.A., *The Ottoman Province of Damascus in the 16th Century.* Beirut 1982

Barbir, K.K., *Ottoman Rule in Damascus, 1708-1758*, Princeton 1980

-, "Wealth, privilege and family structure: the *ᶜaskarî*s of 18th century Damascus according to the *qassâm ᶜaskarî*s inheritance records", in Philipp (ed.), p. 179-96

Barkey, K., *Bandits and Bureaucrats. The Ottoman Route of State Centralization*, Ithaca N.Y. 1994

Barnes, J.R., *An Introduction to Religious Foundations in the Ottoman Empire*, Leiden 1986

Berque, J. et Chevallier, D. (eds.), *Les Arabes par Leurs Archives, XVIe-XXe siècles*, Paris 1976

Berktay, H. and Faroqhi, S., *New Approaches to State and Peasant in Ottoman History*, London 1992

Bodman, H., *Political factions in Aleppo, 1760-1826*, Chapel Hill 1963

Braudel, F. *Civilization and Capitalism, 15th-18th century.* vol. 3, *The Perspective of the World*, London 1985

Brockelmann, C. *Geschichte der arabischen Literatur*, 2 vols, Leiden, 1943; suppl., 3 vols., 1937-1942

Cameron, A., *The Mediterranean World in Late Antiquity*, AD 395-600, London 1993

Chaudhuri, K.N., *Asia before Europe. Economy and Civilisation of the Indian Ocean from the rise of Islam to 1750*, Cambridge 1990

Chevallier, D. (ed.), *L'Espace Social de la Ville Arabe*, Paris 1979

Cohen, A., *Palestine in the 18th century*, Jerusalem 1973

-, *Economic Life in Ottoman Jerusalem*, Cambridge 1989

Cohen, A. and Lewis, B., *Population and Revenue in the Towns of Palestine in the Sixteenth Century*, Princeton 1978

Crecelius, D.N., *The Roots of Modern Egypt. A Study of the Regimes of ʿAli Bey al-Kabir and Muhammad Bey Abu al-Dhahab, 1760-1775*, Minneapolis 1981

-, "Egypt's Reawaking Interest in Palestine during the Regimes of ʿAli Bey al-Kabir and Muḥammad Bey Abû al-Dhahab, 1760-1775", in Kushner (ed.), p. 247-262

Crone, P., *Pre-industrial Societies*, Oxford 1989

Cuno, K.M., *The Pasha's Peasants. Land, Society and Economy in Lower Egypt, 1740-1858*, Cambridge 1992

Darling, L., *Revenue-Raising and Legitimacy; Tax Collection and Finance Administartion in the Ottoman Empire, 1560-1660*, Leiden 1996

Deringil, S., *The Well-Protected Domains; Ideology and the Legitimation of Power in the Ottoman Empire, 1876-1909*, London 1998

Doumani B., *Rediscovering Palestine : merchants and peasants in Jabal Nablus, 1700-1900*, Berkeley 1995

Doumani, B.B., "Palestinian Islamic court records: a source for socioeconomic history", *MESA bulletin* 19 (1985), p. 155-72

Douwes, D. "Knowledge and Oppression; the Nuṣayriyya in the late Ottoman Period", in *La Shīʿa nell'impero ottomano*, Roma 1993

Douwes, D. and Lewis, N.N., "The Trials of the Ismailis of Syria in the First Decade of the 20th Century", *International Journal of Middle East Studies* 21 (1989), p. 215-32

-, "Taxation and Agriculture in the District of Hama, 1800-1831. New Material from the Records of the Religious Court", in Philipp (ed.), p. 261-79

EI2, *Encyclodaedia of Islam*, 2nd edition, Leiden 1954-

Eisenstadt, S.N., *The Political Systems of Empires*, New York 1963

Fahmi, Kh., *All the Pasha's Men; Mehmed Ali, his Army and the Making of Modern Egypt*, Cambridge 1997

Faroqhi, S., McGowan, B., Quartaert, D. and Pamuk, Ş., (eds.) *An Economic and Social History of the Ottoman Empire*, 2. vols., Cambridge USA 1994

Findley, C., *Bureaucratic Reform in the Ottoman Empire*, Princeton 1980

Frank, C. A., *The Transformation of Rural Society. The Syrian Interior 1830-1930*, Ph.D University of Oxford, 1989

Gaulmier, J., "Pèlerinages Populaires à Hama", *Bulletin d'études orientales* 1 (1931), p. 137-52

-, "Notes sur la Proprieté Foncière dans la Syrie Centrale", *L'Asie Française* 309 (1933), p. 130-37

Gellner, E., *Nations and Nationalism*, Oxford 1983

-, *Plough, Sword and Book. The Structure of Human History*, London 1988

Gerber, H., *Social Origins of the Modern Middle East*, Boulder 1987

-, *State, Society, and Law in Islam : Ottoman Law in Comparative Perspective*, Albany 1994

Gibb, H.A.R. and Bowen, H., *Islamic Society and the West (vol. 1) Islamic society in the Eighteenth Century*, 2 parts, London 1950

Göçek, F.M., *Rise of the Bourgeoisie*, Demise of Empire, New York 1996

Ḥamûd, N.R., *al-ᶜAskar fî Bilâd al-Shâm fî al-qarn al-sâdis ᶜashar w-l-sâbiᶜ ᶜashar*, Beirut n.d.

Hansen, B., 1981, "An Economic Model for Ottoman Egypt: the Economics of Collective Tax Responsibility", in Udovitch, 1981, p. 473-520

Hardtmann, M., "Beitrage zur Kenntnis der Syrischen Steppe", *Zeitschrift des deutschen Palästina-Vereins*, 22 (1899), p. 127-49, 153-77 and 23 (1901), p. 1-77, 97-158

Heyd, U., *Ottoman documents on Palestine, 1552-1615. A study of the Firman according to the Mühimme Defteri*, Oxford 1960

Hodgson, M.G.S., *The Venture of Islam; Conscience and History in a World Civilization*, 3 vols., Chicago 1974

Hofman, Y., "The Administration of Syria and Palestine under Egyptian rule", in Maoz (ed.), p. 311-333

Holt, P.M. *Egypt and the Fertile Crescent, 1516-1922*, London 1966

Hourani, A.H., "The Fertile Crescent in the Eighteen Century", in A.H. Hourani, *A Vision of History*, Beirut 1961, p. 35-70

-, "Ottoman Reform and the Politics of Notables", in W.R. Polk and R.L. Chambers (eds.), *Beginning of modernization in the Middle East*, Chicago, p. 41-65

-, "Shaikh Khalid and the Naqshibandi Order", in: *Islamic Philosophy and the Classical Tradition*, ed. Stern, Hourani, Brown, Oxford 1972, pp. 89-104

Hunter, F.R., *Egypt under the khedives, 1805-1879; From Household Government to Modern Bureaucracy*, Pittsburgh 1984

Hütteroth, W.-D., "Ottoman Administration of the Desert Frontier in the Sixteenth Century", Asian and African Studies 19 (1985), p. 145-55

Hütteroth, W.-D., and Abdulfattah, K., *Historical Geography of Palestine, Transjordan and Southern Syria in the late 16th Century*, Erlangen 1977

Inalcik, H., *The Ottoman empire in the classical age, 1300-1600*. London 1973

-, "Centralization and Decentralization in Ottoman Administration", in Naff and Owen (eds.), p. 27-52

-, "Islamization of Ottoman Laws on Land and Land Tax", in Fragner, C. and Schwarz, K. (ed.), *Festgabe an Josef Matuz. Osmanistik-Turkologie Diplomatik*, Berlin 1992

İpşirli, M., "A Preliminary Study of the Public Waqfs of Hama and Homs in the XVIth Century", *Studies on Turkish-Arab Relations*, 1 (1986), p. 119-47

Issawi, C., *The Fertile Crescent, 1800-1914. A documentary economic history*, New York 1988

Islamoglu-Inan, H. (ed.), *The Ottoman Empire and the world-economy*, Cambridge 1987

-, "Peasants, Commercialization and Legitimation of State Power in Sixteenth-Century Anatolia", in Keyder and Tabak (eds.), p. 57-76

Itzkowitz, N., "Men and Ideas in the Eighteenth Century Ottoman Empire", in Naff and Owen (eds.), p. 15-26

Jennings, R.C., "Kadi, Court and Legal Procedure in 17th Century Ottoman Kayseri", *Studia Islamica* 48 (1978), p. 133-172

-, "Limitations of the Judicial Powers of the Kadi in 17th Century Ottoman Kaysari", *Studia Islamica* 50 (1979), p. 151-184

Johansen, B., *The Islamic Law on Land Tax and Rent. The Peasants' Loss of Property Rights as Interpreted in the Hanafite Legal Literature of the Mamluk and Ottoman Periods*, London 1988

al-Jundî, A. *Aᶜlâm al-Adab wa-l-Fann*, 2 vols., Damascus 1954

al-Jundî, M.S. *Târîkh Maᶜarrat al-Nuᶜmân*, 2 vols., Damascus 1965

Kasaba, R., *The Ottoman Empire and the World Economy; the 19th century*, New York 1988

al-Kaylânî, M., *Muḥâfaẓat Ḥamâ*, Damascus 1964

Keyder, C., *State and Class in Turkey. A Study in Capitalist Development*, London 1987

Keyder, C. and Tabak, F, (eds.), *Landholding and Commercial Agriculture in the Middle East*, New York 1991

Khalidi, T., (ed.), *Land Tenure and Social Transformation in the Middle East*, Beirut 1984

Khoury, D. Rizq., *State and Provincial Society in the Ottoman Empire*, Cambridge 1997

Koury, G.J., *The Province of Damascus, 1783-1832*, Ph.D., University of Michigan 1970

Kunt, I.M., *The Sultan's Servants. The Transformation of Ottoman Provincial Government, 1550-1650*, New York 1983

Kurd ᶜAlî, M., *Khiṭaṭ al-Shâm*, 3 vols., Damascus 1983

Kushner, D., (ed.), *Palestine in the late Ottoman Period. Political Social and Economic Transformation*, Jerusalem 1986

Layish, A., "The Sijill of the Jaffa and Nazareth Shariᶜa Courts as a Source for the Political and Social History of Ottoman Palestine", in Ma'oz (ed.), p. 525-32

Lapidus, I.M., *Muslim Cities in the Later Middle Ages*, Cambridge (Mass.) 1984

Lawson, F.H., *The Social Origins of Egyptian Expansionism during the Muhammad 'Ali period*, New York 1992

Leeuwen, R. van, *Notables and Clergy in Mount Lebanon: the Khâzin Sheiks and the Maronite Church (1736-1840)*, Leiden 1994

Lewis, B., *The Emergence of Modern Turkey*, London 1961
-, "Ottoman Land Tenure and Taxation in Syria", *Studia Islamica* 50 (1979), p. 109-124
Lewis, N.N., *Nomads and Settlers in Syria and Jordan, 1800-1980*, Cambridge 1987
Mandaville, J.E., "The Ottoman Court Records of Syria and Jordan", *Journal of the American Oriental Society* 86 (1966), p. 311-9
Manna^c, ^cA., "The *sijill* as Source for the study of Palestine during the Ottoman Period, with Special Reference to the French Invasion", in Kushner (ed.), p. 351-62
-, "Continuity and Change in the Socio-political Elite in Palestine during the late Ottoman Period", in Philipp (ed.), p. 69-89
Mantran, R. et Sauvaget, J., *Règlements Fiscaux Ottomans. Les Provinces Syriennes*, Paris 1951
Ma'oz, M., *Ottoman Reform in Syria and Palestine, 1840-1861.* Oxford 1968
-, (ed.), *Studies on Palestine during the Ottoman Period*, Jerusalem 1975
Marcus, A., *The Middle East on the Eve of Modernity. Aleppo in the Eighteenth Century*, New York 1989
Mardam Bey, Kh., *Aᶜyân al-qarn al-Thâlith ᶜAshar fî al-Fikr wa-l-Siyâsa wa-l-Ijtimâᶜ*, Beirut 1971
Marino, B., *Le Faubourg du Mîdân à Damas à l'Époque Ottomane. Espace Urbaine, Cociété et Habitat (1742-1830)*, Thèse pour le Doctorat Nouveau, Université d'Aix-Marseille I, 1994
Masters, B., *The Origins of Western Economic Dominance in the Middle East. Mercantilism and the Islamic Economy in Aleppo, 1600-1750*, New York 1988
-, "Ottoman Policies toward Syria in the 17th and 18th Centuries", in Philipp (ed.), p. 11-26
Munajjid, Ṣ-D., *Wulât Dimashq fî al-ᶜAhd al-ᶜUthmânî*, Damascus 1949
Mundy, M., "Shareholders and the State. Representing the Village in the late 19th Century Land Registers of the Southern Ḥawrân", in Philipp (ed.), p. 217-38
Naff, T. and Owen, R., (eds.), *Studies in Eighteenth Century Islamic History*, London 1977
Nelson, C. (ed.), *The Desert and the Sown. Nomads in the wider society*, Berkeley 1973
Oppenheim, M. von, *Die Beduinen*, 3 vols., Leipzig, 1939-43
Owen, R., "Introduction [to part II: Resources, Population and Wealth]", in Naff and Owen (eds.), p. 133-51
Owen, R., 1981, *The Middle East in the World Economy, 1800-1914.* London
Parry V.J. and Yapp M.E. (eds.), *War, Technology and Society in the Middle East.* London 1975
Petran, T., *Syria*, London 1972
Philipp, T., *The Syrians in Egypt 1725-1975*, Stuttgart 1985

-, (ed.), *The Syrian Land in the 18th and 19th Century. The Common and the Specific in the Historical Experience*, Stuttgart 1992

-, "Social structure and political power in Acre in the 18th century", in Philipp (ed.), p. 91-108

Piterberg, G., "The Formation of an Ottoman Egyptian Elite in the 18th Century", *International Journal of Middle East Studies* 22 (1990), p. 275-89

Polk, W.R., *The Opening of South Lebanon, 1788-1840; a Study of the Impact of the West on the Middle East*, Cambridge MA 1963

Qaḥḥâla, ʿU.R. *Muʿjam Qabâʾil al-ʿArab al-Qadîma wa-l-Ḥadîtha*, 3 vols., Beirut 1968

al-Qâsimî, M.S. *Qâmûs al-Ṣinâʿât al-Shâmiyya*, Damascus 1988

Rafeq, A.-K, *The Province of Damascus, 1723-1783*, Beirut 1966

-, "Local Forces in Syria in the Seventeenth and Eighteenth Centuries", in Parry and Yapp (eds.), p. 277-307

-, "Maẓâhir min al-Ḥayâ al-ʿAskariyya al-ʿUthmâniyya fî Bilâd al-Shâm min al-Qarn al-Sâdis ʿashar ḥattâ Maṭlaʿ al-Qarn al-Tâsiʿ ʿAshar", *Dirâsât Târîkhiyya*, 1 (1980), p. 66-95

-, "Qâfulat al-Ḥajj al-Shâmî wa-Ahamiyyatihâ fir al-Dawla al-ʿUthmâniyya", *Dirâsât Târîkhiyya*, 6 (1981), p. 5-28

- "The Law-court Registers of Damascus, with Special Reference to Craft Corporations during the First Half of the Eighteenth Century", in Berque et Chevallier (eds.), p. 141-6

-, "The Law-court Registers and their Importance for a Socio-economic and Urban Study of Ottoman Syria", in Chevalier (ed.), p. 51-8

-, "Changes in the Relationship between the Ottoman Central Administration and the Syrian Provinces from the Sixteenth to the Eighteenth Century", in Naff and Owen (eds.), p. 53-73

-, "Economic Relations between Damascus and the Dependent Countryside, 1743-71", in Udovitch (ed.), p. 653-86

-, "Maẓâhir min al-Tanẓîm al-Ḥirafî fî Bilâd al-Shâm fî al-ʿAhd al-ʿUthmânî", *Dirâsât Târîkhiyya* 4 (1981), p. 30-62

-, "Qâfilat al-Ḥajj al-Shâmî wa-Ahammiyyatuhâ fî al-ʿAhd al-ʿUthmânî", *Dirâsât Târîkhiyya* 6 (1981), p. 5-28

-, "Land Tenure Problems and their Social Impact in Syria around the Middle of the Nineteenth Century", in Khalidi (ed.), 371-96

-, "Maẓâhir Iqtiṣâdiyya wa-Ijtimâʿiyya min Liwâʾ Hamâ, 942/1035-943/1536", *Dirâsât Târîkhiyya* 31-2 (1989), p. 17-66

-, "City and Countryside in a Traditional Setting. The case of Damascus in the first quarter of the eighteenth century", in: Philipp (ed.), p. 295-332

Raymond, A., *Artisans et Commerçants au Caire au XVIIIe siècle*, 2. vols., Damascus 1973-4

-, "Les Sources de la Richesse Urbaine au Caire au Dix-huitieme Siècle", in Naff and Owen (eds.), p. 184-204

-, 1981, "The Economic Crisis of Egypt in the Eighteenth Century", in Udovitch (ed.), 1981, p.687-708C-, *Grandes Villes Arabes à l'Époque Ottomane*, Paris 1985

Redhouse, J.W. *Turkish-English lexicon*, Istanbul 1890

Reilly, J.A., "Sharî^{c}a Court Registers and Land Tenure around Nineteenth Century Damascus", *MESA bulletin* 21 (1987), p. 155-69

-, "Properties around Damascus in the Nineteenth Century", *Arabica* 37 (1990), p. 91-114

-, "Damascus Merchants and Trade in the Transition to Capitalism", *Canadian Journal of History* 27 (1992) p. 1-27

Repp, R.C., *The Müfti of Istanbul. A Study in the Developments of the Ottoman Learned Hierarchy*, London 1986

Sâlim, L,M., *al-Ḥukm al-Miṣrî fi-l-Shâm, 1831-1841*, Cairo 1990

Ṣamad, Q., *Târîkh al-Ḍaniyya al-Siyâsî wa-l-Ijtimâ^{c}î fi-l-^{c}Ahd al-^{c}Uthmani*, n.p., n.d.

al-Sayyid Marsot, A.l., "The Wealth of the Ulama in Late Eighteenth Century Cairo", in Naff and Owen (eds.), p. 205-216

-, *Egypt in the Reign of Muhammad Ali*, Cambridge 1984

Schatkowski-Schilcher, L., *Families in Politics. Damascene Factions and Estates of the 18th and 19th centuries*, Stuttgart 1985

Seikaly, S.M., "Land tenure in 17th Century Palestine: the Evidence from the *al-Fatâwâ al-Khayriyya*", in Khalidi (ed.), p. 397-408

Sertoğlu, M., *Resimli Osmanli Tarihi Ansiklopedisi*, Istanbul 1958

Shanin, T. (ed.), *Peasants and Peasant Societies*, London 1988

Shaw, S.J., *Between Old and New. The Ottoman Empire under Sultan Selim III*, Cambridge (Mass.) 1971

-, *History of the Ottoman Empire and Modern Turkey*, vol. 1, Cambridge 1976

Shaw, S.J. and Shaw, E.K., *History of the Ottoman Empire and Modern Turkey*, vol. 2, Cambridge 1977

Singer, A., *Palestinian peasants and Ottoman Officials. Rural Administration around Sixteenth-Century Jerusalem*, Cambridge 1994

Spooner, B., "Desert and Sown: a New Look at an Old Relationship", in Naff and Owen (eds.), p. 236-49

Sugar, P.F., *Southeastern Europe under Ottoman rule, 1354-1804*, Seattle 1977

Sunar, I., "State and Economy in the Ottoman Empire", in Islamoglu-Inan (ed.), p. 63-87

Tabak, F., "Agrarian Fluctuations and Modes of Labor Control in the Western Arc of the Fertile Crescent, c. 1700-1850", in Keyder and Tabak (eds.), p. 135-54

al-Ṭawîl, M.A.Gh., *Târîkh al-^{c}Alawiyyîn*, Beirut n.d.

Thomas, L.V., *A Study of Naima*, New York 1972

Thorner, D., "Peasant Economy as a Category in History", in Shanin (ed.), p. 62-8

Tilly, Ch., *Coercion, Capital and European States, AD 990-1990*, Cambridge (Mass.) 1990

Tischler, H.L., Whitten, Ph. and Hunter, D.E.K., *Introduction to Sociology*, New York 1986

Udovitch, A.L., (ed.) *The Islamic Middle East, 700-1900. Studies in Economic and Social History*, Princeton 1981

Venzke, M.L. "Special Use of the Tithe as a Revenue-raising Measure in the Sixteenth-Century *Sanjaq* of Aleppo, *Journal of the Economic and Social History of the Orient* 29 (1986), p. 239-334

Wallerstein, I., Decdeli, H. and Kasaba, R., "The Incorporation of the Ottoman Empire into the World-Economy", in Islamoglu-Inan (ed.), p. 88-97

Weurlesse, E., *Le Pays des Alaouites*, 2 vols., Tours 1940

-, *L'Oronte. Étude de fleuve*, Paris 1941

Winter, M., *Egyptian society under Ottoman rule, 1517-1798*, London 1992

Wittfogel, K.A., *Oriental despotism. A comparative study of total power*, New Haven 1957

Yannî, J., *Târîkh Sûriyâ*, Beirut 1881

Yûsuf, ʿA.W., "al-Rîf al-Ḥamawî fî al-qarn al-sâdis ʿashar", *Dirâsât Târîkhiyya* 2 (1979), p. 42-61

Zakariyâ, A.W., *ʿAshâʾir al-Shâm*, Damascus 1983

-, *Jawla Athariyya*, Damascus 1984

Ze'evi, D., *An Ottoman Century. The District of Jerusalem in the 1600s*, Albany 1996

Ziyâda, Kh., *al-Ṣura al-Taqlîdiyya li-l-Mujtamaʿ al-Madanî*, Tripoli 1983

-, *Arkiyûlûjiyâ al-Muṣṭalaḥ al-Wathâ'iqî*, Tripoli 1987

Zürcher E.J., *Turkey. A Modern History*. London 1993

Index

ᶜAbdallah Pasha (of Acre) 58, 120, 122, 189–190
ᶜAbdallah Pasha al-ᶜAẓm 57, 87, 93–96, 98–100, 104–105, 108, 116
Acre 7, 16, 53–54, 57, 59, 86–89, 99, 103, 120–122
agriculture 18–25, 184–187, 205–210
Aḥmad (Pasha) al-Jazzâr, see Jazzâr Pasha
ᶜAjlânî family 82, 109
ᶜAkkâr 113–114
Alawites 15, 70, 80, 116, 142–143, 153, 170, 197
Aleppo 7, 16, 19, 20, 22, 66, 77, 81, 102, 105, 155, 198, 200, 206
ᶜAlî Bey al-Asᶜad 114, 118, 120–122
ᶜAlî Bey al-Kabîr 52, 56
ᶜAlwânî family 70–71, 74, 83, 173
ᶜAmq Valley 17
Anatolia 7, 19, 25, 111
ᶜAnaza 15, 28–34, 39–43, 48, 97, 117–118, 200, 206–207
ᶜarab (tribes) 18, 20–43, 47, 51, 69, 97, 117, 137, 184–185, 187, 206–209
Arabia 27–28,
Asᶜad (Pasha) al-ᶜAẓm 50–51, 87, 159, 164, 167
ᶜÂṣî River 14, 17, 28, 32, 43, 173
Atâsî family 84
ᶜAẓm family 45–52, 57, 67–69, 72–75, 86–88, 91–99, 119–122, 132, 158, 169, 173–175, 181–182, 198, 201, 208
authority 3–6, 166–167
aᶜyân 63–66, 84, 86, 148, 200–201

Baghdad 17, 18, 56
Baḫrî family 71, 168 n. 59, 198
Bakrî family 82
Balqa 17
Banî Khâlid (*ᶜarab* tribe) 36, 38
Banî Sḫakhr (*ᶜarab* tribe) 48
Barâdâ River 17
Barâzî family 68–69, 75, 78, 115, 118–119, 169, 174–175
Bashâkim (*ᶜarab* tribe) 36–37,
Bashîr al-Shihâb II 113, 189, 195, 197
beduin, see *ᶜarab* and ᶜAnaza
Beirut 16
Bilâd al-Shâm 16–17
Biqa valley 16, 96
Burckhardt 32

cereals 19, 77–78, 159–160
Christians 71–72, 109, 143–145, 188–189, 193
coercion 1–2, 194
confiscation 164–165
conscription 197
crafts 137–138, 157

Ḍâhir al-ᶜUmar, see Ẓâhir al-ᶜUmar
Damascus 7, 16, 17, 20, 22, 31, 49, 55, 57, 64, 75, 77, 81, 86–96, 99–103, 105–111, 155, 159–161, 176, 190, 195
Dandashlî clan 98, 113, 208
dawla, see state
Druzes 113, 115, 153, 188, 193

economy 38–40, 53–55, 156–158
Egypt 7, 52, 55, 56, 61, 95, 188–189

expenditure (for the army) 145–150, 196
expenditure (for the pilgrimage) 128–129
Euphrates 16, 19, 28

Fadᶜân (ᶜAnaza) 30, 32–34, 37–38, 40–41, 117–118, 208
faddân 135–136
famine 19–20, 124
Faraj Aghâ 14, 15, 122–124, 178–183, 199–200, 208
fees 131–132, 137, 175–178
finances 154–156, 162–165,173, 178–182, 193–194
France (French) 52, 55, 56–57, 88, 95

Ghâb Valley 16–17, 25, 117

Ḥadîdiyyîn (ᶜ*arab* tribe) 37–38, 42,
ḥajj, see pilgrimage
Hama 7, 16, 17, 20, 22, 34–38, 39, 47–50, 66–84, 97–99, 110, 116–124, 125–151, 160, 169–170, 177–187, 190, 198–205, 207–209
Hamad 17, 35,
Ḥasana (ᶜAnaza) 30, 31–34, 38–40, 117–118
Ḥasya 46 , 67
Hawran 17, 19, 20, 24, 88, 113, 115, 159
Hijaz 7, 20, 30, 52–53, 88, 100–102, 154, 188, 206
Hinâdî (ᶜ*arab*) 112–113
Ḥiṣn al-Akrâd 67
Homs 16, 17, 20, 36, 44, 47–49, 67–68, 84, 98, 109, 125, 131, 190

Ibrâhîm Deli Pasha 87, 88, 89–90, 92–93, 105, 163
Ibrâhîm Pasha (of Egypt) 111, 113, 190, 195, 198–199
Ibrâhîm Pasha al-Ḥalabî 87–88, 94, 98, 105
Islamic law 3, 79–81, 153–154
Ismâᶜîl (Pasha) al-ᶜAẓm 45–48,
Ismailis 18, 70, 116, 170

janissaries, see military
Jazira 19
Jazzâr Pasha 52–54, 56–59, 87–89, 91–99, 103, 108, 112, 115, 160, 166, 175
Jews 143, 193–194 n. 16,
Jijaklî family 68–69, 75, 78, 169, 173, 201, 208
jizya 143–145
Jordan valley 16, 24
Jundî family 67–68, 84, 97, 98, 113, 120
justice 3–5, 44, 153–154, 194

Kaylânî family 70–75, 81–82, 98, 110, 123–124, 169, 173–175, 178, 199–201, 208
khuwwa, see protection money
Kunj Yûsuf (Pasha) 88, 100–101, 103, 105–106, 108, 116, 160, 189
Kurds 24, 25, 69, 111, 114

Latakia 16, 101, 197
Lebanon (Mount Lebanon) 51, 59, 89, 113, 115, 188–189
loans 160–162, 175
local administration 63–72, 75–84, 131–132; 167–171, 194–195, 198–201
locusts 20, 124, 184

Maᶜarra 45, 67–68, 131
Maghreb 111, 114
Maḥâsinî family 82
Maḥkama, see religious court
Mahmud II 60–61, 102, 109, 149, 183

mamlûk 56, 58
market 133, 158–160
Mawâlî tribe 26–28, 31–32, 34–5, 42, 46, 69, 78, 88, 90, 93, 97, 103, 116, 130, 207–208
Mecca 16, 30, 45, 52–3, 95
Medina 16, 30, 45, 52–3
merchants 66, 75, 122–123, 148, 173
migration 20, 24–25, 27–29, 31–34
military 2–6, 63–64, 66–70, 76–78, 90–91, 105–111, 111–115, 184–185
mîrî 128–130
monopolies 156, 158–160
muftî 81–83, 92–93
Muḥammad ᶜAlî Efendi al-Kaylânî 82, 201
Muḥammad ᶜAli Pasha 7, 42, 53–54, 59–62, 101, 102, 110–111, 120, 126, 160, 166, 188–196, 208
Muḥammad Khalîl Efendi al-Murâdî 89, 91
Muḥammad al-Khurfân 69, 78, 90, 103, 207–208
Muḥammad Pasha al-ᶜAẓm 57, 87, 91
Muḥammad Salîm Pasha 110
Mullâ Ismâᶜîl 68, 90, 115–119
Murâdî family 82, 92, 109, 198
Mustafa II 58
Muṣṭafâ Aghâ Barbar 57, 96, 98, 100, 120–122, 189, 194–195, 196

Nablus 16, 24, 59, 113, 125
Najd 30, 32
nomadism 21
Nuᶜaym (ᶜ*arab* tribe) 36,
Nuṣayrîs see Alawites

Palestine 51, 52, 105, 197
Palmyra 17, 31, 32,
pastoralism 20–25, 28
patronage 165–167
peasants 3, 20–25, 28, 55, 150, 156–157, 184–187, 206
pilgrimage 45, 48, 49, 52–53, 55, 87, 95, 100–101, 155, 168
plague 20, 124, 184
policing 25–27
protection money 22, 32 (n. 45), 42, 206
provisions (to the army) 145–150, 197–198

Qadariyya order 70

reforms 58–62, 193–194
religious court 8–9, 79–84, 125–126
revenue 4–5, 126, 162, 174, 201–205
revolts 88–91, 97–99, 107–111, 117–118, 197
Ruwâla (ᶜAnaza) 30, 32–34, 38,

Salamiyya 17, 18, 26, 209
Sardiyya (ᶜ*arab* tribe) 48
Saᶜûd family 30–31,
Selim III 58–59, 102, 135
Shâmlî family 69, 105, 123, 199
sharᶜ, see Islamic law
Sibaᶜa (ᶜAnaza) 32–34, 37–38, 40–41, 117–118, 208
Sidon 7, 50, 51, 160
state 1–3, 85, 156–158, 194
Sulaymân Pasha (al-ᶜA^dil) 58, 100–103, 105
Sulaymân (Pasha) ibn Salîm al-ᶜAẓm 121–122
sultanic law 4–5
Syrian Desert 16–17, 21

taxation 3, 76, 77, 126–151, 175–178, 183, 185, 201–205, 208
tax farming 133–135, 168–171, 171–172
Ṭayfûr family 68–69, 75, 78, 174–175, 199–200, 208

trade 54–56
Tripoli 16, 47, 49, 51 (n. 23), 57, 96, 98, 114, 120–122, 190
Turcoman tribes 15–16, 24–26, 46, 48, 49, 68, 142, 170
Turkî (ᶜ*arab* tribe) 33, 37–38, 118
Turkumânî family 68–69, 169, 174

ulema 66, 70–75

village desertion 17–20, 184–187, 209
village economy, see agriculture
violence, see military and revolts

Wahhâbî movement 29–31, 33, 52–53, 55, 88, 95, 100–102
waqf 71, 73–74, 144, 164
Wuld ᶜAlî (ᶜAnaza) 30, 32–34, 40–41, 48–49, 118

Ẓâhir al-ᶜUmar 51, 53–54, 56, 160

www.ingramcontent.com/pod-product-compliance
Ingram Content Group UK Ltd.
Pitfield, Milton Keynes, MK11 3LW, UK
UKHW020820240326
469204UK00019B/96

9 781784 537340